LEARNING *from the* WRITINGS
The HOPE-FILLED TEACHINGS *of* NICHIREN DAISHONIN

DAISAKU IKEDA

World Tribune
Press

Published by
World Tribune Press
606 Wilshire Blvd.
Santa Monica, CA 90401

Printed in the United States of America.

SUSTAINABLE Certified Fiber
FORESTRY   Sourcing
INITIATIVE
Label applies to the text stock www.sfiprogram.org

This book is printed on Glatfelter Thor PCW paper.
It contains 30% post-consumer waste and is
SFI (Sustainable Forestry Initiative) certified.

Design by Lightbourne, Inc.

ISBN 978-1-932911-96-1

10 9 8 7 6 5 4

Contents

Editor's Note

This series of lectures by SGI President Ikeda was published in SGI-USA's *Living Buddhism* from the July–August 2008 issue through the September–October 2009 issues.

Please also see *The Writings of Nichiren Daishonin*, as follows:

"The Drum at the Gate of Thunder," WND-1, pp. 948–51
"On Prolonging One's Life Span," WND-1, pp. 954–56
"Reply to Sairen-bo," WND-1, pp. 309–14
"Hell Is the Land of Tranquil Light," WND-1, pp. 456–59
"On the Buddha's Prophecy," WND-1, pp. 398–404
"Winter Always Turns to Spring," WND-1, pp. 535–37
"The Dragon Gate," WND-1, pp. 1002–04
"The Strategy of the Lotus Sutra," WND-1, pp. 1000–01
"Lessening One's Karmic Retribution," WND-1, pp. 199–201
"Letter to Misawa," WND-1, pp. 894–98
"The Essentials for Attaining Buddhahood," WND-1, pp. 746–49
"Many in Body, One in Mind," WND-1, pp. 618–19
"On Repaying Debts of Gratitude," WND-1, pp. 690–745
"Letter to Jakunichi-bo," WND-1, pp. 993–95
"A Warning against Begrudging One's Fief," WND-1, pp. 823–26

GZ, page number(s)—refers to the *Gosho zenshu*, the Japanese-language compilation of letters, treatises, essays and oral teachings of Nichiren Daishonin.

LSOC, page number(s)—refers to *The Lotus Sutra and Its Opening and Closing Sutras*, translated by Burton Watson (Soka Gakkai: Tokyo, 2009).

OTT, page number(s)—refers to *The Record of the Orally Transmitted Teachings*, translated by Burton Watson (Soka Gakkai: Tokyo, 2004).

WND, page number(s)—refers to *The Writings of Nichiren Daishonin*, vol. 1 (WND-1) (Tokyo: Soka Gakkai, 1999) and vol. 2 (WND-2) (Tokyo: Soka Gakkai, 2006).

LEARNING *from the* WRITINGS

The HOPE-FILLED TEACHINGS *of* NICHIREN DAISHONIN

SGI PRESIDENT IKEDA'S LECTURE SERIES

The HOPE-FILLED TEACHINGS
of NICHIREN DAISHONIN

(1)

"The Drum at the Gate of Thunder"

"It Is the Heart That Is Important"—Continuously Strive
To Deepen and Strengthen the Bonds of Mentor and Disciple

Introduction to New Lecture Series

"In adversity, it is necessary to cry out, 'Hope! Hope! And yet again hope!'"[1]—this was the message that the French writer Victor Hugo sent from his place of exile to compatriots suffering under an oppressive regime. No matter how adverse the circumstances, as long as we have hope, we will never be defeated; as long as we have hope, we can keep moving forward.

Nichiren Buddhism is a teaching of hope. It is a great philosophy, affirming that we possess within ourselves the infinite power to surmount all hardships and break through all obstacles. Nichiren Buddhism also teaches the practice by which we can tap this infinite power in our lives, backed by solid examples of actual proof. As such, it is an inspirational teaching that has the power to generate unceasing hope in the hearts of all people.

The writings of Nichiren Daishonin fully elucidate this philosophy of hope as well as its practice and proof. They are a source of illumination that endlessly encourages and inspires. Nichiren composed these hope-filled writings for his followers and for all humankind in the midst of daunting and often life-threatening struggles. My mentor, Josei Toda, the second Soka Gakkai president, once said: "Nichiren, while himself experiencing serious illness and harsh persecution, exhorts us to forge ahead and shape our own destiny right in the midst of such obstacles. We are truly fortunate in this regard. I, too, have learned this from Nichiren, who engaged in a life-and-death struggle to impart his teachings."

Let us strive to read with our lives—that is, to put into practice—even a line or two of Nichiren's writings, which overflow with his spirit. Basing ourselves on his teachings and pursuing study to strengthen our Buddhist practice are traditions of the Soka Gakkai.

As we head toward the 80th anniversary of the Soka Gakkai's founding (in 2010), let us together study one writing each month in this series, focusing mainly on letters sent to individual followers, with the spirit to learn from the towering life-state of the Buddha of the Latter Day of the Law.

For this first lecture, we will study "The Drum at the Gate of Thunder," a letter addressed to the lay nun Sennichi.

THE PASSAGE FOR STUDY IN THIS LECTURE

Those who make offerings to the Lotus Sutra will receive the same benefit as they would by making offerings to all the Buddhas and bodhisattvas in the ten directions, because all the Buddhas of the ten directions originate from the single character *myo*. Suppose a lion has a hundred cubs. When the lion king sees its cubs attacked by other beasts or birds of prey, he roars; the hundred cubs will then feel emboldened, and the heads of those other beasts and birds of prey will be split into seven pieces. The Lotus Sutra is like the lion king, who rules over all other animals.

A woman who embraces the lion king of the Lotus Sutra never fears any of the beasts of hell or of the realms of hungry spirits and animals. All the offenses committed by a woman in her lifetime are like dry grass, and the single character *myo* of the Lotus Sutra is like a small spark. When a small spark is set to a large expanse of grass, not only the grass but also the big trees and large stones will all be consumed. Such is the power of the fire of wisdom in the single character *myo*. Not only will all offenses vanish, but they will become sources of benefit. This is what changing poison into amrita means. For example, black lacquer will turn white when white powder is added. A woman's offenses are like the lacquer, and the words Nam-myoho-renge-kyo, like the white powder.

When one dies, if one is destined to fall into hell, one's appearance will darken, and one's body will become as heavy as a stone that requires the strength of a thousand men to move. But in the case of a good person, even if she should be a woman seven or eight feet tall and of dark complexion, at the hour of death, her countenance will become pure and white, and her body will be as light as a goose feather and as soft and pliable as cotton.

It is a thousand *ri* [2] across the sea and mountains from Sado Province to this province [of Kai where Mount Minobu is located]. You, as a woman, have held fast to your faith in the Lotus Sutra; and over the years you have repeatedly sent your husband here to visit me in your place. Surely the Lotus Sutra, Shakyamuni, Many Treasures, and the Buddhas of the ten directions know of your devotion. For example, though the moon is forty thousand yojanas high in the heavens, its reflection appears instantly in a pond on earth; and the sound of the drum at the Gate of Thunder is immediately heard a thousand, ten thousand *ri* in the distance. Though you remain in Sado, your heart has come to this province.

The way of attaining Buddhahood is just like this. Though we live in the impure land, our hearts reside in the pure land of Eagle Peak. Merely seeing each other's face would in itself be insignificant. It is the heart that is important. Someday let us meet at [the pure land of] Eagle Peak, where Shakyamuni Buddha dwells. (*The Writings of Nichiren Daishonin*, vol. 1, p. 949)

LECTURE

"It is the heart that is important" (WND-1, 949), Nichiren Daishonin declares. The strongest bond in the mentor-disciple relationship in Buddhism is that of the heart. The hearts of mentor and disciple who aspire for the widespread propagation of the Mystic Law can connect instantly, transcending any distance that may lie between them. Just as when the moon appears in the heavens, "its reflection appears instantly in a pond on earth" (WND-1, 949).

This letter "The Drum at the Gate of Thunder" is like a great painting depicting the heart-to-heart exchange between mentor and disciple separated by a vast distance. Nichiren wrote this letter while living on Mount Minobu on October 19, 1278, when he was 57. He addressed it to the lay nun [3] Sennichi, who lived on Sado Island, far away across the mountains and the sea.

Previously, during Nichiren's exile on Sado, the lay nun Sennichi and her husband, Abutsu-bo, converted to his teachings. They were sincere and pure-hearted followers who risked their lives to support and assist him. Even after

Nichiren moved to Mount Minobu, this husband and wife played a leading role in efforts to propagate the Mystic Law on Sado, striving to fulfill the noble mission that Nichiren had entrusted to them. Furthermore, during a period of several years until his death, Abutsu-bo, despite his advanced age, made the long, perilous journey from Sado to visit Nichiren at least three times.

In summer 1278, a few months before this letter was written, Abutsu-bo had once again journeyed to Mount Minobu, motivated to seek out and support his mentor, Nichiren. Later that same year, as winter approached, Nichiren received offerings from the lay nun Sennichi. In this letter, which he composed to thank her for them, Nichiren also praises her unwavering sincerity in having sent Abutsu-bo to visit him almost every year. He encourages the lay nun wholeheartedly, saying to the effect: "Since you are a woman who embraces the lion king of sutras, there is nothing whatsoever that you need to fear. Shakyamuni, Many Treasures, and the Buddhas of the ten directions and three existences surely know of your devotion."

This letter resounds with the wondrous spirit of the unity of mentor and disciple; it reflects the faith of the disciple who sincerely seeks the mentor and the compassion of the mentor who strives to deeply encourage the disciple.

Those who make offerings to the Lotus Sutra will receive the same benefit as they would by making offerings to all the Buddhas and bodhisattvas in the ten directions, because all the Buddhas of the ten directions originate from the single character *myo*. Suppose a lion has a hundred cubs. When the lion king sees its cubs attacked by other beasts or birds of prey, he roars; the hundred cubs will then feel emboldened, and the heads of those other beasts and birds of prey will be split into seven pieces. The Lotus Sutra is like the lion king, who rules over all other animals.

A woman who embraces the lion king of the Lotus Sutra never fears any of the beasts of hell or of the realms of hungry spirits and animals. (WND-1, 949)

BOUNDLESS BENEFIT RESIDES IN MAKING OFFERINGS TO THE LOTUS SUTRA

The benefit of making offerings to the Lotus Sutra is boundless. Through that benefit, we can triumph over any obstacle and devilish function. And nothing is stronger than a person whose life is instilled with this confidence.

The Lotus Sutra—epitomized by the single character *myo*—is the source of the enlightenment of all Buddhas of the ten directions and three existences. The sutras teach that countless Buddhas have appeared in the universe from the

Dr. Lokesh Chandra, director of the International Academy of Indian Culture (second from right), presents a white shawl to SGI President Ikeda after the joint commencement ceremony for Soka University and Soka Women's College at the Soka University Auditorium in Hachioji, Tokyo, March 21, 2008.

infinite past and will continue to do so into the infinite future. The Lotus Sutra is the teacher by which all Buddhas attain enlightenment (see WND-1, 948). Therefore, making offerings to the Lotus Sutra is equivalent to making offerings to all Buddhas throughout time and space, and the benefit that derives from doing so is immeasurable.

In the first part of this writing, Nichiren Daishonin cites the names of each of the Buddhas of the ten directions who are described in the sutras.[4] He also explains that the Buddhas of the three existences—that is, of past, present and future—are depicted in a sutra as "the thousand Buddhas of the past Glorious Kalpa, the thousand Buddhas of the present Wise Kalpa, and the thousand Buddhas of the future

Constellation Kalpa"[5] (WND-1, 948). In this way, he describes the existence of myriad Buddhas and bodhisattvas over the vast expanse of time and space that is expressed as "the ten directions and three existences." Why does Nichiren here present such a grand and magnificent view of the universe?

In terms of the worldview of the day, the letter's recipient, the lay nun Sennichi, was an elderly woman of no particular distinction living on a remote northerly island of Japan, which was itself a tiny, isolated archipelago. But in terms of faith, her spirit to steadfastly support and assist Nichiren, leader of the widespread propagation of the Mystic Law, was admirable beyond compare and shone with sublime nobility. By describing the existence of countless Buddhas in the universe, Nichiren no doubt seeks to highlight her good fortune and benefit, which are as vast as the universe. He is saying to the effect: "To make offerings to the Lotus Sutra is to make offerings to all Buddhas and bodhisattvas of the ten directions. Therefore, they are all sure to protect you. You will absolutely never become deadlocked. You need not worry about anything. You can serenely savor a state of life as eternal and vast as the universe."

THE BENEFIT INHERENT IN THE CHARACTER *MYO*: THE THREE MEANINGS OF *MYO*

Nichiren Daishonin states that this is so "because all the Buddhas of the ten directions originate from the single character *myo*" (WND-1, 949). The "single character *myo*" refers to the *myo* of *myoho,* the Mystic Law or Wonderful Law, and the *myo* of Myoho-renge-kyo, the title of the Lotus Sutra.

While various principles are expounded in the 28-chapter Lotus Sutra, in the final analysis, these are all for the purpose of expressing, teaching and transmitting the mystic principle of *myo*. One who fully understands and embodies this mystic principle becomes a Buddha. The Lotus Sutra is thus the teacher of all Buddhas. And it is in order to enable all people of the evil age of the Latter Day of the Law to awaken to the power of *myo* that Nichiren revealed and propagated

Nam-myoho-renge-kyo of the Three Great Secret Laws[6]—the teaching implicit in the depths of the Lotus Sutra.

In his writing "The Daimoku of the Lotus Sutra," Nichiren explains that *myo* has three meanings: "to open," "to be fully endowed" and "to revive." Let us now look at each of these:

(1) "The character *myo* means to open" (WND-1, 145). This means that the Lotus Sutra is the key that opens the storehouses of all the sutras preached by the Buddha, making it possible for the treasures that lie within those sutras to be utilized.

(2) "*Myo* means to be fully endowed, which in turn has the meaning of 'perfect and full'" (WND-1, 146). This means that just as all treasures emerge from a wish-granting jewel[7] as small as a mustard seed, and just as all plants and flowers bloom due to the light of the sun, so each single character of the Lotus Sutra contains all teachings and benefits within it.

(3) "*Myo* means to revive, that is, to return to life" (WND-1, 149). This means that the Lotus Sutra can impart fresh life and hope to all people—even those who had been deemed incapable of attaining enlightenment in the pre-Lotus Sutra teachings—and enable them to attain Buddhahood without fail.

The Mystic Law is the fundamental and perfect Law that encompasses all phenomena (the principle of "full endowment") and has the power to open or bring out the inherent value of all things (the principle of "opening"). As such, it also has the power to revitalize and invigorate even those facing the most adverse and intractable circumstances and enable them to attain Buddhahood (the principle of "reviving").

By chanting Nam-myoho-renge-kyo and teaching others to do the same, we can concretely manifest the power of "the single character *myo*" in our own lives. That is the wonderful benefit of Nichiren Buddhism. We carry out our Buddhist practice in order to profoundly engrave "the single character *myo*" in our lives and to master its meaning through experience. This is also the point of our activities for *kosen-rufu*.

President Toda composed the following poem:

> *Now the time has arrived*
> *for the widespread propagation*
> *of the correct teaching,*
> *we stake our lives*
> *on the single character* myo.

When we strive to further *kosen-rufu* without begrudging our lives, we can fully receive the benefit of "the single character *myo*" in every facet of our beings.

THE BENEFIT OF WOMEN WHO EMBRACE THE LION KING OF SUTRAS

In this relatively short letter, Nichiren begins quite a few sentences with words like *for example, suppose* and *to illustrate* to clarify his meaning. We can interpret this as reflecting his deep compassion to explain the principles of Buddhism in the most easily accessible and readily understandable form for his recipient.

In the analogy that begins "Suppose a lion has a hundred cubs," he clarifies how the limitless benefits of making offerings to the Lotus Sutra actually manifest in our lives. Here, the Lotus Sutra, endowed with the infinite power of "the single character *myo*," is likened to a lion king, while those who embrace and make offerings to the Lotus Sutra are likened to lion cubs. In contrast, those who reside in the unfortunate states of hell, hunger and animality— the lower three of the Ten Worlds—are likened to "beasts or birds of prey." When the lion king roars, no matter what beasts or birds of prey may threaten, the hundred lion cubs are filled with courage and can defeat them. In the same way, individuals who make offerings to the Lotus Sutra can acquire the immeasurable power of "the single character *myo*" and win over those in negative life-states such as hell, hunger and animality.

The Lotus Sutra is the lion king of the sutras. Therefore, Nichiren encourages the lay nun Sennichi, saying, "A woman who embraces the lion king of the Lotus Sutra never fears any of the beasts of hell or of the realms of hungry spirits and animals" (WND-1, 949). Here, he specifically says "a woman." In the male-dominated warrior society of the day, women were generally in a weak and disadvantaged position. We can speculate that the lay nun, as one of Nichiren's leading followers on Sado Island, may have encountered or heard of other women suffering due to illness, old age or family problems, and may have sought Nichiren's advice on such matters. Or perhaps, he may have sensed some wavering or vacillation in her heart, which prompted him to write these words. Whatever the case, he warmly encourages her, assuring her that a woman who embraces the Lotus Sutra, the lion king of sutras, has absolutely nothing to fear.

Indeed, this passage might also be interpreted as a frank acknowledgment of the strong faith of women. For we generally find that it is women—more so than men, who often let egoism and appearances hold them back—who demonstrate the infinite power of the Mystic Law at a crucial moment, just as the teachings instruct. The power of belief leads to a state of mind free of fear or doubt, which is the very essence of what it means to have faith. No devilish function can possibly defeat a woman who has attained such a state of mind. A woman of deep faith who correctly practices the Mystic Law possesses the wisdom to instantly distinguish between right and wrong. She has the essential courage to sweep away the three poisons—greed, anger and foolishness. She is endowed with an all-nurturing

Absolutely nothing can stand in the way of women who know "the greatest of all joys," which comes from chanting Nam-myoho-renge-kyo. The presence and example of women whose lives have been revitalized through such joy can become a powerful source of inspiration for many others.

compassion. Inspired by the example of a teacher awakened to the Mystic Law, her wisdom, courage and compassion fuse together in a firm, unwavering resolve. Such a woman will never be swayed by the maneuvers of any devilish function.

President Toda used to say, "The realization of *kosen-rufu*—its success or failure—will depend on the efforts of women." Absolutely nothing can stand in the way of women who know "the greatest of all joys," which comes from chanting Nam-myoho-renge-kyo (see *The Record of the Orally Transmitted Teachings*, p. 212). The presence and example of women whose lives have been revitalized through such joy can become a powerful source of inspiration for many others.

All the offenses committed by a woman in her lifetime are like dry grass, and the single character *myo* of the Lotus Sutra is like a small spark. When a small spark is set to a large expanse of grass, not only the grass but also the big trees and large stones will all be consumed. Such is the power of the fire of wisdom in the single character *myo*. Not only will all offenses vanish, but they will become sources of benefit. This is what changing poison into amrita[8] means. For example, black lacquer will turn white when white powder is added. A woman's offenses are like the lacquer,

and the words Nam-myoho-renge-kyo, like the white powder.

When one dies, if one is destined to fall into hell, one's appearance will darken, and one's body will become as heavy as a stone that requires the strength of a thousand men to move. But in the case of a good person, even if she should be a woman seven or eight feet tall and of dark complexion, at the hour of death, her countenance will become pure and white, and her body will be as light as a goose feather and as soft and pliable as cotton. (WND-1, 949)

THE POWER OF THE MYSTIC LAW TO CHANGE POISON INTO MEDICINE

The encouragement to the lay nun Sennichi continues. Nichiren Daishonin indicates, again by means of analogy, that the Mystic Law has the power to change the "poison" of all offenses and all misfortunes into "medicine"—transforming that which is negative in our lives into something positive.

The sum of all the offenses a person commits in a lifetime is likened to a large expanse of dry grass, while the power of "the single character *myo*" that can instantly eradicate these myriad offenses is likened to a small spark. He uses these similes to indicate that this single character of the Lotus Sutra can function to erase the many offenses a person has committed over a lifetime.

Such is the immense power of the Mystic Law. Because of this, we can live with assurance and peace of mind.

The "offenses of a lifetime," can be understood to mean the problems and sufferings we encounter in the course of our lives. We earnestly chant Nam-myoho-renge-kyo each day to overcome all our problems and have everything go well in our lives without making mistakes we might regret. When we follow this solid path in life, then no matter what adverse circumstances or difficult problems we may encounter, all our worries, anxieties and mistakes will be burned away in the fire of wisdom in the same way that flames from a small spark can consume whole stretches of dry grass. Moreover, Nichiren says that when a large expanse of dry grass is set aflame, then even "big trees and large stones" will be consumed in that fire. In other words, as long as we keep challenging ourselves in faith to resolve our problems through the fire fueled by our efforts to chant Nam-myoho-renge-kyo and teach others to do the same, we can also eventually burn away even heavy, deep-rooted negative karma and break through the fundamental darkness[9] that is the source of all misery and unhappiness. When we do so, our lives are certain to blossom with the great benefit of transforming our karma and attaining Buddhahood in this lifetime.

In this writing, Nichiren says: "Not only will all offenses vanish, but they will become sources of benefit. This is what changing poison into amrita means" (WND-1, 949). The great Mahayana Buddhist scholar Nagarjuna[10] interpreted the Sanskrit word *sad* (*myo*) of the Lotus Sutra (Skt *Saddharma-pundarika-sutra*) as the benefit of changing poison into medicine. This power enables us to change the three paths—earthly desires, karma and suffering[11]—into the three virtues—the Dharma body, wisdom and emancipation.[12] It refers, in other words, to the doctrine of attaining Buddhahood in one's present form.

In addition, a transformation in the karma or destiny of one person opens the way to a transformation in the karma or destiny of all humankind. Following in the lay nun Sennichi's footsteps, our women's division and young women's division members today are leading the way in our efforts to realize this fundamental transformation. Commenting on the development of democracy, Walt Whitman, standard-bearer of the American Renaissance, expressed high expectations for the activities of women. He declared that they are "great...in all departments,"[13] and also exclaimed, "Great, great, indeed, far greater than they know, is the sphere of women."[14] The activities of women who have "embraced the lion king of the Lotus Sutra," therefore, are sure to change the world in an important and significant way. Our network of Soka women is a treasure of the world fulfilling that momentous mission.

A CORRECT AND STEADFAST MIND AT THE MOMENT OF DEATH IS THE PROOF OF ATTAINING BUDDHAHOOD

The analogies continue. Nichiren Dai-shonin says that just as black lacquer will turn white when white powder is added, the Mystic Law has the power to eradicate any offense. As proof of this, he comments on the difference in appearance at the moment of death of a person who has sincerely lived in accord with the Mystic Law and one who has slandered the Law and is destined to fall into a state of hell.

Since this is a well-known passage in which Nichiren discusses the appear-ance of the deceased, allow me to confirm an important point regarding the moment of death. While he uses such statements as "her countenance will become pure and white" and "her body will be as light as a goose feather and as soft and pliable as cotton" to describe the appearance of deceased individuals who have upheld the Mystic Law to the end of their lives, what is most important at the moment of death is a person's heart or state of mind—in other words, their having "a correct and steadfast mind at the moment of death." [15] When it comes to physical appearance, individuals of course differ widely, and this is definitely not an absolute standard for determining whether someone has attained Buddha-hood. Consequently, there is no point in

getting caught up in what people's appearance is like after they die.

When he says that a deceased per-son's "countenance will become pure and white," we can take this to refer to an inner radiance manifested in the per-son's expression—the joyful expression, for instance, of someone departing for the next existence embraced in the voices of friends and loved ones chant-ing for his or her happiness; the bright, gentle expression of a person who exudes an ineffable serenity; the noble expression of a person who shines with the triumph of a lofty mission fulfilled, imparting courage and hope to all beholders.

Some people die young. Some peo-ple die in unforeseen accidents. And some people die after long battles with illness. But whatever the case, there is no need to worry. What matters is a person's heart at the final moment, not the manner of death. What matters is whether that person has persevered in faith to the very end. In one writing, Nichiren cites the Nirvana Sutra, which states, "A mad elephant can only destroy your body; it cannot destroy your mind [i.e., your heart]" [16] (see "On the Protection of the Nation," WND-2, 135). In modern terms, "mad ele-phants" might correspond to things like traffic accidents. Regardless of how people may die, if they have formed a deep connection with the Mystic Law and devoted themselves wholeheartedly to their mission in this world, they are sure to shine with a magnificent inner brilliance at the moment of death. On this, we can absolutely rest assured. It is the manifestation of an inscrutable causality. A person's heart is always what is most important.

It is a thousand *ri* across the sea and mountains from Sado Province to this province [of Kai where Mount Minobu is located]. You, as a woman, have held fast to your faith in the Lotus Sutra; and over the years you have repeatedly sent your husband here to visit me in your place. Surely the Lotus Sutra, Shakyamuni, Many Treasures, and the Buddhas of the ten directions know of your devotion. For example, though the moon is forty thousand yojanas[17] high in the heavens, its reflection appears instantly in a pond on earth; and the sound of the drum at the Gate of Thunder[18] is immediately heard a thousand, ten thousand *ri* in the distance. Though you remain in Sado, your heart has come to this province.

The way of attaining Buddhahood is just like this. Though we live in the impure land, our hearts reside in the pure land of Eagle Peak.[19] Merely seeing each other's face would in itself be insignificant. It is the heart that is important. Someday let us meet at [the pure land of] Eagle Peak, where Shakyamuni Buddha dwells. (WND-1, 949)

OUR HEART OF FAITH CAN TRANSCEND ANY DISTANCE

Nichiren Daishonin writes, "Though you remain in Sado, your heart has come to this province." He is telling the lay nun Sennichi that even though she hasn't set foot outside of Sado, which is far away across mountains and sea, her heart has reached him at Mount Minobu. Nichiren may well have sensed that she felt sad at the thought that she might never see him again in her lifetime. But in our Buddhist practice, there is no need to lament. Based on faith in the Mystic Law, our hearts can instantaneously cross any distance. Nichiren's encouragement conveys the message, "You are fighting alongside me in spirit." We can easily imagine how much courage and hope this must have given the lay nun.

Next, he states, "Though we live in the impure land, our hearts reside in the pure land of Eagle Peak." He explains that although the *saha* world in which they dwell is an impure land, the hearts of those who embrace the correct teaching reside in the pure land of Eagle Peak, which is to say, the Land of Eternally Tranquil Light.[20] But even when one attains the enlightened state of Buddhahood, it doesn't mean he or she will stop having problems or can avoid living in an impure land. Nevertheless, if we, as ordinary human beings, establish a state of absolute and indestructible happiness in the depths of our lives, we will never be consigned to misery. By saying "Our hearts reside in the pure land of Eagle Peak," he is explaining that we can bring forth within us the supremely noble state of Buddhahood that will not be swayed by any problem or circumstance.

"Merely seeing each other's face would in itself be insignificant," indicates that faith is not determined by meeting face-to-face with the mentor. "It is the heart that is important," he asserts. And one's heart is expressed in one's actions. In the case of the lay nun Sennichi, her devotion is revealed in her sending Abutsu-bo to visit Nichiren almost every year. It is an expression of her unchanging commitment to faith. In the succinct statement "It is the heart that is important," Nichiren conveys to her that he is fully aware of her sincere dedication and that this dedication is the way to attaining Buddhahood.

THE BONDS OF MENTOR AND DISCIPLE IN BUDDHISM ARE ETERNAL AND EVERLASTING

Nichiren Daishonin concludes this writing by saying, "Someday let us meet at [the pure land of] Eagle Peak, where Shakyamuni Buddha dwells." These words are a declaration that the lay nun's faith is genuine and that she can definitely attain Buddhahood in this lifetime and meet Nichiren at the pure land of Eagle Peak. The bonds of mentor and disciple in Buddhism are everlasting.

Abutsu-bo and the lay nun Sennichi demonstrated a tireless spirit to seek out the teachings and philosophy of Nichiren. And their son Tokuro Moritsuna, who as a fellow practitioner of the Lotus Sutra inherited his parents' spirit, carried on his father's tradition and visited Nichiren at Mount Minobu. All three are exemplary disciples who strove with the same commitment as Nichiren during his lifetime.

In a discussion with members of the student division, I once responded as follows to a question about the oneness, or unity, of mentor and disciple: "It means to have a mentor in your heart while standing on your own two feet. President Toda resides in my heart. This is not something you speak out loud; it's a matter of the heart. This is because unity is something that exists inside you."

At all times, no matter where I am, I feel as if I am constantly engaging in dialogue with President Toda as I go about my activities. Our unity exists within me. The unity of mentor and disciple transcends distance and time. The hearts of mentor and disciple compose an eternal history of united struggle.

Upholding the great philosophy of Nichiren Buddhism that teaches that the heart is most important, let us apply ourselves with even greater sincerity and dedication in our ongoing efforts for *kosen-rufu*.

NOTES:

1. Translated from French. Victor Hugo, *Pendant l'exil: 1852–70* (During the Exile: 1852–70), in *Actes et Paroles* (Acts and Words) (Paris: Albin Michel, 1938), vol. 2, p. 114.

2. A thousand *ri* here simply indicates a very long distance.

3. Lay nun: A female Buddhist believer who has shaved her head in the manner of a Buddhist nun, but continues to live in society as a layperson.

4. Nichiren writes: "The Buddhas of the ten directions are the Buddha Good Virtue in the east, the Buddha Sorrow-Dispelling Virtue in the southeast, the Buddha Sandalwood Virtue in the south, the Buddha Giver of Treasure in the southwest, the Buddha Infinite Brightness in the west, the Buddha Flower Virtue in the northwest, the Buddha Banner-like Virtue in the north, the Buddha Three Vehicle Practice in the northeast, the Buddha Vast Myriad Virtue of the zenith, and the Buddha Brilliant Virtue of the nadir" (WND-1, 948). These Buddhas of the ten directions are enumerated in *The Commentary on the Ten Stages Sutra*. But since the expression "the Buddhas of the ten directions" is used here to indicate all Buddhas throughout the universe, these ten should be regarded as representing all the Buddhas in their respective directions.

5. The Glorious Kalpa, the Wise Kalpa and the Constellation Kalpa are the *kalpas* of past, present and future, respectively. Each major *kalpa* consists of four medium *kalpas*—the *kalpa* of formation, the *kalpa* of continuance, the *kalpa* of decline and the *kalpa* of disintegration. *The Record of the Three Thousand Buddhas of the Three Kalpas* mentions the advent of a thousand Buddhas in succession in each of these three major *kalpas*.

6. Three Great Secret Laws: The core principles of Nichiren Buddhism: (1) the object of devotion of the essential teaching [the Gohonzon], (2) the invocation, or *daimoku* of the essential teaching [Nam-myoho-renge-kyo] and (3) the sanctuary of the essential teaching [where we enshrine the Gohonzon].

7. A mythological jewel capable of granting wishes. It symbolizes the virtue and power of the Buddha and the Buddhist scriptures.

8. Amrita: A legendary, ambrosia-like liquid. Amrita is said to remove sufferings and confer immortality.

9. Fundamental darkness: Also, fundamental ignorance or primal ignorance. The most deeply rooted illusion inherent in life, said to give rise to all other illusions. Fundamental darkness means the inability to see or recognize the truth, particularly the true nature of one's life. Nichiren interprets fundamental darkness as ignorance of the ultimate Law, or ignorance of the fact that one's life is essentially a manifestation of the Law, which he identifies as Nam-myoho-renge-kyo.

10. Nagarjuna (n.d.): A Mahayana scholar of southern India, thought to have lived between the years 150 and 250. Nagarjuna wrote many important treatises, including *The Treatise on the Middle Way*, and organized the theoretical foundation of Mahayana

thought, having a major impact on Buddhism's development in China and Japan.

11. Three paths—earthly desires, karma and suffering: They are called *paths* because one leads to the other. Earthly desires, which include greed, anger, foolishness, arrogance and doubt, give rise to actions that create evil karma. The effect of this evil karma then manifests itself as suffering. Suffering aggravates earthly desires, leading to further misguided action, which in turn brings on more evil karma and suffering. In this way, the three paths function to prevent a person from attaining Buddhahood.

12. Three virtues—the Dharma body, wisdom and emancipation: Three attributes of a Buddha. The Dharma body means the truth that the Buddha has realized, or the true aspect of all phenomena; wisdom is the capacity to realize this truth; and emancipation means the state of being free from the sufferings of birth and death.

13. Walt Whitman, *Democratic Vistas* (New York: The Liberal Arts Press, 1949), p. 29.

14. Whitman, *Democratic Vistas*, pp. 12–13.

15. "A steadfast and correct mind at the moment of death": To maintain unwavering belief in the Mystic Law until the last moment of one's life. It means that when we continue to follow the Buddha way, confident that we will attain Buddhahood in this lifetime, we can greet death with a sense of profound fulfillment.

16. This passage means that even if the body should be destroyed in some untoward circumstance like being trampled by a mad elephant, the mind or the essence of one's being, which has accumulated great good fortune and benefit through our upholding the Mystic Law in this lifetime, can never be destroyed.

17. *Yojana*: A unit of measurement used in ancient India, said to equal the distance that the royal army could march in a day. One *yojana* is considered to be about 7 kilometers, although there are several other approximations, such as 9.6, 18 and 24 kilometers.

18. Drum at the Gate of Thunder: The Gate of Thunder was a gate located in a region known as K'uai-chi (or Kuei-chi) in what is now Shaoxing in China's Zhejiang Province. The sound of the drum from this place was said to reach all the way to the distant capital of Lo-yang (present-day Luoyang).

19. Eagle Peak is the place where Shakyamuni preached the Lotus Sutra. It also symbolizes the Buddha land or the state of Buddhahood, as in the expression "the pure land of Eagle Peak."

20. Land of Eternally Tranquil Light: Also, Land of Tranquil Light or Land of Eternal Light. It refers to the Buddha land, which is free from impermanence and impurity. In many sutras, the *saha* world is described as an impure land filled with delusions and sufferings, and the Buddha land as a pure land free from these and far removed from this *saha* world. In contrast, the Lotus Sutra reveals the *saha* world to be the Buddha land, or the Land of Eternally Tranquil Light, and explains that the nature of a land is determined by the minds of its inhabitants.

STUDY GUIDE

The following is a summary of points from SGI President Ikeda's lecture.

- "The Drum at the Gate of Thunder," written to the lay nun Sennichi, emphasizes the heart of the mentor-disciple relationship.

- This letter was written at a time when Nichiren Daishonin lived in Mount Minobu and the lay nun Sennichi and her husband, Abutsu-bo, lived far away on Sado Island. The couple consistently supported Nichiren during and after his exile on Sado.

- In this letter, Nichiren thanks the lay nun for her support and sincerity and stresses the significance of making offerings to the Lotus Sutra.

- Because she offered her support to Nichiren and thereby made offerings to the Lotus Sutra—the source of enlightenment for all Buddhas—Nichiren praised her as being worthy of the admiration and protection of the Buddhas of the ten directions.

THE THREE MEANINGS OF *MYO*

- The "single character *myo*," refers to the *myo* of Myoho-renge-kyo, the title of the Lotus Sutra.

- While various principles are expounded in the 28-chapter Lotus Sutra, in the final analysis these are all for the purpose of expressing, teaching and transmitting the principle of *myo*.

- *Myo* has three meanings: to open, to be fully endowed and to revive.

- *To open* means that the Lotus Sutra is the key to fully accessing and utilizing the treasures within all the sutras.

- *To be fully endowed* means that each character of the Lotus Sutra contains all teachings and benefits within it.

- *To revive* means that the Lotus Sutra can revitalize one's life-state and impart hope, and lead all people to enlightenment.

- By chanting Nam-myoho-renge-kyo and teaching others to do the same, we manifest all these qualities of *myo* in our lives. We carry out our Buddhist practice to deeply engrave "the single character *myo*" in our lives and to master its meaning through experience.

ЛEN WHO EMBRACE THE LION KING OF SUTRAS

- Nichiren encourages the lay nun Sennichi, writing, "A woman who embraces the lion king of the Lotus Sutra never fears any of the beasts of hell or of the realms of hungry spirits and animals" (WND-1, 949).

- The power of belief leads to a state of mind free of fear or doubt, which is the very essence of what it means to have faith. No devilish function can possibly defeat a woman who has attained such a state of mind.

- Inspired by the example of a teacher awakened to the Mystic Law, a woman's wisdom, courage and compassion fuse together in a firm, unwavering resolve. Such a woman can inspire countless others.

TO CHANGE POISON INTO MEDICINE

- Just as a spark can easily catch an entire field of dry grass on fire, the single character *myo* can function to erase all the offenses a person has committed in his or her life.

- "Offenses of a lifetime" can be understood to mean the problems and sufferings we encounter.

- Through chanting Nam-myoho-renge-kyo, we can burn away all our worries, anxieties and mistakes with the fire of wisdom and lead lives free of regret.

- We can change the three paths— earthly desires, karma and suffering —into the three virtues—the Dharma body, wisdom and emancipation.

- We can enjoy the greatest benefit of transforming our karma and attaining Buddhahood in this lifetime.

A CORRECT AND STEADFAST MIND AT THE MOMENT OF DEATH

- Nichiren states that at the moment of death, there are differences between the appearance of a person who has sincerely practiced the Mystic Law and one who has slandered the Law. While he uses specific statements regarding certain physical attributes to differentiate the two, it should be understood that these descriptions are used to refer to the inner states of life.

- Physical appearances differ from person to person, and physical appearances cannot be a standard for determining whether the deceased has attained enlightenment.

- What is important at the moment of death is a person's state of mind, or having "a correct and steadfast mind at the moment of death" (see "The Heritage of the Ultimate Law of Life," WND-1, 217).

- Regardless of how a person may die, if they have formed a deep connection with the Mystic Law and devoted themselves wholeheartedly to their mission in this world, they are sure to shine with a magnificent inner brilliance at the moment of death. What matters in the final moment is a person's heart.

OUR HEART OF FAITH TRANSCENDS DISTANCE

- Nichiren encourages the lay nun Sennichi that despite great physical distance, they share the deep bond of mentor and disciple. In telling her they will meet again at Eagle Peak, he assures her that, even if separated by distance or even death, they will always be together because of their shared commitment in faith.

- Nichiren stresses, "It is the heart that is important" (WND-1, 949).

- The unity of mentor and disciple means to have the mentor in our heart while standing on our own two feet. It is not something that is spoken out loud. Unity exists within a person's heart; it transcends distance and time.

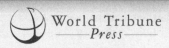

(2)

"On Prolonging One's Life Span"

Faith for Leading a Long and Healthy Life

The Passage for Study in This Lecture

When I prayed for my mother, not only was her illness cured, but her life was prolonged by four years. Now you [the lay nun Toki] too have fallen ill, and as a woman, it is all the more timely for you to establish steadfast faith in the Lotus Sutra and to see what it will do for you. In addition, you can go to Nakatsukasa Saburo Saemon-no-jo [Shijo Kingo], who is not only an excellent physician but a votary of the Lotus Sutra.

Life is the most precious of all treasures. Even one extra day of life is worth more than ten million *ryo* of gold. The Lotus Sutra surpasses all the other sacred teachings of the Buddha's lifetime because of the "Life Span" chapter. The greatest prince in the land of Jambudvipa [the entire world] would be of less consequence than a blade of grass if he died in childhood. If he died young, even a person whose wisdom shone as brilliantly as the sun would be less than a living dog. So you must hasten to accumulate the treasure of faith and quickly conquer your illness.

I could ask Shijo Kingo on your behalf, but, while some people would prefer to be approached by an intermediary, others may feel it reflects a lack of earnestness on the part of the individual concerned. It is extremely difficult to fathom another person's mind. I have experienced such difficulties on several occasions. Shijo Kingo is one who would feel offended if the request came from anyone but the person directly concerned, so in his case, it would not be advisable for me to intercede. Just ask his assistance yourself, frankly and sincerely, without an intermediary. When he came to see me in the tenth month of last year, he told me how grieved he was about your illness. He said that you were probably not overly concerned then because your illness was not yet serious, but that it would surely become critical by the first or second month of this year. His words deeply saddened me. He also said that Toki [Jonin, your husband] depends on you as a staff to lean on and a pillar for support. He was very concerned about you. He is a man who never gives in to defeat and who greatly values his friends.

If you are unwilling to make efforts to heal yourself, it will be very difficult to cure your illness. One day of life is more valuable than all the treasures of the major world system, so first you must muster sincere faith. This is the meaning of the passage in the seventh volume of the Lotus Sutra that states that burning a finger as an offering to the Buddha and the Lotus Sutra is better than donating all the treasures of the major world system. A single life is worth more than the major world system. You still have many years ahead of you, and moreover you have encountered the Lotus Sutra. If you live even one day longer, you can accumulate that much more benefit. How truly precious your life is!

Write down your name and age yourself and send your messenger with it to me so that I can pray to the gods of the sun and moon. Your son Iyo-bo is also extremely worried about you, so he will offer the recitation of the verse section of the "Life Span" chapter to those gods. (*The Writings of Nichiren Daishonin*, vol. 1, p. 955)

LECTURE

There is no greater treasure than life. The teachings of Buddhism exist so that we can live our lives to the fullest. We practice faith in the Mystic Law so that we can lead long and healthy lives.

In the letter we are studying this time, "On Prolonging One's Life Span,"[1] Nichiren Daishonin encourages the lay nun Toki,[2] who for some time had been troubled by ill health, that she can definitely transform her karma through strong faith in the Mystic Law.

For me, "On Prolonging One's Life Span" calls to mind many memories of my mentor, second Soka Gakkai president Josei Toda. On September 27, 1957, Mr. Toda spoke on this writing at a lecture open to all members. I recall attending that meeting and listening to his talk. That was during the same month he made his historic antinuclear declaration[3] in which he proclaimed, "We, the citizens of the world, have an inviolable right to live." Everyone has a right to live. That my mentor lectured on "On Prolonging One's Life Span," a writing that underscores the preciousness and sanctity of life, in the very same month, is significant.

After Mr. Toda's death, I ensured that recordings of his lectures and addresses were preserved in the form of phonograph records so that they could be passed on to future generations. These records were a compilation of my mentor's heartfelt guidance. His lecture on "On Prolonging One's Life Span" was in fact the first record in the series to be completed.

In that lecture, after reading from the text, Mr. Toda declared vigorously: "Suffering from illness is a means by which you can eradicate your negative karma. Live long lives, placing your faith in the Gohonzon! You mustn't die young!" His powerful voice still resonates deeply in my heart.

It was also around that time that Mr. Toda spoke of resuming the morning study sessions of what I fondly refer to as "Toda University," which had been discontinued for a time due to his poor health. My mentor was deeply and solemnly committed to fostering and educating people, to raising genuine successors who could accomplish *kosen-rufu*, even if the effort cost him his life.

As Nichiren says, "One day of life is more valuable than all the treasures of the major world system"[4] (WND-1, 955). Day after day, President Toda gave every last ounce of his being to train me. Profoundly moved by how much effort he was making on my behalf, I studied furiously and applied myself to Soka Gakkai activities with single-minded determination.

His proposal to restart our study sessions came in the autumn of the year just before I turned 30.

Today, I forge ahead each day with the same feeling President Toda had at that time, exerting myself to the fullest.

How can we make the most of this precious day that will never come again? For what purpose will we use our precious lives in this existence? In this installment, let us look at passages from "On Prolonging One's Life Span" and study the secret to changing our karma or destiny and the essence of faith for leading a long and healthy life.

When I prayed for my mother, not only was her illness cured, but her life was prolonged by four years. Now you [the lay nun Toki] too have fallen ill, and as a woman, it is all the more timely for you to establish steadfast faith in the Lotus Sutra and to see what it will do

for you. In addition, you can go to Nakatsukasa Saburo Saemon-no-jo [Shijo Kingo],[5] who is not only an excellent physician but a votary of the Lotus Sutra.

Life is the most precious of all treasures. Even one extra day of life is worth more than ten million *ryo* of gold.[6] The Lotus Sutra surpasses all the other sacred teachings of the Buddha's lifetime because of the "Life Span" chapter. The greatest prince in the land of Jambudvipa [the entire world] would be of less consequence than a blade of grass if he died in childhood. If he died young, even a person whose wisdom shone as brilliantly as the sun would be less than a living dog. So you must hasten to accumulate the treasure of faith and quickly conquer your illness. (WND-1, 955)

ENCOURAGEMENT TO THE AILING LAY NUN TOKI

The lay nun Toki had long been plagued by illness. She had been a widow with a son when she married Toki Jonin, and the challenges and stresses of her new life may have taken their toll on her in various ways. It appears that as her ill health dragged on, she had grown pessimistic about her prospects for recovery. In this writing, however, Nichiren Daishonin asserts that she can definitely prolong her life based on the teachings of Buddhism.

The main theme of this letter is that the power of faith in the Mystic Law can transform even fixed karma. *Karma* means actions in the form of thoughts, words and deeds. Each action becomes a cause, the effect of which manifests at some point in the future as either a positive or negative outcome, depending on the nature of the action. The type of karma in which effects are destined to appear at a set time and in a set form is called "fixed" or "immutable" karma, while the type of karma in which effects are not destined to appear in this way is called "unfixed" or "mutable" karma. In this writing, the term *fixed karma* is used specifically with reference to one's life span.

In the passages preceding those we are studying in this installment, Nichiren emphasizes that, just as a skilled physician can cure even a serious illness, we can change any fixed karma and extend our life spans through the "highly effective medicine" (*The Lotus Sutra and Its Opening and Closing Sutras*, p. 269) of the Lotus Sutra. After citing several examples from the Buddhist scriptures to illustrate this point, he assures the lay nun Toki that it is the most natural thing in the world for a woman living in the Latter Day of the Law to change her fixed karma by practicing the teachings of the Lotus Sutra.[7]

Nichiren then gives a further example, explaining how he had prayed for his own mother's illness to be cured. This constitutes great actual proof of the principle of "prolonging one's life through faith" as taught in the Lotus Sutra.[8]

Nichiren addresses the lay nun Toki in an ardent appeal to deeply touch her life and rouse her into action. He says in effect: "My mother cured her illness through the power of the Mystic Law and extended her life by four years. You, too, as a woman just like her, should muster strong faith in the Lotus Sutra. You also have Shijo Kingo, an outstanding physician who is a fellow practitioner of the Lotus Sutra, to turn to. A single day of life is more valuable than countless treasures. The Lotus Sutra is the foremost among all of Shakyamuni's teachings because it contains the 'Life Span' chapter that expounds the eternity of the Buddha's life. Therefore, you mustn't die an untimely death. You mustn't die young. Quickly summon your faith, and cure your illness as soon as possible!" (see WND-1, 955).

"You have to live on! You must survive without fail!"—With this impassioned cry, Nichiren earnestly appeals to the lay nun Toki, seeking to lift her out of the morass of suffering into which she had sunk.

Nichiren Daishonin on Illness

The lion king is said to advance three steps, then gather himself to spring, unleashing the same power whether he traps a tiny ant or attacks a fierce animal. In inscribing this Gohonzon for her protection, Nichiren was like the lion king. This is what the sutra means by "the power [of the Buddhas] that has the lion's ferocity." Believe in this mandala with all your heart. Nam-myoho-renge-kyo is like the roar of a lion. What sickness can therefore be an obstacle? ("Reply to Kyo'o," *The Writings of Nichiren Daishonin*, vol. 1, p. 412)

THE "LIFE SPAN" CHAPTER REVEALS THE ETERNITY OF LIFE

Nothing is more precious than life. Nichiren Daishonin says, "Life is the most precious of all treasures" (WND-1, 955). And toward the end of this letter, he adds, "A single life is worth more than the major world system" (WND-1, 955). No doubt Nichiren emphasizes the value of life in order to awaken the lay nun Toki's will to live. "Please strive to live even one day longer" is the message he seeks to convey.

Life itself is infinitely precious. Even a single day of life, to use Nichiren's analogies, is worth more than "ten million *ryo* of gold" or "all the treasures of the major world system." A single day of life is valuable beyond measure. For that very reason, he encourages the lay nun Toki to live as long as she possibly can.

The "Life Span of the Thus Come One" chapter of the Lotus Sutra, which is the essence of Shakyamuni's teaching, clarifies the infinite value of life, truly recognizing that the sanctity of life is the heart of Buddhism. Those who believe in the Lotus Sutra, therefore, should strive to live out their precious lives for as long as they can.

The title of this chapter in the Lotus Sutra literally means "to fathom or measure the Buddha's life span." Among all the Buddhist sutras, only the "Life Span" chapter of the Lotus

Sutra reveals the eternal nature of the Buddha's life, and further teaches that this does not apply exclusively to the Buddha. The eternal life expounded in the "Life Span" chapter also applies to our own lives. We can each awaken to this great, eternal life within us just as we are. The "Life Span" chapter teaches this through the example of Shakyamuni as the Buddha who attained enlightenment in the remote past. Later, Nichiren expounded Nam-myoho-renge-kyo so that all people could experience this eternal and infinitely precious life as the reality of their own beings.

We have a wonderful opportunity in this existence to awaken to the eternity of life taught in Buddhism, to live based on this profound truth, to forge a state of indestructible happiness and help others do the same.

Mr. Toda often told people suffering from illness, "I've taught you this Buddhist practice so that you can become happy in terms of your eternal life, transcending birth and death."

"You can definitely cure your illness!"—This was Mr. Toda's great conviction. When we continue to strive in faith for the happiness of ourselves and others, we will without fail come to discover the eternal nature of our lives. We will enjoy actual proof in some form or another of having overcome the hindrance of illness. That is why when Mr. Toda gave guidance to those who were swayed by illness and had lost their resolve in faith, he was very strict in correcting their attitude.

Life is tenacious; it is endowed with the impulse to survive and the power to heal. The "highly effective medicine" for drawing forth these innate properties is the Mystic Law. Ultimately, it is we ourselves who cure our illness, while the decision to undertake this battle to do so arises from faith. Nichiren indicates this in his reference to the "treasure of faith" (WND-1, 955).

To see illness as an opportunity to transform our karma—this strong spirit and resolve can break through all obstacles and devilish functions and open wide the path to happiness. Like a rocket blasting out of the earth's atmosphere, the passionate conviction of faith that comes from viewing illness as an opportunity to transform our karma can become a powerful engine propelling us forward not only in this existence but throughout eternity, enabling us to freely savor everlasting happiness.

PROMPTLY AND UNHESITATINGLY SEEKING TREATMENT

"You must . . . quickly conquer your illness" (WND-1, 955), Nichiren Daishonin tells the lay nun Toki. Once we understand how precious a single day of life is, there is no reason to vacillate about seeking treatment when we are ill. Don't put yourself in a situation where you

later have cause for regret because you were reluctant or hesitant to take action. Nichiren urges the lay nun Toki to act promptly. Buddhism always conforms with reason. A Buddhist text states: "Hasten to do good. . . . The mind of one who is sluggish about doing good finds amusement in evil."[9] In Nichiren's use of the word *quickly*, I can't help but feel his profound compassion and urgent wish that the lay nun Toki get well as soon as possible and not miss this opportunity to transform her karma.

I could ask Shijo Kingo on your behalf, but, while some people would prefer to be approached by an intermediary, others may feel it reflects a lack of earnestness on the part of the individual concerned. It is extremely difficult to fathom another person's mind. I have experienced such difficulties on several occasions. Shijo Kingo is one who would feel offended if the request came from anyone but the person directly concerned, so in his case, it would not be advisable for me to intercede. Just ask his assistance yourself, frankly and sincerely, without an intermediary. When he came to see me in the tenth month of last year, he told me how grieved he was about your illness. He said that you were probably not overly concerned then because your illness was not yet serious, but that it would

surely become critical by the first or second month of this year. His words deeply saddened me. He also said that Toki [Jonin, your husband] depends on you as a staff to lean on and a pillar for support. He was very concerned about you. He is a man who never gives in to defeat and who greatly values his friends. (WND-1, 955)

A DISCIPLE'S WELL-BEING IS ALWAYS THE MENTOR'S FOREMOST CONCERN

Next, Nichiren Daishonin urges the lay nun Toki to seek treatment from Shijo Kingo, an accomplished physician, and offers concrete advice about how to approach him. With a keen understanding of Kingo's character, he advises her that rather than requesting Kingo's help through an intermediary, she should take up the matter with him herself and sincerely request his assistance.

Of course, if Nichiren had asked Kingo to help, he certainly wouldn't have refused. But it may be that the lay nun Toki was the type of person who was reluctant to ask for favors. We can take it that Nichiren, knowing the temperaments of both followers and respecting their differences, was explaining the way for them to maintain harmonious relations so that they would readily and warmly support one another.

Nichiren put a great deal of thought and effort into writing this letter, offering extremely detailed advice and suggestions so that the lay nun Toki would actually take the step of seeking treatment for her ailment. His conduct provides a model for Buddhist leaders that we should strive to emulate. It is important to unceasingly value and care

To see illness as an opportunity to transform our karma—this strong spirit and resolve can break through all obstacles and devilish functions and open wide the path to happiness.

for each person. Only by translating this ideal into concrete action can we ensure the happiness of all humanity and the realization of world peace.

BUDDHISM IS FOUND IN COMPASSIONATE ACTION

To what extent can we pray for and offer encouragement to each person? To what extent are we willing to rack our minds to open a way forward for each youth? These efforts may or may not be seen by others, but Buddhism is found only in such compassionate action.

Mr. Toda once declared that religion should focus on helping people become independent and lead strong and vigorous lives. His own conduct perfectly accorded with this. With an earnestness surpassing even that of a parent, he devoted himself to raising new practitioners into people who could confidently take action for *kosen-rufu* even while grappling with their own personal problems.

Once, when a men's division member was ill and sought guidance from him, Mr. Toda immediately set about helping him: "I think you may be vitamin deficient. You have to do something about this. There's a good hospital near my house. You should go there right away to have an injection. I'll go there with you."

Another time, there was a schoolteacher who was being unjustly persecuted at his workplace because of his faith and was threatened with being transferred. As soon as Mr. Toda heard this, he went off to the school that freezing winter morning to personally resolve the situation. "I don't want to see my disciples suffer," he remarked. "If there's anything I can do to help them, I will gladly do it."

In this letter, Nichiren Daishonin writes to lay nun Toki, "[Shijo Kingo's] words saddened me deeply." We can imagine these warm sentiments, filled with such concern for her well-being, touching her deeply and inspiring her to summon fresh resolve.

The Soka Gakkai is a beautiful realm of comrades working together for *kosen-rufu*—a realm built through the all-out struggles of the first three Soka Gakkai presidents, united by the bonds of mentor and disciple and carrying on Nichiren's spirit. Through the efforts of dedicated disciples striving to fulfill the mentor's vision, our SGI network, a precious treasure of humanity, will no doubt spread even more widely throughout the world and far into the future.

If you are unwilling to make efforts to heal yourself, it will be very difficult to cure your illness. One day of life is more valuable than all the treasures of the major world system, so first you must muster sincere faith. This is the meaning of the passage in the seventh volume of

the Lotus Sutra that states that burning a finger as an offering to the Buddha and the Lotus Sutra is better than donating all the treasures of the major world system. A single life is worth more than the major world system. You still have many years ahead of you, and moreover you have encountered the Lotus Sutra. If you live even one day longer, you can accumulate that much more benefit. How truly precious your life is!

Write down your name and age yourself and send your messenger with it to me so that I can pray to the gods of the sun and moon. Your son Iyo-bo[10] is also extremely worried about you, so he will offer the recitation of the verse section of the "Life Span" chapter to those gods. (WND-1, 955)

THE VALUE OF EVEN A SINGLE DAY OF LIFE

A single day of life has a brilliance that nothing can replace; it has immense value and is a paean of joy. To rob someone of life is a grave offense that goes against the fundamental law of the universe. Mr. Toda strictly admonished, "Under no circumstances must you ever kill another."

In our attitude toward illness, we need to be fearless, yet at the same time we must not make light of the situation.

Becoming ill in itself is certainly not a sign of defeat. Even the Buddha, who is said to have "few ills and few worries"

(LSOC, 254), struggles with sickness from time to time. Accordingly, there will be times when we are confronted with illness. The important point above all is not to be defeated mentally or emotionally by the prospect of being ill. Faith is the source of the fighting spirit to stand up to illness. Therefore, as we noted earlier, Nichiren Daishonin first of all talks about the "treasure of faith."

Next, it is only natural that we exert ourselves in practical and concrete ways to get well. To simply think, *I'm practicing Buddhism, so I'll be OK*, or to dismiss an illness as "nothing to worry about," reflects a mistaken understanding of faith and amounts to disrespect for one's own life. It is vital that we take action to "quickly conquer our illness." Therefore, Nichiren admonishes the lay nun Toki not to begrudge making efforts to cure her illness.

The Mystic Law is the fundamental power for defeating the hindrances of illness and death. "Nam-myoho-renge-kyo is like the roar of a lion" ("Reply to Kyo'o," WND-1, 412), Nichiren writes. Of key importance in conquering illness are a positive fighting spirit, an effective curative treatment and a vigorous life force. And in this regard, chanting Nam-myoho-renge-kyo is especially crucial in terms of strengthening ourselves mentally and emotionally, getting the most out of the treatment available to us and summoning forth a strong life force.

In this writing, Nichiren says that we

should "use" our bodies, our lives, which are more valuable than even the universe, to praise and make offerings to the Lotus Sutra. To illustrate this point, he cites a passage from the Lotus Sutra about "burning a finger as an offering." In our Buddhist practice in the Latter Day of the Law, however, the greatest offering we can make to the Mystic Law with our bodies or lives is in the form of our voices chanting and our earnest and sincere efforts to share and spread the Mystic Law.

Therefore, Nichiren says: "If you live even one day longer, you can accumulate that much more benefit. How truly precious your life is!" (WND-1, 955). How valuable and precious is each single day that we can chant Nam-myoho-renge-

kyo and work to further the flow of *kosen-rufu*! How wonderful is each day that we can take part in constructing an eternal realm of peace and happiness based on the Mystic Law, united in spirit with our mentor and together with the Soka Gakkai!

The struggle with illness becomes an opportunity for us to realize this glorious truth. As Nichiren says, "Illness gives rise to the resolve to attain the way" ("The Good Medicine for All Ills," WND-1, 937). If a practitioner who upholds faith in the Mystic Law becomes ill, it definitely has some profound meaning. It could be said that confronting illness is one route to awakening to the eternity of life. President Toda often said, "A person who has overcome a major illness knows how to

Chanting Nam-myoho-renge-kyo is especially crucial in terms of strengthening ourselves mentally and emotionally, getting the most out of the treatment available to us and summoning forth a strong life force.

deeply savor life." Also, those who wage a struggle against illness with such confidence are champions of faith for living long and healthy lives.

A member of the doctors division remarked that people who chant Nam-myoho-renge-kyo in their battle against illness always brim with appreciation and smiles, an attitude that is itself a sign of their victory over their illness.

Of course, people suffer all kinds of sicknesses and diseases, and the severity or degree of their illness varies. In some cases, a person may become bedridden or physically incapacitated. But those who, through chanting, are battling or have battled illness, shine from the depths of their beings. They have nothing to worry about, because their lives are infused with Nam-myoho-renge-kyo. They are assured beyond a doubt of enjoying good fortune and benefit throughout eternity.

MAKE THE 21ST CENTURY A CENTURY OF LIFE

Nichiren Daishonin asks the lay nun Toki to write down her name and age in her own hand and forward it along for him to use in praying for her recovery to the Buddhist gods[11]—the protective functions of the universe.

In a letter to her husband, Toki Jonin, on another occasion, Nichiren writes, "I am as concerned about the illness of your wife, the lay nun Toki, as though it were I myself who is ailing, and day and night I pray to the heavenly gods that she will recover" ("Prayer for the Lay Nun's Recovery," WND-2, 666). He prayed for the well-being of his followers as if their sufferings were his own. In another letter to Toki Jonin, he also says, "I am praying to Heaven that the life of your wife, the lay nun, will be prolonged well into the future" ("Praying for the Prolonging of the Lay Nun's Life," WND-2, 1082).

He constantly prayed for the good health and longevity of his disciples. Such was his immense compassion. And the lay nun Toki—earnestly seeking to reply to Nichiren who had shown such deeply moving concern for her—courageously persevered in faith just as he instructed. Through this united struggle of mentor and disciple, she extended her life by more than 20 years. Hers was a triumphant example of splendidly transforming her karma and going on to live to a healthy, ripe old age. It is recorded that even after Nichiren's passing, the lay nun Toki continued to practice strongly until the end of her days, visiting and seeking guidance in faith from his successor, Nikko Shonin.

Emulating Nichiren's spirit, whenever I learn of a fellow practitioner or one of their family members falling ill, I sincerely chant Nam-myoho-renge-kyo for their recovery. Each day, my wife and I offer strong and deep prayers for the good health, longevity, prosperity and safety of all our members everywhere.

Let us make the 21st century a century of life! Let us make it a century of good health and longevity! May all of you, our infinitely precious members, who are shining examples of such an era, live out each irreplaceable day to the fullest, winning over all obstacles and creating immeasurable and boundless value! My wife and I are always wholeheartedly praying for this every day, and we will continue to do so throughout our lives.

NOTES:

1. Nichiren Daishonin composed this letter at Mount Minobu in 1279, when he was 58. It is addressed to the lay nun Toki.

2. The lay nun Toki: The wife of Toki Jonin. When she married Toki Jonin, she had been widowed by her first husband and had a son from that marriage. Her marriage with Toki Jonin produced two more children—a boy and a girl. When Toki Jonin became a lay priest, she became a lay nun, calling herself Myojo (Wonderful Eternity). Though suffering from illness herself, she looked after Toki Jonin's mother until the end of the latter's life. Her two sons became priest-disciples of Nichiren.

3. This refers to the Declaration for the Abolition of Nuclear Weapons made by second Soka Gakkai president Josei Toda before a gathering of 50,000 Soka Gakkai youth at the Mitsuzawa Stadium in Yokohama, on September 8, 1957. This declaration became the starting point of the Soka Gakkai's activities for peace.

4. The "Medicine King" chapter of the Lotus Sutra says: "If there are those who have made up their minds and wish to gain supreme enlightenment, they would do well to burn a finger or one toe of their foot as an offering to the buddha towers. It is better than offering one's realm and cities, wife and children, or the mountains, forests, rivers, and lakes in the lands of the major world system, or all of their precious treasures" (LSOC, 326). Based on this passage, Nichiren states that the value of even one day of life exceeds that of all the treasures in the major world system. According to ancient Indian cosmology, one major world system comprises one billion worlds, and hence it is also referred to as the thousand-millionfold world.

5. Shijo Kingo: One of Nichiren's leading followers. His full name and title were Shijo Nakatsukasa Saburo Saemon-no-jo Yorimoto. As a samurai retainer, he served the Ema family, a branch of the ruling Hojo clan. Kingo was well versed in both medicine and the martial arts. He is said to have converted to Nichiren's teachings around 1256. When Nichiren was taken to Tatsunokuchi to be beheaded in 1271, Shijo Kingo accompanied him, resolved to die by his side.

6. *Ryo* (Jpn): A unit of weight in Japan that was modeled after that of ancient China. One *ryo* was equivalent to about 37.5 grams, though the exact amount of one *ryo* differed according to the historical period.

7. Nichiren writes: "In this age [of the Latter Day of the Law], it is as natural for a woman to change her fixed karma by practicing the Lotus Sutra as it is for rice to ripen in fall or chrysanthemums to bloom in winter" (WND-1, 955).

8. This is based on the passage in the "Life Span" chapter of the Lotus Sutra that reads, "We beg you to cure us and let us live out our lives!" (LSOC, 269). This is in the section that tells the parable of the outstanding physician, who imparts "good medicine" (Myoho-renge-kyo) to his children who have "drunk poison" (succumbed to delusion) and implore him to cure their illness. The episode is a metaphor for the Buddha bestowing the Mystic Law on all living beings in order to fundamentally free them from suffering.

9. *The Dhammapada: Sayings of the Buddha,* translated by Thomas Cleary (New York: Bantam Books, 1994), p. 43.

10. Iyo-bo (1252–1317): The son of the lay nun Toki. He became Nichiren's disciple and took the name Nitcho, one of the six senior priests.

11. Rather than primary objects of belief or devotion, Buddhism views gods as functioning to support and protect the Buddha, the Law and practitioners.

STUDY GUIDE

The following is a summary of points from SGI President Ikeda's lecture.

■ The lay nun Toki, to whom this letter was written, had faced illness for a long time. Nichiren Daishonin sought to encourage her, saying that she could improve her health and prolong her life based on faith in Nam-myoho-renge-kyo.

■ Karma is created through our thoughts, words and deeds. At some point in the future, our actions impact our lives either positively or negatively, depending on the nature of our actions.

■ *Fixed* or *immutable karma* appears at a set time and in a set form, while karma that does not adhere to a set time or form is called *unfixed* or *mutable.*

■ In this writing, Nichiren uses the term *fixed karma* in reference to one's life span.

■ Even fixed karma can be changed through the power of faith in the "highly effective medicine" (*The Lotus Sutra and Its Opening and Closing Sutras*, p. 269) of the Lotus Sutra.

THE "LIFE SPAN" CHAPTER REVEALS THE ETERNITY OF LIFE

■ A single day of life is more valuable than all the treasures of the universe.

■ Nichiren wished to impart a passionate will to live to his disciples, especially the lay nun, who had grown weary of her health troubles.

■ The "Life Span of the Thus Come One" chapter of the Lotus Sutra expounds the essence of all Shakyamuni Buddha's teachings—the eternal nature of the Buddha's life, which applies equally to all life.

■ Through practicing Nichiren's teachings and chanting Nam-myoho-renge-kyo, all people can experience the vast expanse of life as perceived by the Buddha.

■ Nichiren Buddhist practice exists to help people transcend suffering and experience eternal happiness.

■ SGI President Ikeda: "Life is tenacious; it is endowed with the impulse to survive and the power to heal. The 'highly effective medicine' for drawing forth these innate properties is the Mystic Law. Ultimately, it is we ourselves who cure our illness, while the decision to undertake this battle to do so arises from faith."

■ Illness can be an opportunity to transform our karma, to strengthen our resolve to break through all obstacles and devilish functions, and savor everlasting happiness.

A DISCIPLE'S WELL-BEING IS ALWAYS THE MENTOR'S FOREMOST CONCERN

- Understanding the temperaments of his disciples and respecting their differences, Nichiren urged the lay nun Toki to seek the assistance of Shijo Kingo, a physician and dedicated practitioner.

- He explained the way for them to maintain harmonious relations so that they would readily and warmly support one another.

- Nichiren's conduct provides a model for Buddhist leaders that we should strive to emulate. It is important to unceasingly value and care for each person.

THE VALUE OF EVEN A SINGLE DAY OF LIFE

- Illness itself is not a sign of defeat. What matters most is not to let the prospect of illness defeat us mentally or emotionally.

- Through conviction in our Buddhist practice, we can bring out a vigorous life force to win over illness and find the wisdom to seek practical and effective care.

- We cannot be dismissive about illness, thinking that since we practice Buddhism, everything will work itself out. Rather, we must have faith and take action.

- A single day of life is a great treasure. Nichiren says, "If you live even one day longer, you can accumulate that much more benefit" (WND-1, 955).

- Every day, we have the opportunity to chant Nam-myoho-renge-kyo and take action based on our Buddhist practice for ourselves and for the sake of others.

- Nichiren also says, "Illness gives rise to the resolve to attain the way" (WND-1, 937). Fighting illness can awaken in us a profound appreciation for the value of life, the eternity of life and the hope-inspiring power of the Mystic Law.

- Based on Nichiren's urgent and clear encouragement and the shared struggle of mentor and disciple, the lay nun Toki transformed her karma, extended her life by more than 20 years and continued to practice strongly until the end of her days.

(3)

"Reply to Sairen-bo"

Striving With a Shared Commitment for Kosen-rufu—The Eternal Bonds of Mentor and Disciple

The Passage for Study in This Lecture

In your letter you mention that you became a disciple of mine and pledged to follow me at the beginning of the second month, and that from now on, though you may not measure up to others, you would be most pleased and honored if I would continue to count you among my disciples.

The sutra says, "Those persons who had heard the Law dwelled here and there in various Buddha lands, constantly reborn in company with their teachers" [see *The Lotus Sutra and Its Opening and Closing Sutras*, p. 178]. It also says, "If one stays close to the teachers of the Law, one will speedily gain the bodhisattva way. By following and learning from these teachers one will see Buddhas as numerous as Ganges sands" [see LSOC, 208].

A commentary states, "Originally one followed this Buddha and for the first time conceived the desire to seek the way. And by following this Buddha again, one will reach the stage where there is no retrogression." Another commentary states, "In the beginning one followed this Buddha or bodhisattva and formed a bond with him, and so it will be through this Buddha or bodhisattva that one will attain one's goal."

When I consider these passages of the sutra and the commentaries, I wonder if you and I have not been pledged to each other as teacher and disciple from countless kalpas in the past. You and I have been born together in this defiled age of the Latter Day of the Law, in the country of Japan in the southern continent of Jambudvipa, and with the utmost reverence we chant with our mouths Nam-myoho-renge-kyo, the ultimate reason for which the Buddhas appear in the world; we believe in it in our hearts, embrace it with our bodies, and delight in it with our hands. Has all of this not come about solely because of some bond of karma we share from the past?

When I look at the situation in Japan, I find that the devil king of the sixth heaven has entered into the bodies of wise persons, transforming correct teachers into erroneous teachers, and good teachers into bad teachers. This is what the sutra means when it says, "Evil demons will take possession of others" [LSOC, 233].

Although I, Nichiren, am not a man of wisdom, the devil king of the sixth heaven has attempted to take possession of my body. But I have for some time been taking such great care that he now no longer comes near me. Therefore, because the power of the heavenly devil is ineffectual against me, he instead possesses the ruler and his high officials, or foolish priests such as Ryokan, and causes them to hate me.

Be that as it may, one should understand that, at present, when it comes to teachers, there is a difference between correct teachers and erroneous teachers, between good teachers and bad teachers. One should shun those who are erroneous or evil, and associate with those who are correct and good. Even if their virtue is known throughout the country and their wisdom is as bright as the sun and moon, one should recognize that teachers who slander the Lotus Sutra are evil teachers and erroneous teachers, and refrain from approaching them. (*The Writings of Nichiren Daishonin*, vol. 1, pp. 309–10)

So day and night I ponder the important doctrines, and hour by hour, moment by moment, I savor the principle that allows us to attain Buddhahood. And because I pass the time in this fashion, though months and years go by, it does not seem long at all, and the hours that have elapsed do not seem like many. It is similar to the case described in the sutra when the two Buddhas Shakyamuni and Many Treasures, seated side by side in the treasure tower, nodded in approval over the wonderful principles of the Lotus Sutra, and although fifty small kalpas had elapsed, because of the supernatural powers of the Buddha, it seemed to the great crowd assembled there like no more than half a day.

Among all the persons since the beginning of our present kalpa who have incurred the wrath of their parents or their rulers and have been exiled to distant islands, there can be none who overflow with joy as we do. Therefore, wherever we dwell and practice the single vehicle [the Lotus Sutra], that place will be the Capital of Eternally Tranquil Light. And, without having to take a step, those who are our disciples and lay supporters can view Eagle Peak in India and day and night will go to and from the Land of Eternally Tranquil Light that has

existed for all time. What a truly inexpressible joy it is!

So delightful is the thought that I will now make a promise to you. If you should be released quickly from exile and return to the capital, although the lord of Kamakura may continue to refuse pardon to Nichiren, I will call upon the heavenly deities, and when I have returned to Kamakura, I will write to you in Kyoto. If I should be pardoned first and return to Kamakura, I will call upon the heavenly gods to make certain that you are able to return home to the capital. (WND-1, 312–13)

LECTURE

The bonds of mentor and disciple in Buddhism are eternal, extending across the three existences—past, present and future. This is because both mentor and disciple dedicate their lives to the original wish deep in their hearts to widely propagate the Mystic Law for the benefit of all people. This original wish is the great desire or vow of the Buddha, and it serves as the driving force behind the altruistic practice of bodhisattvas. Mentor and disciple in Buddhism are comrades in a shared struggle, who devote themselves to fulfilling their vow to guide all humanity to happiness.

In the letter we are studying this time, "Reply to Sairen-bo," Nichiren Daishonin clarifies that he and Sairen-bo—whom he had met during his exile on Sado Island—share an eternal bond of mentor and disciple from countless *kalpas*[i] in the past. "Reply to Sairen-bo" is thought to have been composed on April 13, 1272. For reasons unclear, Sairen-bo, a learned priest of the Tendai school of Buddhism, had also been exiled to Sado. He was already there when Nichiren arrived toward the end of 1271. Sairen-bo met Nichiren and subsequently converted to his teachings in February 1272.

Sairen-bo also appears to have encountered persecution because of his association with Nichiren, who had incurred the enmity of the government and lived under constant threat of attack by Pure Land (Nembutsu) believers and others. The Daishonin begins this letter by urging Sairen-bo to exercise caution, saying, "Take great care when you come to see me after dark" (WND-1, 309). These words reflect Nichiren's sincere concern for Sairen-bo's safety.

Nichiren had just been transferred from Tsukahara to Ichinosawa earlier that same month,[2] and it seems that the local official under whose custody he had been placed was initially extremely antagonistic toward him. Speaking of this in another writing, Nichiren states, "The headman…treated me with greater malice than if I had been a lifelong enemy of [his] parents or a foe from some previous existence" ("Letter to the Lay Priest Ichinosawa," WND-1, 529). Also, the area abounded with people looking for any opportunity to kill him.[3]

As Nichiren's disciple, Sairen-bo also ran the risk of encountering such adversities, but his spirit to seek the Dai-shonin's teachings never wavered. He knew the joy of having found and of receiving instruction from the correct teacher. For that reason, he could endure any hardship. Nichiren was undefeated by his exile to an inhospitable land where he was exposed to the elements year-round and never knew which day might be his last. We can well imagine that

Nichiren's steadfast perseverance in the struggle to refute the erroneous and reveal the true inspired Sairen-bo and heightened his elation in having chosen to live as Nichiren's disciple.

Others who became Nichiren's followers on Sado—such as the lay priest Abutsu-bo and his wife, the lay nun Sen-nichi; and the lay priest and lay nun of Ko—demonstrated the same unwavering spirit as Sairen-bo. Considered from a secular standpoint, it would have been safer not to go anywhere near Nichiren, who was kept under close watch by the government and targeted for attack by Pure Land believers. But the joy of encountering a great teacher and struggling together with him completely outweighed any fear or misgivings about facing persecution themselves.

Through overcoming hardships alongside him, Nichiren's disciples on Sado came to appreciate deeply that no way of life was more profound than striving with the same spirit as one's mentor for the sake of Buddhism. Having come into direct contact with Nichiren's immense spirit, his expansive state of life and the depth of his charac-ter and integrity, they must have been genuinely happy to support and assist this truly great teacher of the Law.

By practicing Buddhism as taught by a teacher who has overcome immense persecution and who embodies the Law, we can experience the true power of the Buddha and the power of the Law[4] in our own lives. Disciples who could

SGI President Ikeda sings together with Soka Junior and Senior High School students in Kodaira, Tokyo, March 16, 2004.

recognize what a priceless treasure this teaching is appeared on Sado, Nichiren's place of exile.

In your letter you mention that you became a disciple of mine and pledged to follow me at the beginning of the second month, and that from now on, though you may not measure up to others, you would be most pleased and honored if I would continue to count you among my disciples.

The sutra says, "Those persons who had heard the Law dwelled here and there in various Buddha lands, constantly reborn in company with their teachers" [see LSOC, 178]. It also says, "If one stays close to the teachers of the Law, one will speedily gain the bodhisattva way. By following and learning from these teachers one will see Buddhas as numerous as Ganges sands" [see LSOC, 208].

A commentary states, "Originally one followed this Buddha and for the first time conceived the desire to seek the way. And by following this Buddha again, one will reach the stage where there is no retrogression."[5] Another commentary states, "In the beginning one followed this Buddha or bodhisattva and formed a bond with him, and so it will be through this Buddha or bodhisattva that one will attain one's goal."[6]

When I consider these passages of the sutra and the commentaries, I wonder if you and I have not been pledged to each other as teacher and disciple from countless kalpas in the past. You and I have been born together in this defiled age of the

Latter Day of the Law, in the country of Japan in the southern continent of Jambudvipa,[7] and with the utmost reverence we chant with our mouths Nam-myoho-renge-kyo, the ultimate reason for which the Buddhas appear in the world; we believe in it in our hearts, embrace it with our bodies, and delight in it with our hands. Has all of this not come about solely because of some bond of karma we share from the past? (WND-1, 309)

THE PATH OF A DISCIPLE

Sairen-bo always maintained a sincere seeking spirit in faith. Nichiren Daishonin writes to him, "You mention that . . . though you may not measure up to others, you would be most pleased and honored if I would continue to count you among my disciples" (WND-1, 309). As we can glean from this, Sairen-bo regarded it as an unequalled source of fulfillment to be considered Nichiren's disciple and was deeply committed to remaining true to the path he had chosen to walk with his mentor.

The path of a disciple is a great path of unflagging seeking spirit and unceasing gratitude. Walking this path throughout one's life is the ideal of human existence as taught in Buddhism. To deviate from it can lead one to fall into a misguided path of arrogance and ingratitude.

At a general meeting of the Soka Kyoiku Gakkai (forerunner of the Soka Gakkai) before World War II—at which

In Nichiren Buddhism, the promise of mentor and disciple means being born together in the same world in this latter age of the widespread propagation of the Law and chanting and teaching others about Nam-myoho-renge-kyo—the supreme teaching of Buddhism and the ultimate reason for which Buddhas appear in the world.

the organization's first president, Tsunesaburo Makiguchi, was present—Josei Toda, then general director, remarked: "Nikko Shonin had not the least desire to surpass or outdo Nichiren Daishonin. Likewise, our duty is to faithfully follow President Makiguchi's teachings, put them into practice and manifest them in our daily lives.... Disciples must follow the path of the disciple. In both word and deed, we have to implement President Makiguchi's teachings in our lives."[8]

In Buddhism, the teacher or mentor represents an exemplary role model for how we should live our lives. To place our faith in a correct teacher means practicing exactly as that person teaches. By doing so, we can break out of our narrow, self-limiting life-state to live a more profound and expansive existence.

In any field of endeavor, people of the highest caliber are sure to have, in some form or another, a teacher or mentor who serves as a role model or inspiration for them; they have invariably walked the path of a student or disciple.

It is the way of mentors to wish for the success of their disciples and to hold each of them dear. It is the way of mentors to give their all to imparting everything they know to their disciples. The relationship between mentor and disciple constitutes an infinitely beautiful realm of the heart and a lofty spiritual bond.

THE PROFOUND KARMIC TIES OF MENTOR AND DISCIPLE—BORN TOGETHER IN LIFETIME AFTER LIFETIME

In response to Sairen-bo's communication of his joy in having become a disciple, Nichiren Daishonin cites a passage from "The Parable of the Phantom City" chapter of the Lotus Sutra and goes on to discuss the profound tie or pledge that links mentor and disciple: "Those persons who had heard the Law dwelled here and there in various Buddha lands, constantly reborn in company with their teachers" (see LSOC, 178). This passage clarifies that the bond shared by Shakyamuni and his voice-hearer disciples was not limited to that lifetime alone but was a relationship or connection existing from a time in the distant past, major world system dust particle *kalpas* ago.[9] It indicates that the disciples have constantly been born in various Buddha lands together with their teacher Shakyamuni, carrying out bodhisattva practice alongside him.

These voice-hearer disciples of Shakyamuni—voice-hearers in form, but in truth bodhisattvas—rejoice when they "recall" how they had in fact carried out bodhisattva practice together with their teacher over countless previous lifetimes.

Lives dedicated to the deepest human wish for the happiness of self and others, striving in a spirit of the oneness of mentor and disciple, from

41

the infinite past into the eternal future—nothing could be more sublime than this.

Next, Nichiren cites a passage from "The Teacher of the Law" chapter, which explains that to follow and learn from a teacher will bring one to see Buddhas as numerous as the sands of the Ganges River (see WND-1, 309); that is to say, it is the path of eternal happiness. Nichiren also cites the words of the great teachers T'ien-t'ai and Miao-lo of China, which underscore the importance of following the path of mentor and disciple if one hopes to attain the Buddha way.

Based on these passages from the sutra and related commentaries, he says to Sairen-bo, "I wonder if you and I have not been pledged to each other as teacher and disciple from countless kalpas in the past" (WND-1, 309). He thus suggests that they share deep karmic ties as mentor and disciple. The bond of the mentor-disciple relationship in Buddhism is forged by a pledge that continues over the three existences—past, present and future.

Next, Nichiren says, "You and I have been born together in this defiled age of the Latter Day of the Law" (WND-1, 309). Although this statement is addressed specifically to Sairen-bo, we can read it to include all of us. Precisely because this is the "defiled age of the Latter Day of the Law," a time of unprecedented spiritual pollution and confusion, everyone in the depths of his

or her life seeks the great teaching of hope of the Mystic Law. In that sense, the Latter Day is the time for the propagation of this ultimate Law that can free people from suffering at the most fundamental level and lead them to genuine happiness.

In Nichiren Buddhism, the promise of mentor and disciple means being born together in the same world in this latter age of the widespread propagation of the Law and chanting and teaching others about Nam-myoho-renge-kyo— the supreme teaching of Buddhism and the ultimate reason for which Buddhas appear in the world. What a noble and glorious promise this is! And we dedicate our lives to propagating the Mystic Law in this way, Nichiren says, as a result of "some bond of karma we share from the past" (WND-1, 309), stretching back immeasurable *kalpas* ago. What a profound and powerful spiritual bond we share!

Let's dedicate ourselves to fulfilling the promise of mentor and disciple and advance together for *kosen-rufu*. If we stay true to this promise from the remote past, we will without a doubt savor a lofty state of life and make our way triumphantly on the path of our mission—forever as Bodhisattvas of the Earth and forever in rhythm with the Mystic Law.

When I look at the situation in Japan, I find that the devil king of the sixth

VOICE-HEARERS

The term *voice-hearer* (Skt *shravaka*) originally meant those disciples who were alive during the time of Shakyamuni and could hear his voice as he taught the Law. Mahayana sutras other than the Lotus Sutra describe them as disciples who had "heard" the teaching of the four noble truths[1] and aspired to attain the state of arhat (a state of having completed all learning) and then the nirvana of no remainder (a state in which the body and mind are extinguished). Such sutras condemn the voice-hearers as being unable to attain enlightenment, because, in their pursuit of personal emancipation, they overlook compassionate practice for others.

The Lotus Sutra clarifies the true nature of the voice-hearers, referring to them not as Buddhists seeking release through annihilation, but rather as those who "take the voice of the Buddha way and cause it to be heard by all." The Lotus Sutra predicts that they, too, will attain enlightenment.

In the doctrine of the Ten Worlds, the seventh world is the realm of the voice-hearers, also known as the world of learning. In Nichiren Buddhism, the world of learning is the state in which individuals are dedicated to self-improvement through study of their predecessors, as compared to the realm of cause-awakened ones in which they seek understanding through their own observations and efforts.

Nichiren Daishonin considered it highly significant that only the Lotus Sutra guarantees the enlightenment of the voice-hearers; without this, the Ten Worlds could not be considered mutually inclusive and Buddhism could not be considered capable of leading all people to happiness.

---

1. Four noble truths: A fundamental doctrine of Buddhism clarifying the cause of suffering and the way of emancipation. The four noble truths are the truth of suffering, the truth of the origin of suffering, the truth of the cessation of suffering and the truth of the path to the cessation of suffering.

heaven has entered into the bodies of wise persons, transforming correct teachers into erroneous teachers, and good teachers into bad teachers. This is what the sutra means when it says, "Evil demons will take possession of others" [LSOC, 233].

Although I, Nichiren, am not a man of wisdom, the devil king of the sixth heaven has attempted to take possession of my body. But I have for some time been taking such great care that he now no longer comes near me. Therefore, because the power of the heavenly devil is ineffectual against me, he instead possesses the ruler and his high officials, or foolish priests such as Ryokan, and causes them to hate me.

Be that as it may, one should understand that, at present, when it comes to teachers, there is a difference between correct teachers and erroneous teachers, between good teachers and bad teachers. One should shun those who are erroneous or evil, and associate with those who are correct and good. Even if their virtue is known throughout the country and their wisdom is as bright as the sun and moon, one should recognize that teachers who slander the Lotus Sutra are evil teachers and erroneous teachers, and refrain from approaching them. (WND-1, 309–10)

True Buddhist teachers set an example of personally battling and triumphing over devilish functions. Those who not only overcome devilish functions in their own lives but also strive to teach and show all people how they can surmount such obstacles are true teachers in Buddhism.

TRUE "GOOD TEACHERS" ARE THOSE WHO HAVE VANQUISHED THE DEVIL KING OF THE SIXTH HEAVEN

There is no greater misfortune than that of supporting and following erroneous or misguided leaders. Nichiren Daishonin tells us that when it comes to teachers, there are correct teachers and erroneous teachers, good teachers and bad teachers, and he says that we need the ability to distinguish among them.

What he is emphasizing here is the frightening aspect of negative influences and evil friends. When our inner darkness or negativity—our fundamental delusion—is activated through evil influences, our tendencies of greed, anger and foolishness intensify, our judgment becomes clouded, and our lives begin a downward spiral into confusion, wrongdoing and misery.

In this writing, Nichiren admonishes that if we associate with evil persons, then we will naturally come to follow their teaching in perhaps two or three out of 10 instances, and will in the end become evil people ourselves (see WND-1, 310).[10] That is how insidious and frightening erroneous teachers and evil teachers can be. For precisely this reason, making resolute efforts to battle evil together with correct teachers and good teachers is crucial in revealing our inherent Buddhahood.

Erroneous and evil teachers are the ultimate negative influences or evil friends. Such individuals are the embodiment of what the sutras call "worms within the lion's body"[11]—influences that destroy Buddhism from within and bring misery to others. Nichiren further explains that erroneous and evil teachers arise because they are "possessed by evil demons" (see LSOC, 233). In other words, the devil king of the sixth heaven—the heavenly devil—enters their bodies, causing them to become deranged. References to the devil king of the sixth heaven entering a person's body simply mean that their own fundamental darkness has been activated.

Fundamental darkness[12] refers to fundamental ignorance of the Law, which manifests as not believing in, doubting and disrespecting the Law. This darkness or negativity is activated in our lives when our faith becomes clouded, our practice weakens, and we cease to feel the power of the Buddha and power of the Law—on account of such things as, for example, becoming attached to erroneous teachings or obsessed with a selfish desire for fame and fortune.

In this writing, based on the principle of evil demons possessing one's body,[13] Nichiren teaches that the devil king of the sixth heaven may possess the bodies of even people of wisdom. He also states that the devil king has tried to take possession of his own body. We can read this as a warning that we mustn't underestimate the devilish functions that pervade the universe. But he indicates that he is now impervious to the devil king, saying: "I have for some time been taking such great care that [the devil king of the sixth heaven] now no longer comes near me. [Consequently,] the power of the heavenly devil is ineffectual against me." His assertion, "I have for some time been taking such great care," means that he has been prepared for an onslaught of obstacles and devils and that he has made and upheld a vow to triumph over them without fail. In this way, Nichiren teaches us that we can definitely beat devilish functions if we are firmly resolved to do so.

THE ESSENTIAL QUALITIES OF "CORRECT AND GOOD TEACHERS"

Who, then, are "correct and good teachers"? What are their essential qualities? Nichiren Daishonin's criteria are perfectly clear: They are teachers who battle the three powerful enemies, and who chant and propagate the Mystic Law without begrudging their lives. Correct teachers are those who will stand up to evil and injustice to protect the people.

In "Reply to Sairen-bo," Nichiren clarifies that the decisive criterion distinguishing good teachers from bad is ultimately their ability to defeat the devil king of the sixth heaven. True Buddhist teachers set an example of

personally battling and triumphing over devilish functions. Those who not only overcome devilish functions in their own lives but also strive to teach and show all people how they can surmount such obstacles are true teachers in Buddhism.

By contrast, individuals who easily give in to devilish functions, no matter how wise or virtuous they might appear, will end up slandering the Law, showing hostility toward the practitioners of the Lotus Sutra and destroying Buddhism. Nichiren unequivocally declares that teachers who try to pass themselves off as having a profound understanding of Buddhism, while never having battled hardships and obstacles themselves, are all erroneous teachers; whereas he himself, having encountered repeated attacks and repression, is a genuine teacher of the Law.[14]

Conquering obstacles and devils and embodying the Law are key qualifications for "correct and good teachers" who can connect people directly to the Law through the example of their own behavior. Such teachers may be described as "correct" in terms of the truth of the Law they uphold, and "good" in terms of their compassion to transmit the Law to others and to impart benefit in the form of "removing suffering and bringing joy" (see *The Record of the Orally Transmitted Teachings*, p. 173).

Here, let's confirm the three main qualities of a "correct and good teacher" as found in this writing. Such a teacher

THE DEVIL KING OF THE SIXTH HEAVEN

In Buddhism, devils (Skt *mara*) represent the destructive impulses that obstruct a person's Buddhist practice. *Mara* is also the name of the devil king who attempts, but fails, to prevent Shakyamuni from attaining Buddhahood and from teaching others the nature of that enlightenment.

The devil king of the sixth heaven is considered the ruler of the Heaven of Freely Enjoying Things Conjured by Others, which is another way of saying he represents power gained through abusive authority and subordination of the weak. Since the Lotus Sutra is a teaching of freedom and self-empowerment of the most profound degree, the devil king seeks to interfere with its development, practice and propagation.

The devil king is also considered a manifestation of the fundamental darkness inherent in life. In Nichiren Buddhism, the fundamental darkness is a state of delusion in which one denies or is ignorant of the essential truth, namely that Nam-myoho-renge-kyo is one's own life. Nichiren Daishonin states: "Both good and evil are inherent even in those at the highest stage of perfect enlightenment. The fundamental nature of enlightenment manifests itself as [the protective forces] Brahma and Shakra, whereas the fundamental darkness manifests itself as the devil king of the sixth heaven" ("The Treatment of Illness", *The Writings of Nichiren Daishonin*, vol. 1, p. 1113).

Fundamental darkness is not destroyed by Buddhahood, nor is Buddhahood destroyed by fundamental darkness, since life at every moment possesses each of the Ten Worlds from hell to Buddhahood. Instead, the continued practice of Buddhism in the face of obstacles establishes Buddhahood as the dominant life-condition, thus minimizing the influence of the devil king.

must be (1) a person of wisdom who sees through the devilish nature that is the fundamental evil inherent in human life and who reveals the Mystic Law that is the fundamental good; (2) a person of courage whose life is dedicated to the correct teaching of Buddhism and who continues fighting against evil without being led astray by the devilish nature; (3) a person of compassion who is always concerned with relieving people's suffering and imparting joy and actively works to realize happiness for oneself and others.

Once people have found or encountered such a "correct and good teacher," all that remains for them to do as disciples is to rise up together with their teacher and earnestly contribute to *kosen-rufu*, as well as to battle resolutely against any negative forces that seek to obstruct that great objective.

In reading the letters Nichiren addressed to Sairen-bo,[15] we find many passages in which he calls on his disciple to join him in the struggle for *kosen-rufu*. It is when the disciple stands up for *kosen-rufu* in accord with the mentor's call and wins in life that mentor and disciple become truly united and one. The lives of mentor and disciple resonate in harmony with one another, and the power of the Buddha and the power of the Law pulse in the life of the disciple.

There is no path to attaining Buddhahood apart from the path of struggling for *kosen-rufu* together with one's mentor.

So day and night I ponder the important doctrines, and hour by hour, moment by moment, I savor the principle that allows us to attain Buddhahood. And because I pass the time in this fashion, though months and years go by, it does not seem long at all, and the hours that have elapsed do not seem like many. It is similar to the case described in the sutra when the two Buddhas Shakyamuni and Many Treasures, seated side by side in the treasure tower, nodded in approval over the wonderful principles of the Lotus Sutra, and although fifty small kalpas had elapsed, because of the supernatural powers of the Buddha, it seemed to the great crowd assembled there like no more than half a day.

Among all the persons since the beginning of our present kalpa who have incurred the wrath of their parents or their rulers and have been exiled to distant islands, there can be none who overflow with joy as we do. Therefore, wherever we dwell and practice the single vehicle [the Lotus Sutra], that place will be the Capital of Eternally Tranquil Light. And, without having to take a step, those who are our disciples and lay supporters can view Eagle Peak in India and day and night will go to and from the Land of Eternally Tranquil Light that has existed for all time. What a truly inexpressible joy it is! (WND-1, 312–13)

THE GREAT JOY OF THE SHARED COMMITMENT OF MENTOR AND DISCIPLE

Nichiren Daishonin writes, "Hour by hour, moment by moment, I savor the principle that allows us to attain Buddhahood" (WND-1, 312). When we follow "correct and good teachers" and practice as they instruct, our lives will come into sync with theirs. The great inner joy of teachers who are one with the Law inspires and animates their disciples. For a disciple, there is no greater joy than following a "correct and good teacher" and engaging together in the struggle to propagate the Mystic Law.

This is the joy of the world of Buddhahood that vanquishes even fundamental darkness. It is the greatest of all joys that can beat back any adversity. Therefore, Nichiren says: "Ah, how assuring! How assuring!" and "If we continue to think in this way, then, though we may be exiles, we have cause to be joyful in both body and mind!" (WND-1, 312). He is expressing that even amid great persecution, it is possible to savor a state of life overflowing with the boundless joy of the Law.

The teaching of the Mystic Law is passed from mentor to disciple when the disciple summons up the courage to propagate that teaching, with a lion's roar echoing the vow of the mentor. The 20-line verse section of the "Encouraging Devotion" chapter of the Lotus Sutra, which describes the three powerful enemies of Buddhism, is a "lion's roar" of bodhisattvas vowing to propagate the Lotus Sutra even at the risk of intense persecution. Nichiren says with regard to this "lion's roar" (Jpn *shishi-ku*): "The first *shi* of the word *shishi,* or 'lion' [which means 'teacher'], is the Wonderful Law that is passed on by the teacher. The second *shi* [which means 'child'] is the Wonderful Law as it is received by the disciples. The 'roar' [*ku*] is the sound of the teacher and the disciples chanting in unison" (OTT, 111).

The life-state in which one savors the boundless joy of the Law endures for eternity. And this eternity is condensed

> The teaching of the Mystic Law is passed from mentor to disciple when the disciple summons up the courage to propagate that teaching, with a lion's roar echoing the vow of the mentor.

in the deep and powerful resolve of a disciple who, acting in unity with the mentor, overcomes hardships and conquers devilish functions. It is in this moment-to-moment state of life that we can savor the immense joy of attaining Buddhahood.

THE PLACE WHERE WE DWELL BECOMES THE "CAPITAL OF ETERNALLY TRANQUIL LIGHT"

Nichiren Daishonin and Sairen-bo had both come to Sado as exiles. That's why Nichiren expresses the joy he shares with his disciple as follows, "Among all the persons since the beginning of our present kalpa who have incurred the wrath of their parents or their rulers and have been exiled to distant islands, there can be none who overflow with joy as we do" (WND-1, 313). And even though he and Sairen-bo found themselves in bitter exile on Sado, he declares, "Wherever we dwell and practice the single vehicle [the Lotus Sutra], that place will be the Capital of Eternally Tranquil Light" (WND-1, 313).

When we uphold the supreme teaching of the Mystic Law, our lives as well as the place where we dwell come to shine with immense brilliance. When we challenge ourselves to propagate the Mystic Law, firmly resolving that the place where we are now is the place of our Buddhist practice and the stage on which we will carry out our human revolution, then that place will become the

Capital of Eternally Tranquil Light—the place where the Buddha dwells.

Nichiren writes, "Day and night [we] will go to and from the Land of Eternally Tranquil Light that has existed for all time" (WND-1, 313). Our daily practice of chanting Nam-myoho-renge-kyo and reciting the sutra is a ceremony of inner rejuvenation in which we return instantly to our eternal abode—our "home" within the eternal dimension of life—to recharge ourselves and get ready to set off spiritedly once more to grapple with our struggles in the real world.

So delightful is the thought that I will now make a promise to you. If you should be released quickly from exile and return to the capital, although the lord of Kamakura[16] may continue to refuse pardon to Nichiren, I will call upon the heavenly deities, and when I have returned to Kamakura, I will write to you in Kyoto. If I should be pardoned first and return to Kamakura, I will call upon the heavenly gods to make certain that you are able to return home to the capital. (WND-1, 313)

THE VICTORY OF MENTOR AND DISCIPLE IS THE VICTORY OF BUDDHISM

Lastly, Nichiren Daishonin encourages Sairen-bo by making a promise reflecting

A YOUTHFUL DIARY:
A Record of the Mentor–Disciple Relationship

The following is an excerpt from SGI President Ikeda's preface to A Youthful Diary, *the personal accounts of his daily life as a youth.*

Around the beginning of 1949, a year and a half after I became a Soka Gakkai member, I began working for the publishing company headed by Josei Toda. Working for him day after day, I came to realize that he never for a moment forgot his teacher, Tsunesaburo Makiguchi, the first Soka Gakkai president. Mr. Makiguchi had been sent to prison along with Mr. Toda and died there during the war at the age of 73. Mr. Toda saw himself as the heir to his teacher's faith and convictions, firmly dedicated to carrying out Mr. Makiguchi's unfulfilled hopes for widespread propagation of Nichiren Daishonin's teachings. The fervency with which he devoted his life to the realization of that goal made him in my eyes a figure of shining nobility. . . .

Deep in my heart was one single thought—how I could best help to fulfill my teacher's goals and ambitions. I saw myself as the vessel of Mr. Makiguchi's and Mr. Toda's hopes. This meant working tirelessly on a practical level to protect the precious Soka Gakkai membership. (pp. vii–viii)

The following entries are included in A Youthful Diary:

Wednesday, November 29 (1950). Sleet.
(Mr. Toda) thoroughly instilled in me that I must carry on and fulfill the task that he, my teacher, has begun.

In the afternoon, he went to the Ministry of Finance and returned shivering. He smiled and said, "How cold the world is!"

"Daisaku," he told me, "I am not defeated. I lost a battle, but that is past. The real fight starts from now."

Resolve blazed up anew within me that I must strive never to let anyone so much as point a finger at Mr. Toda or at the Soka Gakkai.

Thursday, February 22 (1951). Light rain.
Fourteen gathered for a lecture on "The True Aspect of All Phenomena." Mr. Toda asked us several questions concerning the relationship between the first and second parts of "Expedient Means," the second Lotus Sutra chapter. Pained by my own lack of study. Must learn by watching my seniors. . . .

I want us all to carry out splendidly our teacher's noble will. Now Mr. Toda and the Gakkai are being slandered and maliciously spoken ill of. But a profound emotion wells up from deep within my heart—just let them see us after 10 or 20 years, after we have grown!

his confidence that they will both eventually return from exile. This is the mentor calling out to the disciple, "Let's win together!" What a deep source of encouragement and inspiration these words must have been to Sairen-bo.

Two years after this letter was written, Nichiren was pardoned and returned to Kamakura. It is recorded that Sairen-bo was also pardoned and returned to the capital, Kyoto. The disciple cherishing a tireless seeking spirit toward the mentor, and the mentor continuing to believe in and to pray for the victory of the disciple—these deep and vibrant life-to-life bonds triumphed in the end.

The closing section of this letter also resounds as a compassionate and inspiring call, urging Sairen-bo to the effect: "Please go on to become a worthy or sage! Please follow in my footsteps!"

The mentor's aspirations for the disciple spur the disciple's awareness and sense of responsibility. The disciple's victory becomes the victory of the mentor and the victory of Buddhism.

The mentor-disciple relationship is the very heart of Buddhism. The Lotus Sutra is the teaching of the way of mentor and disciple. Nichiren's conduct, too, is pervaded with the bonds of mentor and disciple. And walking the great path of mentor and disciple is also the fundamental spirit of the Soka Gakkai, an organization dedicated to realizing the Buddha's decree. Mentor and disciple in the Soka Gakkai share the mission to transform the karma or destiny of humankind based on the principles and ideals of Nichiren Buddhism. As long as this fundamental spirit of mentor and disciple never changes, the Soka Gakkai will continue to develop without end.

Mr. Toda taught that everything depends on the disciples. He stood up alone to carry on and make accessible to all people the great path of the correct teaching that his mentor, Mr. Makiguchi, had laid down his life to protect and pass on to future generations. I likewise dedicated myself to supporting and assisting my mentor, Mr. Toda. Working together with my fellow members and overcoming all manner of adversities, I have extended our great path of mentor and disciple to 192 countries and territories. I have actualized all of Mr. Toda's dreams and plans and have demonstrated his victory to the entire world.

Because Mr. Toda won, Mr. Makiguchi was victorious. Similarly, I am confident that my victory is Mr. Toda's victory.

I have established the successful formula for accomplishing *kosen-rufu* based on upholding the Soka spirit of mentor and disciple.

And I can now report triumphantly to Mr. Toda with all of you that we have completed the foundations of worldwide *kosen-rufu*. Nothing could bring me greater joy.

This lecture was published in the November 2007 issue of The Daibyakurenge, *the Soka Gakkai study journal.*

NOTES:

1. *Kalpa*: (Skt) In ancient Indian cosmology, an extremely long period of time.

2. In April 1272, Nichiren was moved to new quarters on the estate of the lay priest Ichinosawa from the dilapidated hut known as the Sammai-do at Tsukahara, where he had lived for five months following his arrival on Sado the previous year.

3. For example, in a letter addressed to the lay nun Sennichi, titled "The Sutra of True Requital," Nichiren writes: "The lay priest Ichinosawa on several occasions saved my life by hiding me in a corridor of his residence" (WND-1, 934).

4. The power of the Buddha and the power of the Law: Two of the four powers of the Mystic Law (the other two being the power of faith and the power of practice), whose interaction enables one to have one's prayers answered and attain Buddhahood. The power of the Buddha means the power inherent in the lives of Buddhas, while the power of the Law means the boundless power of the Mystic Law, Nam-myoho-renge-kyo.

5. T'ien-t'ai, *The Profound Meaning of the Lotus Sutra*.

6. Miao-lo, *The Annotations on "The Words and Phrases of the Lotus Sutra."*

7. Jambudvipa: One of four continents situated in the four directions around Mount Sumeru, the mountain that stands at the center of the world, according to the ancient Indian worldview. Jambudvipa is the southern continent.

8. Translated from Japanese. Josei Toda, *Toda Josei Zenshu* (Collected Writings of Josei Toda) (Tokyo: Seikyo Shimbunsha, 1983), vol. 3, pp. 383–84.

9. Major world system dust particle *kalpas*: An immensely long period of time described in "The Parable of the Phantom City" chapter of the Lotus Sutra to indicate how much time has passed since Shakyamuni preached the sutra to his voice-hearer disciples as the 16th son of the Buddha Great Universal Wisdom Excellence.

10. Nichiren writes: "No matter how honest and upright you may be, or how you may strive to be known as a worthy person in the secular or the religious world, if you associate with evil persons, then as a natural result you will find that in two or three instances out of ten you are following their teachings, and in the end you, too, will become an evil person" (WND-1, 310).

11. Worms within the lion's body: An analogy for those who, despite being followers of Buddhism, destroy its teachings, just as worms born from the carcass of the lion devour the lion. This analogy appears in the Benevolent Kings Sutra, the Brahma's Net Sutra, the Lotus-like Face Sutra and elsewhere. It is intended to point out that members of the Buddhist Order, rather than non-Buddhists, are capable of destroying Buddhism.

12. Fundamental darkness: Also, fundamental ignorance or primal ignorance. The most deeply rooted illusion inherent in life, said to give rise to all other illusions. Fundamental darkness means the inability to see or recognize the truth, particularly the true nature of one's life. Nichiren interprets fundamental darkness as ignorance of the ultimate Law, or ignorance of the fact that one's life is essentially a manifestation of the Law, which he identifies as Nam-myoho-renge-kyo.

13. The "Encouraging Devotion" chapter of the Lotus Sutra states: "Evil demons will take possession of others / and through them curse, revile and heap shame on us. / But we, reverently trusting in the Buddha, / will put on the armor of perseverance" (LSOC, 233).

14. Also in "Reply to Sairen-bo," Nichiren writes: "Each of the proponents of the various schools I have mentioned above declares that he beyond all others has grasped the meaning of and is practicing the Lotus Sutra. But none of them have been exiled to the province of Izu as I was…, or exiled to the island of Sado as I was…, or been led to the place of decapitation at Tatsunokuchi or faced the countless other difficulties that I have. If the sutra passages [that predict such difficulties] are true, then you should realize that I am the correct teacher, the good teacher, and that the scholars of the other schools are all erroneous teachers and evil teachers" (WND-1, 311).

15. Among Nichiren's letters addressed to Sairen-bo are such important writings as: "The Heritage of the Ultimate Law of Life," "The Oral Tradition regarding the Enlightenment of Plants," "On Prayer," "The True Aspect of All Phenomena," "The Entity of the Mystic Law" and "On the Eighteen Perfections."

16. Lord of Kamakura: This refers to Hojo Tokimune, the regent of the military government in Kamakura.

STUDY GUIDE

The following is a summary of points from SGI President Ikeda's lecture.

- The bonds of mentor and disciple are eternal and based on the vow of the Buddha to widely propagate the Mystic Law for the benefit of all people.

- Despite the fact that Nichiren Daishonin had incurred enmity from the government and was under constant threat of attack by Pure Land believers and others, Sairen-bo, a former Tendai school priest, became Nichiren's disciple in February 1272.

- Sairen-bo and Nichiren's other disciples on Sado felt great joy in and deeply understood the profundity of striving for the sake of Buddhism with the same spirit as their mentor.

THE PATH OF A DISCIPLE

- Essential to Buddhist practice is the disciple's unflagging seeking spirit and unceasing gratitude. To deviate from this path can lead to arrogance and ingratitude.

- To place our faith in a correct teacher means practicing exactly as that person teaches. By doing so, we can break out of our narrow, self-limiting life-state to live a more profound and expansive existence.

MENTOR AND DISCIPLE BORN TOGETHER IN LIFETIME AFTER LIFETIME

- The Lotus Sutra states, "Those persons who had heard the Law / dwelled here and there in various Buddha lands, / constantly reborn in company with their teachers" (see *The Lotus Sutra and Its Opening and Closing Sutras*, p. 178). Shakyamuni and his voice-hearer disciples, it is said, spent lifetime after lifetime carrying out bodhisattva practice together. Similarly, Nichiren suggests that he and Sairen-bo share the same kind of deep karmic bond as mentor and disciple.

- In Nichiren Buddhism, the mentor and disciple pledge to be born together in the Latter Day of the Law—a time of unprecedented spiritual pollution and confusion—to chant and teach others about Nam-myoho-renge-kyo and to lead all people to happiness.

"GOOD TEACHERS" HAVE VANQUISHED THE DEVIL KING

■ We need the ability to distinguish erroneous and evil teachers from correct and good teachers. In associating with evil people, our tendencies toward greed, anger and foolishness are intensified, our judgment becomes clouded, and we become increasingly engulfed by confusion, wrongdoing and misery.

■ Fundamental darkness, or fundamental ignorance of the Mystic Law, manifests as not believing in, doubting and disrespecting the Law.

■ The devil king of the sixth heaven (a personification of fundamental darkness) may influence even the very wise. Nichiren, however, states that the devil king no longer harms him. Because he has been prepared for an onslaught of obstacles and devils, and has resolved and upheld his vow to triumph over them, he has rendered the devil king's power ineffectual.

THE ESSENTIAL QUALITIES OF "CORRECT AND GOOD TEACHERS"

■ A "correct and good teacher" must be (1) a person of wisdom who sees through the fundamental evil inherent in human life and reveals the Mystic Law that is the fundamental good; (2) a person of courage who is dedicated to the correct teaching of Buddhism and continues fighting against evil; (3) a person of compassion who is concerned with relieving people's suffering and imparting joy and actively works to realize happiness for self and others.

■ When the disciple stands up for *kosen-rufu* in accord with the mentor's call and wins in life, mentor and disciple become truly united. There is no path to attaining Buddhahood apart from this relationship.

THE GREAT JOY OF THE MENTOR AND DISCIPLE'S SHARED COMMITMENT

■ Nichiren writes, "Hour by hour, moment by moment, I savor the principle that allows us to attain Buddhahood" ("Reply to Sairen-bo," *The Writings of Nichiren Daishonin*, vol. 1, p. 312). The great joy of teachers who are one with the Law inspires their disciples. This joy endures for eternity and is condensed in the powerful resolve of a disciple who, acting in unity with the mentor, overcomes hardship and conquers devilish functions.

THE "CAPITAL OF ETERNALLY TRANQUIL LIGHT"

■ Nichiren writes, "Day and night [we] will go to and from the Land of Eternally Tranquil Light that has existed for all time" (WND-1, 313). The place where we challenge ourselves to expand our abilities and teach others about Buddhism becomes the Land of Eternally Tranquil Light.

■ Our daily practice of chanting Nam-myoho-renge-kyo and reciting the sutra is a ceremony in which we instantly return to the place where we recharge ourselves and get ready to face the realities and struggles of everyday life.

THE VICTORY OF MENTOR AND DISCIPLE
IS THE VICTORY OF BUDDHISM

■ The mentor-disciple relationship is the very heart of Buddhism. Walking the great path of mentor and disciple is the fundamental spirit of the Soka Gakkai, which is dedicated to transforming the destiny of humankind based on the principles and ideals of Nichiren Buddhism.

THE FOUNDATIONS OF FAITH

Nichiren Daishonin's complete written works are now available in English. A challenging and fascinating world of encouragement and philosophy awaits you.

The Writings of Nichiren Daishonin, vol. 1
M/O #1100

The Writings of Nichiren Daishonin, vol. 2
M/O #1101

The Record of the Orally Transmitted Teachings
M/O #1103

Available at your local SGI-USA community center bookstore or from the Mail Order Center: (800) 626-1313 or mailorder@sgi-usa.org

"Hell Is the Land of Tranquil Light"

A Buddha in Both Life and Death—Attaining Buddhahood in One's Present Form Means Savoring Joy in Both Life and Death

The Passage for Study in This Lecture

I have received your offering of various articles. Nothing would please me more than to know that you have communicated with the late Ueno [your husband Nanjo Hyoe Shichiro], but I know that that is impossible. Unless it was in a dream, it is unlikely that you have seen him. Unless it was an illusion, how could you have seen him? Surely your late husband is in the pure land of Eagle Peak, listening and watching over this saha world day and night. You, his wife, and your children have only mortal senses, so you cannot see or hear him, but be assured that you will eventually be reunited [on Eagle Peak].

The men with whom you have exchanged marriage vows over the course of all your previous lifetimes must outnumber even the grains of sand in the ocean. Your vows this time, however, were ones made with your true husband. The reason is that it was due to his encouragement that you became a practitioner of the Lotus Sutra. Thus you should revere him as a Buddha. When he was alive, he was a Buddha in life, and now he is a Buddha in death. He is a Buddha in both life and death. This is what is meant by that most important doctrine called attaining Buddhahood in one's present form. The fourth volume of the

Lotus Sutra states, "If one can uphold this [sutra], one will be upholding the Buddha's body."

Neither the pure land nor hell exists outside oneself; both lie only within one's own heart. Awakened to this, one is called a Buddha; deluded about it, one is called an ordinary person. The Lotus Sutra reveals this truth, and one who embraces the Lotus Sutra will realize that hell is itself the Land of Tranquil Light. . . .

This teaching is of prime importance, but I will impart it to you just as Bodhisattva Manjushri explained the secret teaching of the attainment of Buddhahood in one's present form to the dragon king's daughter. After hearing it, strive even more earnestly in faith. One who, on hearing the teachings of the Lotus Sutra, makes even greater efforts in faith is a true seeker of the way. T'ien-t'ai states, "From the indigo, an even deeper blue." This passage means that, if one dyes something repeatedly in indigo, it becomes even bluer than the indigo leaves. The Lotus Sutra is like the indigo, and the strength of one's practice is like the deepening blue. (*The Writings of Nichiren Daishonin*, vol. 1, pp. 456–57)

Since your deceased husband was a votary of this [Lotus] sutra, he doubtless attained Buddhahood just as he was. You need not grieve so much over his passing. On the other hand, to grieve is only natural for ordinary people. However, even sages are sometimes sad. Could the lamenting of all the great enlightened disciples of Shakyamuni Buddha at his passing have been meant to show the behavior of ordinary people?

You should by all means perform as much good as you possibly can for the sake of your deceased husband. The words of a wise man of old also teach that "you should base your mind on the ninth consciousness, and carry out your practice in the six consciousnesses." How reasonable it is too! In this letter I have written my long-cherished teachings. Keep them deep within your heart. (WND-1, 458)

LECTURE

In 1950, my mentor, Josei Toda, facing dire circumstances in his business, stepped down as Soka Gakkai general director to shield the Soka Gakkai from any negative repercussions. His lively study lectures at the Soka Gakkai Headquarters, which had been regularly attended by dozens of people, grew more infrequent. Yet he still made time amid this intense period to give lectures to small groups. He solemnly declared: "I will give every ounce of my strength for those of you who wish to study, even if there is only one of you." He also said: "Even if I should fall into hell, that wouldn't matter to me in the least. I would simply share the correct teaching with the inhabitants there and turn it into the Land of Tranquil Light. But my concern is what would happen to you who are still so young in faith."

No matter how trying the hardships that beset him, no matter how exhausted he was, Mr. Toda would summon all his compassion and energy to encourage those who sought him out—whether it be a member struggling with karma and wishing to receive guidance in faith, or a young person eager to learn about Buddhism.

Mr. Toda eventually broke through his business difficulties, and, in 1951, he was inaugurated as president of the Soka Gakkai. A short time before that,

he moved his company office to a room in the Ichigaya Building near Ichigaya Station in Tokyo. He also established a branch office of the Soka Gakkai Headquarters in a separate small room in the same building. There, he devoted many hours each day to giving guidance and encouragement to members who came to see him.

Nichiren Buddhism enables those experiencing the greatest suffering to gain the greatest happiness. The Mystic Law has the power to change even hell into the Land of Tranquil Light.[1]

I have heard a wonderful testimony about this related by a former receptionist at the Ichigaya Building. A women's division member who was a close friend of hers conveyed the woman's remarks to me.

The former receptionist vividly recalled the situation back in those days. A great many people would come to visit the room that served as our branch office. Moreover, people who arrived seemingly weighted down by problems and worries would leave looking like completely different people, bright smiles lighting their faces. This transformation always amazed her, she said.

Both Tsunesaburo Makiguchi and Josei Toda, the first and second presidents of the Soka Gakkai, taught a way of life of striving continuously to kindle flames of courage and great confidence in people's hearts—illuminating this friend or that family's future—so that they could come to view karma as mission. To thoroughly encourage each individual, to inspire all to stand up together in pursuit of the noblest mission, worldwide *kosen-rufu*—that is the fundamental spirit that pervades the mentor-disciple relationship in the Soka Gakkai. As long as this spirit is passed on, the Soka Gakkai will without doubt continue to develop eternally.

In this installment, we'll study the writing "Hell Is the Land of Tranquil Light" and learn from Nichiren's earnest, lifelong struggle to encourage his followers.

I have received your offering of various articles. Nothing would please me more than to know that you have communicated with the late Ueno [your husband Nanjo Hyoe Shichiro],[2] but I know that that is impossible. Unless it was in a dream, it is unlikely that you have seen him. Unless it was an illusion, how could you have seen him? Surely your late husband is in the pure land of Eagle Peak,[3] listening and watching over this saha world[4] day and night. You, his wife, and your children have only mortal senses, so you cannot see or hear him, but be assured that you will eventually be reunited [on Eagle Peak].

The men with whom you have exchanged marriage vows over the course of all your previous lifetimes must outnumber even the grains of sand in the ocean. Your vows this time, however, were ones made with your true husband. The reason is that it was due to his encouragement that you became a practitioner of the Lotus Sutra. Thus you should revere him as a Buddha. When he was alive, he was a Buddha in life, and now he is a Buddha in death. He is a Buddha in both life and death. This is what is meant by that most important doctrine called attaining Buddhahood in one's present form.[5] The fourth volume of the Lotus Sutra states, "If one can uphold this [sutra], one will be upholding the Buddha's body" [*The Lotus Sutra and Its Opening and Closing Sutras*, p. 220]. (WND-1, 456)

BOTH LIFE AND DEATH ARE PERVADED WITH JOY

Nichiren Daishonin writes: "When he was alive, he was a Buddha in life, and now he is a Buddha in death. He is a Buddha in both life and death" (WND-1, 456). The great teaching of Nichiren Buddhism makes it possible for us to reveal our inherent Buddhahood within this present lifetime and to eternally undergo the cycle of birth and death with complete freedom and boundless hope.

If our lives are filled with joy, then our death will also be filled with joy.

SGI President Ikeda enjoys a discussion with John Dewey Society
president Jim Garrison (left) at the Nagano Training Center,
Nagano Prefecture, Japan, August 12, 2008.

And if our deaths are filled with joy, then our next lives will also be filled with joy. Nichiren teaches that the cycle of birth and death is a continuum of joy and that the essence of life lies in dedicating ourselves to actually making that joy the reality of our existence and helping others do the same.

The writing "Hell Is the Land of Tranquil Light" is a letter addressed to the lay nun Ueno, widow of Nanjo Hyoe Shichiro. Scholars are divided over exactly when this letter was composed. Some suggest it was written immediately after Hyoe Shichiro's death in 1265. Others speculate that it was written around 1274, after Nichiren returned from Sado and went to live at Mount Minobu, during which time he resumed corresponding frequently with the Nanjo family.

Hyoe Shichiro was the first member of the Nanjo family to convert to Nichiren's teachings. A retainer of the Kamakura shogunate whom Nichiren valued greatly, he died from a serious illness in 1265. He had sincerely followed Nichiren's guidance and maintained faith in the Mystic Law to the end of his life. His surviving family members carried on their own Buddhist practice with the same pure spirit of faith.

At the time of Hyoe Shichiro's death, his second son, Tokimitsu[6]—who later became the head of the Nanjo family— was 7 years old. In addition, Hyoe Shichiro's wife was then pregnant with their fifth son. No doubt she had to put aside her own feelings of loss and grief as she struggled valiantly to protect and raise her family on her own.

61

Nichiren could sense the irrepressible grief and sadness in this mother's heart, and he encouraged her in an effort to relieve her suffering. In this letter, he comments that even should she see her husband in a dream, it would not be possible for her to receive any communication from him in reality. Nichiren tells her that, from the standpoint of Buddhism, her husband is in the pure land of Eagle Peak, constantly watching over his family. And he assures her that in the end they will be reunited there.

He warmly consoles the lay nun Ueno, saying that all those united by the deep bonds of faith—be they fellow practitioners, family members or friends—are certain to be reunited.

THE PURE LAND OF EAGLE PEAK IS THE ETERNAL "HOME" OF LIFE ITSELF

The pure land of Eagle Peak of which Nichiren Daishonin speaks certainly does not indicate some imaginary other world such as the paradise of the Pure Land of Perfect Bliss in the west[7] that is expounded in the Pure Land (Nembutsu) school of Buddhism. Simply put, the pure land of Eagle Peak represents the realm of Buddhahood within the universe itself. In Nichiren's writings, we find the words: "One's body and mind at a single moment pervade the entire realm of phenomena"[8] ("The Object of Devotion for Observing the Mind,"

WND-1, 366). The life of a person who dies after having steadfastly upheld the Mystic Law will enter a vast and boundless state encompassing the entire universe and be pervaded by great joy. Mr. Toda described this as "merging with the realm of Buddhahood within the universe."

In Nichiren's writings, we frequently find passages such as: "Let us meet in the pure land of Eagle Peak" ("Letter to the Lay Nun of Ko," WND-1, 596), and "Without fail both mother and child will go to the pure land of Eagle Peak" ("Reply to the Honorable Konichi," WND-2, 964).

The pure land of Eagle Peak represents the realm of Buddhahood that can be reached by all who maintain faith in the Mystic Law to the very end of their lives. There, mentor and disciple, fellow members, parents and children, spouses, family members—and, indeed, all those who are joined by deep life-to-life bonds—can share a joyous reunion.

The Bodhisattvas of the Earth appear in this strife-filled *saha* world from the realm of Buddhahood to carry out the mission of leading people to enlightenment. And after fulfilling their mission in this life, they return once more to the realm of Buddhahood within the universe. This is the pure land of Eagle Peak. It is the eternal "home"—on the profound dimension of life—of courageous Bodhisattvas of the Earth who are forever committed to widely propagating the Mystic Law; it is a realm of comrades from time without beginning.

To be a "Buddha in life" means to bring forth our innate Buddhahood based on this awareness and to stand up valiantly on the stage of our mission in the midst of life's painful realities to work for our own happiness and that of others. To be a "Buddha in death" means to enter the eternal path of boundless joy of the Law[9] after having completed our mission in this lifetime and to embark on our next journey on the bodhisattva path to continue fulfilling our vow to lead others to enlightenment.

The purpose of this present existence is to attain the lofty spiritual state in which we truly sense that we are Buddhas in both life and death and that both life and death are pervaded by joy. Or rather, each moment of this existence is a struggle to achieve this state of life.

In this writing, Nichiren cites a passage from the Lotus Sutra: "If one can uphold this [sutra], one will be upholding the Buddha's body" [LSOC, 220].[10] Just as this passage states, Nanjo Hyoe Shichiro could enter the eternal path of birth and death in the realm of Buddhahood because he persevered in his Buddhist practice and established the life-state of Buddhahood in the course of that existence. Nichiren thus assures the lay nun Ueno, his message implying: "Your late husband is certainly a Buddha as indicated in the Lotus Sutra. Your husband won! Now it's your turn to win!"

Neither the pure land nor hell exists outside oneself; both lie only within one's own heart. Awakened to this, one is called a Buddha;

deluded about it, one is called an ordinary person. The Lotus Sutra reveals this truth, and one who embraces the Lotus Sutra will realize that hell is itself the Land of Tranquil Light....[11]

This teaching is of prime importance, but I will impart it to you just as Bodhisattva Manjushri[12] explained the secret teaching of the attainment of Buddhahood in one's present form to the dragon king's daughter.[13] After hearing it, strive even more earnestly in faith. One who, on hearing the teachings of the Lotus Sutra, makes even greater efforts in faith is a true seeker of the way. T'ien-t'ai states, "From the indigo, an even deeper blue." This passage means that, if one dyes something repeatedly in indigo, it becomes even bluer than the indigo leaves. The Lotus Sutra is like the indigo, and the strength of one's practice is like the deepening blue. (WND-1, 456–57)

THE BENEFICIAL POWER OF THE MYSTIC LAW: TRANSFORMING HELL INTO THE LAND OF TRANQUIL LIGHT

Both the pure land and hell exist within us. To suppose that they exist somewhere else is an illusion. That is Nichiren Daishonin's teaching.

Here, he goes on to encourage the lay nun Ueno by shifting his focus from her late husband's attainment of Buddhahood to her own.

Those who uphold the Lotus Sutra can actualize in their own lives the principle that "hell is itself the Land of Tranquil Light." In another writing, Nichiren tells Shijo Kingo that if it were necessary in order to protect him, he would accompany him even to hell, writing, "For if you and I should fall into hell together, we would find Shakyamuni Buddha and the Lotus Sutra there" ("The Three Kinds of Treasure," WND-1, 850). The implication here is that if Nichiren Daishonin and Shakyamuni Buddha were both present, hell would no longer be hell; it would become a Buddha land. And if that were so, then the wardens of hell[14] would not attack the followers of the Buddha, nor would King Yama, the king of hell, have any choice but to become a protector of the Lotus Sutra.

The Lotus Sutra is a teaching of changing the place we are right now into a Buddha land. Faith in the Lotus Sutra means undertaking the challenge to do just that. Consequently, Nichiren's followers who persevere in the practice of the Lotus Sutra will not possibly suffer in the world of hell. They are guaranteed to enjoy a state of life of complete freedom.

Nichiren wanted to deeply impress this point on the lay nun Ueno. Though she perhaps had already heard several times before about this principle that "hell is itself the Land of Tranquil Light," he no doubt wanted

ATTAINING BUDDHAHOOD MEANS REVEALING OUR TRUE SELVES

From SGI President Ikeda's lecture series on
"On Attaining Buddhahood in This Lifetime"

Myoho-renge-kyo is the name of the ultimate mystic truth, and Nam-myoho-renge-kyo is the name of the life-state of Buddhas who embody and reveal this truth. Thus, when we chant Nam-myoho-renge-kyo with conviction, the infinite benefit of Myoho-renge-kyo unfolds in our lives. This is what it means to bring forth the world of Buddhahood.

At work here is the principle of "cause and effect in a single moment of life in which faith is the cause and manifesting the life-state of Buddhahood is the effect. When we continue chanting Nam-myoho-renge-kyo through times of both suffering and joy while striving for our own happiness and that of others, we can establish as the core and innermost essence of our lives the benefit of the cause and effect for attaining Buddhahood—which are themselves contained within the practice of chanting. When we do so, the indomitable state of Buddhahood emerges within us. This is the meaning of "attaining Buddhahood in this lifetime."

In his treatise "The Object of Devotion for Observing the Mind," Nichiren Daishonin states: "Shakyamuni Buddha, who has attained perfect enlightenment, is our own flesh and blood. His practices and the resulting virtues are our bones and marrow" (*The Writings of Nichiren Daishonin*, vol. 1, p. 365). He explains that to embrace Myoho-renge-kyo is in itself attaining enlightenment. The power of chanting Nam-myoho-renge-kyo enables us to actualize cause and effect in a single moment of life—that is, faith (cause) leading to the manifestation of our Buddhahood (effect).

Considered in this light, one's voice chanting Nam-myoho-renge-kyo is the voice of unshakable faith and seeking spirit that breaks through the inner darkness of ignorance and illusion and sweeps away obstacles and devilish functions. It is also the courageous lion's roar that issues forth from the Buddhahood one reveals as a result of chanting. (November–December 2006 *Living Buddhism*, pp. 79–80) her to grasp it on a more profound level and to manifest it in her own life. These passages also convey his sincere wish that she exert herself in her Buddhist practice with stronger resolve.

ATTAINING BUDDHAHOOD IN ONE'S PRESENT FORM IS A PRINCIPLE OF JOY AND HOPE

The reason why Nichiren Daishonin spoke of the principle that "hell is itself the Land of Tranquil Light" was to reassure the lay nun Ueno that her late husband had most certainly attained Buddhahood. It was also to teach her that Buddhahood existed in her own life—a realization that was a source of supreme hope and inspiration—even as she struggled intrepidly to raise her young children on her own.

To further encourage her, Nichiren discusses the episode in the Lotus Sutra where the dragon king's daughter attains Buddhahood in her present form. At the behest of Shakyamuni Buddha in the "Devadatta" chapter, Bodhisattva Manjushri explains the beneficial power of the Mystic Law to Bodhisattva Wisdom Accumulated. At that time, to provide concrete evidence that the Mystic Law has the power to enable people to attain Buddhahood in their present form, he calls forth and introduces the dragon king's daughter.

But individuals such as Bodhisattva Wisdom Accumulated and Shariputra, one of Shakyamuni's leading disciples, were not inclined to believe that Buddhahood could be attained by women. Nor, they thought, could it be achieved in one's present form. In front of men harboring such disbelief, the dragon girl vows to Shakyamuni: "I unfold the doctrines of the great vehicle [the Lotus Sutra] / to rescue living beings from suffering" (LSOC, 227), and then demonstrates actual proof of attaining Buddhahood in her present form. As for the multitudes who witness this

The Lotus Sutra is a teaching of changing the place we are right now into a Buddha land. Faith in the Lotus Sutra means undertaking the challenge to do just that.

feat, the sutra states: "Their hearts were filled with great joy" (LSOC, 228). Brimming with delight, they entered the path of attaining Buddhahood. Meanwhile, all the doubters were dumbstruck with admiration at the dragon girl's achievement and forced to silently accept its reality. The thrilling drama of the dragon girl attaining Buddhahood illuminated the assembly with a brilliant light of hope and set off waves of joy.

The principle of attaining Buddhahood in our present form has the power to call forth hope and joy in the lives of all people. In this writing, Nichiren teaches this fundamental principle to the lay nun Ueno in order to inspire hope in her heart.

NICHIREN BUDDHISM: ACTUALIZING THE PRINCIPLES OF THE LOTUS SUTRA

"Strive even more earnestly in faith," Nichiren Daishonin writes to the lay nun Ueno. "One who...makes even greater efforts in faith is a true seeker of the way" (WND-1, 457).

He explains such profound principles as "attaining Buddhahood in one's present form" and "hell is itself the Land of Tranquil Light" to help his disciples deepen their faith. Buddhism is not a game of words or concepts.

The fundamental principles explained in this writing all teach that the source

of supreme hope—Buddhahood—resides within us. If we can accept this as being true of our own lives and maintain firm belief in this, then that very faith and conviction will dispel the darkness or ignorance[15] that obscures our Buddhahood.

Therefore, the important thing is faith. The more we deepen our faith, the more our lives will be dyed with the hues of Buddhahood. To illustrate this, Nichiren cites the words of the Great Teacher T'ien-t'ai of China: "From the indigo, an even deeper blue."

The leaves of the indigo plant are a green color with a faint bluish tint. But if something is soaked many times in the dye extracted from these leaves, it will become a deep, vibrant blue. Our practice for attaining Buddhahood in this lifetime is the same. The Lotus Sutra, which expounds this principle, can be likened to the leaves of the indigo plant, while practicing Nichiren Buddhism is like being repeatedly soaked in the dye produced from these leaves. In other words, when we deepen our faith through hearing the teachings and strive ever harder in our Buddhist practice, we can manifest our Buddhahood in our actual lives and attain enlightenment in this existence.

The purpose of studying Nichiren's writings is not only to understand his spirit and deepen our own faith. It is also important because by learning about the profound principles of Buddhism, we can gain the solid conviction

...urce of hope and peace resides within our own hearts, and based on this we can strive earnestly for the happiness of ourselves and others. Study also helps us summon the courage to challenge difficulties as we learn from Nichiren's example as one who triumphed over enormous trials and obstacles. This is the key to practical Buddhist study—study that we can apply to our daily lives. Let us always bear this deeply in mind.

Since your deceased husband was a votary of this sutra, he doubtless attained Buddhahood just as he was. You need not grieve so much over his passing. On the other hand, to grieve is only natural for ordinary people. However, even sages are sometimes sad. Could the lamenting of all the great enlightened disciples of Shakyamuni Buddha at his passing have been meant to show the behavior of ordinary people?

You should by all means perform as much good as you possibly can for the sake of your deceased husband. The words of a wise man of old also teach that "you should base your mind on the ninth consciousness, and carry out your practice in the six consciousnesses."[16] How reasonable it is too! In this letter I have written my long-cherished teachings. Keep them deep within your heart. (WND-1, 458)

FOLLOW THE PATH OF YOUR MISSION, JUST AS YOU ARE

Attaining, or revealing, Buddhahood in one's present form is not about acquiring special, superhuman qualities, but rather it means achieving, as ordinary human beings, an eternal and boundless state of life characterized by the virtues of eternity, happiness, true self and purity.[17]

The benefits and blessings of the Mystic Law are immeasurable. All life— no matter in which of the Ten Worlds it may reside—is originally an entity of the Mystic Law. Therefore, even if at present we are in the state of hell, by changing our focus at that moment, we can immediately manifest our pure and highest state of life as entities of the Mystic Law. This is what it means to attain Buddhahood in our present form.

Naturally, "in our present form" doesn't mean attaining Buddhahood while wallowing in suffering or surrendering to indolence. What's required is a struggle to transform the moment-to-moment focus of our minds. Nichiren Daishonin revealed the Gohonzon, the object of devotion, so that anyone can undertake this struggle.

He gave expression to the supreme state of life he had attained by inscribing it in the form of the Gohonzon. Those who chant Nam-myoho-renge-kyo with faith in the Gohonzon can break through the darkness that shrouds their lives and bring forth from

NICHIREN DAISHONIN ON THE GOHONZON

Though this mandala has but five or seven characters, it is the teacher of all Buddhas throughout the three existences and the seal that guarantees the enlightenment of all women. It will be a lamp in the darkness of the road to the next world and a fine horse to carry you over the mountains of death. It is like the sun and moon in the heavens or Mount Sumeru on earth. It is a ship to ferry people over the sea of the sufferings of birth and death. It is the teacher who leads all people to Buddhahood and enlightenment. This great mandala has never yet been propagated anywhere in Jambudvipa in the more than 2,220 years since the Buddha's passing. ("On Offering Prayers to the Mandala of the Mystic Law," *The Writings of Nichiren Daishonin*, vol. 1, p. 414)

Never seek this Gohonzon outside yourself. The Gohonzon exists only within the mortal flesh of us ordinary people who embrace the Lotus Sutra and chant Nam-myoho-renge-kyo. The body is the palace of the ninth consciousness, the unchanging reality that reigns over all of life's functions. To be endowed with the Ten Worlds means that all ten, without a single exception, exist in one world. Because of this it is called a mandala. Mandala is a Sanskrit word that is translated as "perfectly endowed" or "a cluster of blessings." This Gohonzon also is found only in the two characters for faith. This is what the sutra means when it states that one can "gain entrance through faith alone." ("The Real Aspect of the Gohonzon," WND-1, 832)

A sword is useless in the hands of a coward. The mighty sword of the Lotus Sutra must be wielded by one courageous in faith. Then one will be as strong as a demon armed with an iron staff. I, Nichiren, have inscribed my life in sumi ink, so believe in the Gohonzon with your whole heart. The Buddha's will is the Lotus Sutra, but the soul of Nichiren is nothing other than Nam-myoho-renge-kyo. ("Reply to Kyo'o," WND-1, 412)

At Holy Eagle Peak, Nichiren without question faced the Buddha and received oral instruction from him in these three great laws. The object of devotion is thus the entity of the entire life of the votary of the Lotus Sutra. (*The Record of the Orally Transmitted Teachings*, p. 142) within the state of Buddhahood that is one with the Mystic Law.

Believing in the Gohonzon means believing that the supremely noble state of life that Nichiren manifested also exists within our own lives. This means persevering in faith and practice as a votary of the Lotus Sutra, just as he did. Only by striving in faith with the same spirit that he teaches can we vanquish the ignorance or darkness that clouds our lives.

In this writing, Nichiren declares that Hyoe Shichiro, having been a votary of the Lotus Sutra, most definitely attained Buddhahood in his present form. In other words, by virtue of being a votary of the Lotus Sutra, he had been a "Buddha in life" while alive, and now was a "Buddha in death." As such, Nichiren assures the lay nun Ueno that her late husband had surely enjoyed peace of mind during his lifetime, and after death surely dwelled in the eternal and indestructible realm of Buddhahood within the universe. Based on his profound insight into the true nature of life, Nichiren warmly encourages her to the effect: "There is essentially no reason for you to grieve or lament."

BECOME A WINNER IN THE REAL WORLD

Nichiren Daishonin goes on to say, however, that even though we may understand this intellectually, it is only natural that as ordinary human beings we grieve over the loss of a loved one. He points out that even sages are sad on occasion. This being the case, he encourages the lay nun Ueno to perform as much good as she can so as to benefit her deceased husband. In other words, he is telling her to turn her grief into prayer for the sake of her husband's eternal happiness.

Nichiren always treasured the feelings of his followers. Every single word in this letter warmly embraces the lay nun Ueno. Nichiren's immense heart, as vast as the sky or the ocean, is the heart of the Buddha of the Latter Day of the Law.

He urges the lay nun Ueno to strive in faith as much as she can. For by elevating her sorrow at losing her husband through prayer based on the Mystic Law, she will be making efforts in faith that will ennoble her own life and enable her to actualize the principle of attaining Buddhahood in this lifetime. Offering prayers for the deceased based on the Mystic Law constitutes an admirable part of Buddhist practice.

There is absolutely no need for us to pretend in front of the Gohonzon. We should chant to the Gohonzon just as we are—with joy when we're elated, and with sadness when we're feeling down. We should regard both suffering and joy as facts of life and continue chanting Nam-myoho-renge-kyo steadfastly to the very end. Through the vast power of the Mystic Law, all of our prayers form part of our Buddhist practice. Those who continue to resolutely chant Nam-myoho-renge-kyo, come what may, will achieve true victory. A person who chants with this spirit and manifests the power of the Mystic Law in their lives is truly a "Buddha in life."

Mr. Toda said: "To enjoy complete peace of mind in the depths of one's being is what it means to be a Buddha.... As a result of embracing the Gohonzon, the life of one who is ill, for example, will be transformed into one of complete peace of mind. With this deep underlying serenity, one will find pleasure in the simple act of living.... Don't you think that finding life itself an absolute joy is what it means to be a Buddha? Isn't this what it means to attain the same life-state as Nichiren?"[18]

To explain this state of life to the lay nun Ueno, Nichiren cites the passage: "You should base your mind on the ninth consciousness, and carry out your practice in the six consciousnesses" (WND-1, 458).

The "ninth consciousness" is life that is pure without defilements and one with the Mystic Law, the ultimate truth. It means the Buddha nature innate in all life. Our lives are inherently palaces wherein dwells the "mind king,"[19] the fundamental entity of the mind known as the ninth consciousness. In one writing, we find the expression the "palace of the ninth consciousness, the unchanging reality that reigns over all of life's functions"[20] ("The Real Aspect of the Gohonzon," WND-1, 832). Nichiren inscribed this inherent reality of our lives in the form of the Gohonzon. Therefore, to "base one's mind on the ninth consciousness" means simply chanting Nam-myoho-renge-kyo with faith in the Gohonzon.

The "six consciousnesses" means the five senses (sight, sound, smell, taste and touch), which function in response to the phenomena of the world around us, plus the awareness that integrates these five senses. In other words, the six consciousnesses indicate our actual lives in this world. "To carry out one's practice in the six consciousnesses" means firmly establishing the state of Buddhahood

Through the vast power of the Mystic Law, all of our prayers form part of our Buddhist practice. Those who continue to resolutely chant Nam-myoho-renge-kyo, come what may, will achieve true victory.

within us by making our daily lives our place of practice. This is the principle of "faith manifesting itself in daily life."

It could further be said that "basing one's mind on the ninth consciousness" and "carrying out one's practice in the six consciousnesses" encompasses all of our Soka Gakkai activities. This is because, while grounding our lives solidly in the world of Buddhahood, we go out to spread the Mystic Law and lead people to enlightenment amid society with all its problems and suffering.

Encouraging others in faith requires an earnest, all-out effort. It entails a powerful interaction on the dimension of life itself, invoking the dynamics of the "three thousand realms in a single life-moment" of each person. It is a dedicated challenge in which we polish our own lives so that we can consolidate our Buddhahood, while seeking to elevate the lives of our friends so they may do the same.

What a source of strength and courage this letter must have been to the lay nun Ueno.

Later in life, this admirable mother suddenly lost her fifth son when he was 16 years old. Her second son and head of the family, Tokimitsu, was also struck by a severe illness that nearly cost him his life. Even while battling such painful destiny, the lay nun Ueno continued to seek out Nichiren's teachings. She fought on tenaciously and won a splendid victory.

How wonderful it is to struggle together with a teacher in faith who has a profound understanding of the Buddhist view of life and death. The principle of attaining Buddhahood in one's present form is actualized when both teacher and disciple can savor joy in both life and death.

This lecture was published in the December 2007 issue of The Daibyakurenge, *the Soka Gakkai study journal.*

NOTES:

1. Also, Land of Eternally Tranquil Light or Land of Eternal Light. It refers to the Buddha land, which is free from impermanence and impurity. In many sutras, this *saha* world is described as an impure land filled with delusions and sufferings, and the Buddha land as a pure land free from these and far removed from this *saha* world. In contrast, the Lotus Sutra reveals the *saha* world to be the Buddha land, or the Land of Tranquil Light, and explains that the nature of a land is determined by the minds of its inhabitants.

2. The late Ueno, or Nanjo Hyoe Shichiro, was the steward of Ueno Village in Fuji District and a retainer of the Kamakura government. He was originally a believer in the Pure Land teachings, but

heard Nichiren Daishonin preach and became his follower. He became ill in 1264 and received a letter of encouragement from Nichiren toward the end of that year. He died in 1265.

3. Pure land of Eagle Peak: Eagle Peak is the place where Shakyamuni preached the Lotus Sutra. It also symbolizes the Buddha land or the state of Buddhahood, as in the expression "the pure land of Eagle Peak."

4. *Saha* world: This world, which is filled with suffering. Often translated as the world of endurance. *Saha* means the earth; it derives from a root meaning "to bear" or "to endure." In this context, the *saha* world indicates a world in which people must endure suffering.

5. Attaining Buddhahood in one's present form: This means revealing our inherent Buddhahood just as

we are, without discarding the body of an ordinary person. According to many of the teachings other than the Lotus Sutra, one can attain Buddhahood only after practicing for an incredibly long period of time spanning countless lifetimes and severing any connection with the nine worlds. But the Lotus Sutra teaches that we can attain Buddhahood in our present form, as ordinary people. This principle is often illustrated by the example of the dragon king's daughter who, according to the "Devadatta" chapter, attained Buddhahood in a single moment without changing her dragon form, through the beneficial power of the Mystic Law.

6. Nanjo Tokimitsu (1259–1332): A lay follower of Nichiren Daishonin and the second son of Nanjo Hyoe Shichiro. In addition to supporting Nichiren, Tokimitsu aided Nikko Shonin, Nichiren's direct disciple and subsequent successor, in his propagation efforts in the Fuji area. He also provided crucial assistance to fellow practitioners at the time of the Atsuhara Persecution, which began in 1278.

7. Pure Land of Perfect Bliss in the west: A pure land described in the Pure Land sutras. It is said to be located "a hundred thousand million Buddha lands away in the west" where Amida Buddha lives.

8. A passage from Miao-lo's *The Annotations on "Great Concentration and Insight."* Because the Ten Worlds in their entirety, and all of the three thousand realms, originally exist in people's lives at each moment, when people attain Buddhahood, in accordance with this original principle, their bodies and minds pervade the phenomenal realm and they attain a state of complete freedom.

9. Boundless joy of the Law: The supreme and ultimate happiness of the Buddha, the benefit of the Mystic Law.

10. With regard to this passage from the "Treasure Tower" chapter of the Lotus Sutra, Nichiren states in *The Record of the Orally Transmitted Teachings*: "To uphold the Lotus Sutra is to uphold belief in the fact that our bodies are the Buddha's body…. To uphold the body of the Buddha means to uphold the belief that outside of our own bodies there is no Buddha. That is, the ordinary mortal at…the stage of being a Buddha in theory, is not different from the Buddha at…the stage of ultimate enlightenment" (pp. 96–97).

11. "Hell is itself the Land of Eternally Tranquil Light": This means that the world of hell, a life-state of suffering, can become, just as it is, the Land of Eternally Tranquil Light where the Buddha dwells. "Hell" means a world of extreme suffering, and "the Land of Eternally Tranquil Light" means the world of Buddhahood. That the world of hell is itself the world of Buddhahood figuratively expresses the principle of the mutual possession of the Ten Worlds.

12. Bodhisattva Manjushri: A bodhisattva who appears in the sutras as a leader of bodhisattvas and is regarded as symbolic of the perfection of wisdom.

13. Dragon king's daughter: Also, known as the dragon girl. The 8-year-old daughter of Sagara, one of the eight great dragon kings said to dwell in a palace at the bottom of the sea. She conceives the desire for enlightenment upon hearing Bodhisattva Manjushri preach the Lotus Sutra. She then appears in front of the assembly of the Lotus Sutra and instantaneously attains Buddhahood in her present form.

14. Wardens of hell: Demons in Buddhist mythology who torment transgressors who have fallen into hell. They work for King Yama, the king of hell who is said to judge and determine the rewards and punishments of the dead.

15. In Buddhism, this means ignorance about the true nature of existence. It is deemed the fundamental cause of suffering and delusion. It prevents people from recognizing the true nature of their lives and taking faith in the Mystic Law, which enables all to attain enlightenment.

16. Nine consciousnesses and six consciousnesses: The doctrine of the nine consciousnesses identifies nine types of discernment. Proceeding from shallow to deep, they are the five senses (sight, hearing, smell, taste and touch), mind-consciousness (which integrates the perceptions of the five senses into coherent images), *mano*-consciouness (which corresponds to the inner spiritual world), *alaya*-consciousness (or karmic storehouse), and *amala*-consciousness (which remains free of karmic impurity and is the basis of all life's functions). The ninth consciousness means the most profound *amala*-consciousness. The six consciousnesses means the first six of the nine consciousnesses, or the five senses plus mind-consciousness, the spiritual function that draws judgments and inferences in response to external stimuli.

17. Eternity, happiness, true self and purity: Four noble qualities or virtues of a Buddha's life. *Eternity* means that the Buddha nature is unchanging and everlasting. *Happiness* means tranquility and joy transcending any suffering. *True self* means that the Buddha nature is one's foundation and truth. And *purity* means free of deluded or erroneous conduct.

18. Translated from Japanese. Josei Toda, *Toda Josei zenshu* (Collected Writings of Josei Toda) (Tokyo: Seikyo Shimbunsha, 1982), vol. 2, pp. 446–47.

19. "Mind king" refers to the core of the mind, which controls the various workings of the mind.

20. "Palace of the ninth consciousness, the unchanging reality that reigns over all of life's functions": The ninth consciousness is likened to a palace because it is life's central function, and it is one with the eternal and immutable truth.

STUDY GUIDE

The following is a summary of points from SGI President Ikeda's lecture.

- The lay nun Ueno, to whom Nichiren Daishonin wrote this letter of condolence, was the widow of Nanjo Hyoe Shichiro. At the time of Hyoe Shichiro's death, the lay nun Ueno was pregnant with their fifth son and their second son Tokimitsu was 7 years old.

- Nichiren Buddhism enables those experiencing the greatest suffering to gain the greatest happiness. The Mystic Law has the power to change even hell into the Land of Tranquil Light.

- Nichiren Buddhism makes it possible for us to attain Buddhahood within this present lifetime and to eternally undergo the cycle of birth and death with complete freedom and boundless hope.

- If our lives are filled with joy, then our deaths will also be filled with joy, as will our next lives. Nichiren teaches that the cycle of birth and death is a continuum of joy and that the essence of life lies in dedicating ourselves to making that joy the reality of our existence and helping others do the same.

THE PURE LAND OF EAGLE PEAK IS THE ETERNAL "HOME" OF LIFE ITSELF

- The pure land of Eagle Peak is not some imaginary paradise like the Pure Land of Perfect Bliss believed in by the Pure Land school of Buddhism. Rather, it represents the realm of Buddhahood within the universe itself, reached by all who maintain faith in the Mystic Law to the very end of their lives. Second Soka Gakkai president Josei Toda described this as "merging with the realm of Buddhahood within the universe."

- To be a "Buddha in life" means bringing forth our innate Buddhahood, fulfilling our respective missions while facing life's difficulties and working for our own happiness as well as that of others. To be a "Buddha in death" means experiencing the joy of the Law after completing our missions in this lifetime and embarking on our next missions as bodhisattvas in the lifetime that follows.

  In this present existence, we can come to know that we are Buddhas in both life and death and that both life and death are pervaded by joy. Each moment of this existence is a struggle to achieve this state.

ATTAINING BUDDHAHOOD IN ONE'S PRESENT FORM IS A PRINCIPLE OF JOY AND HOPE

- Both the pure land and hell exist within us. To suppose that they exist somewhere else is an illusion.

- The Lotus Sutra teaches how to change our present circumstances into a Buddha land. Faith in the Lotus Sutra means undertaking the challenge to do this.

- In the Lotus Sutra, the dragon king's daughter demonstrates her Buddhahood, proving that the Mystic Law has the power to enable one to attain Buddhahood in his or her present form. She manifested Buddhahood in her present form to dispel the disbelief of certain bodhisattvas who thought a woman could not attain enlightenment. When she accomplished it, joy welled in the hearts of those who had not believed before.

NICHIREN BUDDHISM: ACTUALIZING THE PRINCIPLES OF THE LOTUS SUTRA

- Nichiren explains such profound principles as "attaining Buddhahood in one's present form" and "hell is itself the Land of Tranquil Light" to help his disciples deepen their faith. Such faith and conviction dispels the darkness or ignorance that obscures Buddhahood.

- Attaining Buddhahood in one's present form is not about acquiring special, superhuman qualities. All life—no matter in which of the Ten Worlds it may reside—is originally an entity of the Mystic Law.

- "In one's present form" doesn't mean attaining Buddhahood while surrendering to suffering. A struggle to transform the moment-to-moment focus of our minds is required.

- Believing in the Gohonzon means believing that the supremely noble state of life that Nichiren manifested

also exists within our own lives. This means persevering in faith and practicing as a votary of the Lotus Sutra, just as he did.

BECOME A WINNER IN THE REAL WORLD

- Though we may understand the Buddhist view of death intellectually, it is only natural that we grieve. Nichiren encourages the lay nun Ueno to turn her grief into prayer for the sake of her husband's eternal happiness.

- There is no need for us to pretend in front of the Gohonzon. We should chant Nam-myoho-renge-kyo to the Gohonzon just as we are, whether joyful or sad.

- Nichiren cites the words: "You should base your mind on the ninth consciousness, and carry out your practice in the six consciousnesses" (WND-1, 458).

- The "ninth consciousness" is the Mystic Law, the ultimate truth. To "base one's mind on the ninth consciousness" means simply chanting Nam-myoho-renge-kyo with faith in the Gohonzon. The "six consciousnesses" means the five senses that function in response to the phenomena of the world around us, plus the awareness that integrates these five senses. "To carry out one's practice in the six consciousnesses" means firmly establishing the state of Buddhahood within us by making our daily lives our place of practice.

(5)

"On the Buddha's Prophecy"

Worldwide *Kosen-rufu*—A Towering Declaration on
Sado Island for the Happiness of All Humankind

The seventh volume of the Lotus Sutra states, "After I have passed into extinction, in the last five-hundred-year period you must spread it [the Lotus Sutra] abroad widely throughout Jambudvipa and never allow it to be cut off." On the one hand, it is deplorable to me that more than 2,220 years have already passed since the Buddha's demise. What evil karma prevented me from being born in his lifetime? Why could not I have seen the four ranks of sages in the Former Day of the Law, or T'ien-t'ai and Dengyo in the Middle Day of the Law? On the other hand, I rejoice at whatever good fortune enabled me to be born in the last five-hundred-year period and to read these true words of the sutra.

Even if I had been born in the Buddha's lifetime, it would have served

no purpose, for those who embraced the four flavors of teachings had not yet heard of the Lotus Sutra. Again, my being born in either the Former or the Middle Day of the Law would have been meaningless, for neither the scholars of the three schools of the south or the seven schools of the north [in China], nor those of the Flower Garland, True Word, or any other schools, believed in the Lotus Sutra.

The Great Teacher T'ien-t'ai states, "In the last five-hundred-year period, the mystic way will spread and benefit humankind far into the future." Does this not describe the time of wide propagation? The Great Teacher Dengyo says, "The Former and Middle Days are almost over, and the Latter Day is near at hand." These words reveal how much he longed for the beginning of the Latter Day of the Law. If we consider the rewards of living in the different ages, it is clear that mine surpass those of Nagarjuna and Vasubandhu, and excel those of T'ien-t'ai and Dengyo. (*The Writings of Nichiren Daishonin*, vol. 1, p. 398)

Question: I have seen that the Buddha's prophecy applies to you; now what do you yourself predict?

Answer: In the light of the Buddha's prophecy, "the last five-hundred-year period" has already begun. I say that without fail Buddhism will arise and flow forth from the east, from the land of Japan....

Twenty-one years have gone by since I, Nichiren, understood this principle [and began propagation]. During this period I have suffered difficulties day after day and month after month. In the last two or three years, among other things, I was almost put to death. The chances are one in ten thousand that I will survive the year or even the month. If anyone questions these things, let that person ask my disciples for details.

What fortune is mine to expiate in one lifetime the offenses of slandering the Law I have accumulated from the infinite past! How delighted I am to serve Shakyamuni Buddha, the lord of teachings, whom I have never seen! I pray that before anything else I can

guide and lead the ruler and those others who persecuted me. I will tell the Buddha about all the disciples who have aided me, and before I die, I will transfer the great blessings deriving from my practice to my parents who gave me life. Now, as if in a dream, I understand the heart of the "Treasure Tower" chapter. As the sutra states: "If you were to seize Mount Sumeru and fling it far off to the measureless Buddha lands, that too would not be difficult. . . . But if after the Buddha has entered extinction, in the time of evil, you can preach this sutra, that will be difficult indeed!"

The Great Teacher Dengyo says: "Shakyamuni taught that the shallow is easy to embrace, but the profound is difficult. To discard the shallow and seek the profound is the way of a person of courage. The Great Teacher T'ien-t'ai trusted and obeyed Shakyamuni and worked to uphold the Lotus school, spreading its teachings throughout China. We of Mount Hiei inherited the doctrine from T'ien-t'ai and work to uphold the Lotus school and to disseminate its teachings throughout Japan." I, Nichiren of Awa Province, have doubtless inherited the teachings of the Law from these three teachers, and in this era of the Latter Day I work to uphold the Lotus school and disseminate the Law. Together we should be called the four teachers of the three countries. Nam-myoho-renge-kyo, Nam-myoho-renge-kyo. (WND-1, 401–02)

LECTURE

"On the Buddha's Prophecy" is one of my favorite writings of Nichiren Daishonin. To me, it powerfully communicates his lofty commitment to actualize Shakyamuni Buddha's prophecy of the future propagation of the Mystic Law throughout the world. And Nichiren's clarion call—urging his followers of future generations to rise into action for the sake of worldwide *kosen-rufu* in the same spirit as the Buddha—resonates eternally in my heart. It would be no exaggeration to say that this writing is the source of the Soka Gakkai spirit, which is directly connected to Nichiren Daishonin.

Second Soka Gakkai president Josei Toda put great emphasis on this writing and often lectured on it. In fact, he also spoke about it during our historic Osaka Campaign (in 1956), out of his wish for the great success of his disciples. I will never forget the profound debt we all owe him.

Mr. Toda specifically chose "On the Buddha's Prophecy" for the topic of his first general lecture in Osaka, held on January 17, 1956. In response to a question he fielded after his lecture on that occasion, he ardently said to the effect: "The Bodhisattvas of the Earth, who in the Lotus Sutra are entrusted with the Law of Nam-myoho-renge-kyo, will be reborn and gather together at the time of *kosen-rufu*. Therefore, you [as Bodhisattvas of the Earth] can't stay poor. Remember, you have the power of Nam-myoho-renge-kyo, the potential to realize infinite good fortune and benefit. You have to tap this power yourselves by chanting and teaching others to do the same."

The immortal history of "Ever-victorious Kansai," the tremendous success that we, as representatives of the people, achieved in the Osaka Campaign—accomplishing what everyone had thought impossible—all arose from the fresh determination and vibrant initiative of our members, Bodhisattvas of the Earth, who had been ignited by Mr. Toda's impassioned declaration.

Let us carefully study "On the Buddha's Prophecy" and once again dedicate ourselves to the great vow of *kosen-rufu*, the Soka Gakkai's starting point, as we set in motion glorious waves of victories from each of our districts.

The ["Medicine King" chapter in the] seventh volume of the Lotus Sutra states, "After I [Shakyamuni] have passed into extinction, in the last five-hundred-year period you must spread it [the Lotus Sutra] abroad widely [i.e., carry out *kosen-rufu*] throughout Jambudvipa [the entire world] and never allow it to be cut off."[1] On the one hand, it is deplorable to me that more than 2,220 years have already passed since the Buddha's demise. What evil karma prevented me from being born in his lifetime? Why could not I have seen the four ranks of sages[2] [people such as the Buddha's voice-hearer disciples Mahakashyapa and Ananda or the Buddhist scholars Nagarjuna and Vasubandhu] in the Former Day of the Law, or [the Great Teachers] T'ien-t'ai and Dengyo in the Middle Day of the Law?[3] On the other hand, I rejoice at whatever good fortune enabled me to be born in the last five-hundred-year period [that marks the start of the Latter Day of the Law] and to read these true words of the sutra.

Even if I had been born in the Buddha's lifetime, it would have served no purpose, for those who embraced the four flavors[4] of teachings [i.e., the Hinayana and provisional Mahayana teachings] had not yet heard of the Lotus Sutra. Again, my being born in either the Former or the Middle Day of the Law would have been meaningless, for neither the scholars of the three schools of the south or the seven schools of the north [in China],[5] nor those of the Flower Garland, True Word, or any other schools [of Buddhism in Japan], believed in the Lotus Sutra.

The Great Teacher T'ien-t'ai states, "In the last five-hundred-year period [that marks the start of the Latter Day], the mystic way [i.e., the Mystic Law] will spread and benefit humankind far into the future."[6] Does this not describe the time of wide propagation [*kosen-rufu*]? The Great Teacher Dengyo says, "The Former and Middle Days are almost over, and the Latter Day is near at hand."[7] These words reveal how much he longed for the beginning of the Latter Day of the Law. If we consider the rewards of living in the different ages, it is clear that mine surpass those of Nagarjuna and Vasubandhu, and excel those of T'ien-t'ai and Dengyo. (WND-1, 398)

THE BUDDHA'S PROPHECY: A TESTAMENT FOR FOLLOWERS OF FUTURE GENERATIONS

"On the Buddha's Prophecy," concerns itself primarily with fulfilling or actualizing the Buddha's prophecy for the future.

On one level, "the Buddha's prophecy" indicates the prophecy of Shakyamuni, but the essential purpose of this writing is to announce the prophecy of Nichiren Daishonin as the Buddha of the Latter Day of the Law.

Shakyamuni's prophecy is contained in the passage from the "Medicine King" chapter of the Lotus Sutra, which Nichiren cites at the beginning of this writing. It conveys the Buddha's will and decree, urging followers in the evil age after his passing—and especially in the Latter Day of the Law—to battle the onslaught of devilish forces and ensure that the widespread propagation of the Lotus Sutra throughout the entire world never ceases.

In this writing, Nichiren states that he alone has actualized Shakyamuni's prophecy. He then predicts that the great Law of Nam-myoho-renge-kyo, which is the essence of the Lotus Sutra, will spread widely throughout the world.

Nichiren composed "On the Buddha's Prophecy" in the intercalary fifth month of 1273, at Ichinosawa on Sado Island, his place of exile. Interestingly, no recipient is specified. This would seem to indicate that this work is an important writing meant as a will and testament addressed to all his followers in the present and future.

Already, while on Sado, he had composed "The Opening of the Eyes" and "The Object of Devotion for Observing the Mind," which clarify the object of devotion, or Gohonzon, in terms of the Person and the Law,

respectively. Based on these profound doctrines, "On the Buddha's Prophecy" explains that Nichiren Buddhism—by enabling people to attain the infinitely noble state of life that is one with the Mystic Law, the fundamental law of the universe—is the supreme teaching for the enlightenment of all humanity in the Latter Day.

THE JOY OF BEING BORN IN THE LATTER DAY OF THE LAW

At the outset, Nichiren Daishonin says that it is regrettable that, as a result of being born in the Latter Day of the Law, he has missed the chance of meeting Shakyamuni Buddha who expounded the Lotus Sutra, or the great Buddhist teachers T'ien-t'ai, Dengyo and others who propagated the sutra during the Former and Middle Days of the Law.

The Latter Day is a period far removed from the time of Shakyamuni. It is an age when his influence as a teacher declines, his teachings lapse into formality and Buddhism as a whole loses its power to lead people to enlightenment. In this writing, Nichiren describes the Latter Day as a time when Shakyamuni's teachings remain in form only and are neither practiced nor produce any proof of benefit (enlightenment).[8] Along with this decline in Buddhism, it is also an age when people's life force wanes and when the age itself becomes polluted. Accordingly, people of Nichiren's day regarded the Latter

Day as a deplorable time to be alive—both in terms of the Law and the age.

However, Nichiren reverses this, saying that being born in the Latter Day is in fact a cause for rejoicing. This is because the Latter Day coincides exactly with the "last five-hundred-year period" that Shakyamuni specifies in the "Medicine King" chapter as the time for the realization of his wish for the widespread propagation of the Mystic Law throughout the entire world. As supporting evidence, Nichiren further cites the words of T'ien-t'ai and Dengyo, which can be read as expressing their wish to be born in this latter age.

On the face of it, the Latter Day is an age of deadlock and decline, but Nichiren says that, in terms of the Law, we are fortunate to live in an age when the correct teaching will spread.

THE ULTIMATE MYSTIC PRINCIPLE AND THE INFINITELY NOBLE LIFE OF THE BUDDHA

How, then, can Nichiren Daishonin say that, in terms of the Law, the Latter Day is in fact a fortunate age?

In "On the Buddha's Prophecy," in addition to outlining the nature of the Latter Day, Nichiren elucidates both the teaching that will be spread during that age and the person who will propagate it. In conclusion, he states: "The heavenly gods and benevolent deities, as well as the bodhisattvas numerous as the dust particles of a thousand worlds who emerged from beneath the ground, will protect him (the person who discards the provisional teachings and correctly upholds the Lotus Sutra) as the votary of the Lotus Sutra. Under their protection, he will [establish and] spread abroad widely (i.e., carry out *kosen-rufu*) throughout Jambudvipa (the entire world) the object of devotion of the essential teaching, or the five characters of Myoho-renge-kyo" (WND-1, 400).

In other words, the teaching that should be spread in the Latter Day of the Law is "the object of devotion of the essential teaching, or the five characters of Myoho-renge-kyo." And the person who will spread it is "the votary of the Lotus Sutra." When these two requirements are met, the Latter Day is transformed from a deplorable and defiled age in which the Buddha's teaching has all but perished into a joyous age of widespread propagation of the Lotus Sutra.

"The object of devotion of the essential teaching, or the five characters of Myoho-renge-kyo" constitutes the ultimate mystic principle for the enlightenment of all people. It is also the infinitely noble life of the Buddha that is one with the mystic principle. Moreover, it is the supreme Law by which all Buddhas gain enlightenment. As such, it can also be called "the seed of Buddhahood," in the sense that it is the cause for attaining this highest state of life.

FROM "THE EMERGENCE OF THE TREASURE TOWER" CHAPTER OF THE LOTUS SUTRA

If there were a person
who took the empty sky in his hand
and walked all around with it,
that would not be difficult.
But if after I have passed into extinction
one can write out and embrace this sutra
and cause others to write it out,
that will be difficult indeed!
If one took the great earth,
placed it on his toenail,
and ascended with it to the
    Brahma heaven,
that would not be difficult.
But if after the Buddha has passed
    into extinction,
in the time of evil,
one can even for a little while
    read this sutra,
that will be difficult indeed!
If, when the fires come at the end
    of the kalpa,
one can load dry grass on his back
and enter the fire without being burned,
that would not be difficult.
But after I have passed into extinction
if one can embrace this sutra
and expound it to even one person,
that will be difficult indeed!
If one were to embrace this storehouse
of eighty-four thousand doctrines,
the twelve divisions of the sutras,
and expound it to others,
causing listeners
to acquire the six transcendental
    powers—
though one could do that,

that would not be difficult.
But after I have entered extinction
if one can listen to and accept this sutra
and ask about its meaning,
that will be difficult indeed!
If a person expounds the Law,
allowing thousands, ten thousands,
    millions,
immeasurable numbers of living beings
equal to Ganges sands
to become arhats
endowed with the six transcendental
    powers,
though one might confer such benefits,
that would not be difficult.
But after I have entered extinction
if one can honor and embrace
a sutra such as this one,
that will be difficult indeed!
For the sake of the Buddha way
in immeasurable numbers of lands
from the beginning until now
I have widely preached many sutras,
and among them
this sutra is foremost.
If one can uphold this,
he will be upholding the Buddha's body.
All you good men,
after I have entered extinction
who can accept and uphold,
read and recite this sutra?
Now in the presence of the Buddha
let him come forward and speak his vow!

(See *The Lotus Sutra and Its Opening
and Closing Sutras*, pp. 218–20)

All people inherently possess the seed of Buddhahood, but the darkness or ignorance that shrouds their lives prevents that seed from readily functioning; hence the need for a teacher who shows the way to conquer that darkness and for a teaching that clearly elucidates the universal existence of this seed. In the Latter Day of the Law, this teacher is "the votary of the Lotus Sutra," and the teaching is "the object of devotion of the essential teaching, or the five characters of Myoho-renge-kyo."

The people of the Latter Day need the direct path to enlightenment that is the Mystic Law—a path that activates the seed of Buddhahood within them. That is why Nichiren first clarified the teacher and the teaching—or the Person and the Law—in "The Opening of the Eyes" and "The Object of Devotion for Observing the Mind,"[9] and then composed "On the Buddha's Prophecy" to issue his declaration for worldwide *kosen-rufu.*

THE VOTARY OF THE LOTUS SUTRA WHO BATTLES DEVILISH FORCES IS THE TEACHER OF THE LATTER DAY

Nichiren Daishonin's identification of the votary of the Lotus Sutra as the teacher who will propagate the Mystic Law in the Latter Day is a point of enormous importance in his teaching of Buddhism. This is because the process of bringing to fruition the seed of Buddhahood, which is the Law of life, and battling the darkness or ignorance that prevents this seed from sprouting all come down to human beings themselves. The person who qualifies as the teacher of the Latter Day of the Law, therefore, must be someone who can demonstrate through personal example that individuals have the power to break through their fundamental darkness and manifest the potential of the seed of Buddhahood (enlightenment). This is the votary of the Lotus Sutra of whom he speaks. The votary is one who actually puts the sutra's teachings into practice. Someone who only studies the Lotus Sutra, or who only reads and recites it out of formality, cannot be considered a votary.

The defining qualities of the votary of the Lotus Sutra are practicing the sutra's teaching with one's life and showing the actual proof of manifesting the potential of the seed of Buddhahood. In particular, to secure the way for all people to bring the seed of Buddhahood to fruition in the reality of their lives, the votary needs to have powerful conviction and make determined efforts to defeat the devilish functions that will invariably arise in the course of this challenge.

Struggles against devilish functions are also the starting point of the Soka Gakkai. Our founding president, Tsunesaburo Makiguchi, proclaimed: "It must be said that actual proof of

Shakyamuni's prediction three millennia ago of the defiled and evil age of the Latter Day of the Law, a fearful and evil age such as the present, is borne out not so much by such serious crimes as robbery and murder . . . or by great social ills. Rather, it is due to high-ranking priests and the so-called accomplished, wise and learned who, while occupying positions of high office and high standing in society and appearing to possess discernment, integrity and virtue, are in fact jealous and disparaging of persons of great good. They acquiesce to and abet persons of great evil, and in this way, put their energy into protecting their positions and maintaining the status quo."

In the Latter Day, people of seemingly upstanding character and reputation in society will harbor jealousy and resentment toward people of integrity, and they will seek to ingratiate themselves with people who are corrupt and authoritarian. That such a paradoxical situation will inevitably arise is one of the main reasons why it is so hard to propagate the correct teaching of Buddhism in this defiled age.

It is the mission of the votary of the Lotus Sutra, the teacher of the Latter Day of the Law, to ceaselessly challenge this difficulty.

Because the first three Soka Gakkai presidents persevered in this struggle, they could take the lead for *kosen-rufu* in the modern age.

Question: I have seen that the Buddha's prophecy applies to you [Nichiren]; now what do you yourself predict?

Answer: In the light of the Buddha's prophecy, "the last five-hundred-year period" [that marks the start of the Latter Day of the Law] has already begun. I say that without fail [the correct teaching of] Buddhism will arise and flow forth from the east, from the land of Japan. (WND-1, 401)

The defining qualities of the votary of the Lotus Sutra are practicing the sutra's teaching with one's life and showing the actual proof of manifesting the potential of the seed of Buddhahood.

NICHIREN DAISHONIN'S PROPHECY: THE WESTWARD TRANSMISSION OF BUDDHISM

Nichiren Daishonin's own prophecy is clear. A direct question is posed about his prediction for the future, and he answers unhesitatingly. His prediction is that of the westward transmission of Buddhism[10]—that is to say, worldwide *kosen-rufu*. He declares that the great Law, Nam-myoho-renge-kyo, which has the power to lead all people to enlightenment throughout the 10,000 years and more of the Latter Day, has now appeared. And he prophesies that it will open the way for the happiness of humanity and lead to the construction of a world of peace and prosperity. He writes: "The moon appears in the west and sheds its light eastward,[11] but the sun rises in the east and casts its rays to the west. The same is true of Buddhism. [The Buddhism of Shakyamuni] spread from west to east [making its way from India to Japan] in the Former and Middle Days of the Law, but [the great Law of Nam-myoho-renge-kyo] will travel from east [Japan] to west in the Latter Day" (WND-1, 401).

Regarding this passage, Mr. Toda wrote: "If we were to fail to actualize this prediction, then wouldn't we, as the Buddha's disciples, be guilty of making a lie of the Buddha's prophecy? That is a truly frightening and sobering thought." In response to the prophecy

of the westward transmission of Buddhism, Mr. Toda called for the realization of *kosen-rufu* in Asia and encouraged us youth to take our place on the global stage to propagate Nichiren Buddhism far and wide. Our great alliance for peace based on the Mystic Law has today spread to 192 countries and territories. Making Mr. Toda's spirit my own, I opened a path to the world.

Mr. Makiguchi earnestly took to heart the declaration of the westward transmission of Buddhism and worldwide *kosen-rufu*, and nurtured a fervent wish to enable people across the globe to actualize the principle of "attaining Buddhahood in one's present form." Mr. Toda inherited this wish of his mentor. Before he died, he told me about a dream he had of going to Mexico. "They were all waiting," he said. "Everyone was waiting. They were all seeking Nichiren Buddhism. I want to go—to travel the world on a journey for *kosen-rufu.*" These words will resonate forever in my mind.

Each time I have ventured overseas, I have done so with the spirit of taking Mr. Toda with me and showing him firsthand the development of worldwide *kosen-rufu*. With that sentiment, I have visited countries around the globe and reached out in dialogue to countless people. When traveling abroad, I have always carried with me a photograph of my mentor. And now I can confidently report to him my victory. I have actualized the cherished wish of my two great predecessors. I have completed the sound and solid foundations of worldwide *kosen-rufu*. I can vividly imagine Mr. Toda's warm, happy smile.

The second act of worldwide *kosen-rufu* is an age when infinite brilliant flowers of value creation based on Buddhism come into bloom through the magnificent endeavors of our members, Bodhisattvas of the Earth. I have fully prepared the stage for them. People from diverse fields around the globe have high hopes for the SGI's activities for peace and culture.

This victory, glory and good fortune is shared by all our members throughout the world, and will flow on to their children and descendants in future generations. I extend my heartfelt gratitude to everyone.

Twenty-one years have gone by since I, Nichiren, understood this principle [and began propagation]. During this period I have suffered difficulties day after day and month after month. In the last two or three years, among other things, I was almost put to death. The chances are one in ten thousand that I will survive the year or even the month. If anyone questions these things, let that person ask my disciples for details.

What fortune is mine to expiate in one lifetime the offenses of slandering the Law I have accumulated from the

infinite past! How delighted I am to serve Shakyamuni Buddha, the lord of teachings, whom I have never seen! I pray that before anything else I can guide and lead the ruler and those others who persecuted me. I will tell the Buddha about all the disciples who have aided me, and before I die, I will transfer the great blessings deriving from my practice to my parents who gave me life. (WND-1, 402)

THE SERENE MIND OF THE BUDDHA OF THE LATTER DAY OF THE LAW

"This principle" refers to the appearance of the votary of the Lotus Sutra, who will undertake the widespread propagation of the Law in the Latter Day just as Shakyamuni predicts in the sutra. Nichiren Daishonin had been aware of this principle for 21 years, since establishing his teaching (in 1253).

Throughout that time, he endured steadily intensifying persecution and was ultimately exiled to Sado. Though never knowing whether he would survive to see another day, Nichiren here records his resolve to exert even greater effort to spread the correct teaching and lead people to enlightenment. In those days, being sentenced to exile on Sado was second in severity only to execution. No one, it was said, ever returned from exile. Therefore, his assertion, "The chances are one in ten thousand that I will survive the year or even the month," is certainly not hyperbole.

From his instruction, "If anyone questions these things, let that person ask my disciples for details," we can surmise that he may well have considered that this writing could be his last. Living in the harsh conditions he did and under constant threat of death by starvation, cold or assassination—he may have intended this treatise to convey the necessary teachings to his successors and encourage his disciples.

Discussing "On the Buddha's Prophecy," Mr. Toda wrote: "In this writing, we can palpably sense the serene state of mind of Nichiren Daishonin, the Buddha of the Latter Day of the Law. . . . Buddhahood is a state of absolute happiness. A state of being that at each moment is like a translucent ocean or a cloudless sky, utterly invincible and fearless—this is how I perceive Nichiren's state of life during his exile on Sado."

NICHIREN'S COMPASSIONATE STRUGGLE TO TRANSFORM THE DESTINY OF HUMANKIND

The struggle of *kosen-rufu*—which is a struggle against obstacles and devilish functions—abounds with the power to transform the destiny of each person. This in turn can lead to a transformation in the destiny of a country, and a transformation in the destiny of all humankind. Because this is a struggle in which we dedicate our lives to fulfilling the great vow of the Buddha and seek to bring forth Buddhahood in ourselves and others, it constitutes the great path to elevating the life-state of all humankind. Describing the joy of manifesting one's Buddhahood, Nichiren Daishonin says: "What fortune is mine . . ." "How delighted I am. . . ."

Also, through striving for *kosen-rufu* with the aim of realizing happiness

The second act of worldwide *kosen-rufu* is an age when infinite brilliant flowers of value creation based on Buddhism come into bloom through the magnificent endeavors of our members, Bodhisattvas of the Earth.

for ourselves and others, our own compassionate life force is strengthened. In this writing, Nichiren shows great compassion toward the ruler, his disciples and his parents. His statement, "I pray that before anything else I can guide and lead the ruler and those others who persecuted me," can be read as the ultimate expression of compassion. He also voices his wish to report to Shakyamuni about his praiseworthy disciples who have sincerely aided and supported him, and to transfer the great blessings of Buddhahood to his parents, thereby repaying his debt of gratitude to them.

Pervaded with joy, appreciation and compassion, these resounding declarations flow forth from the Daishonin's towering state of life as the votary of the Lotus Sutra who has battled through and triumphed over all obstacles. Indeed, we can regard them as the jubilant expression of Buddhahood, as great proclamations of victory by the Buddha of the Latter Day, whom no onslaught of persecution could defeat.

Now, as if in a dream, I understand the heart of the "Treasure Tower" chapter [of the Lotus Sutra]. As the sutra states: "If you were to seize Mount Sumeru[12] and fling it far off to the measureless Buddha lands, that too would not be difficult…. But if after the Buddha has entered extinction, in the time of evil,

you can preach this sutra, that will be difficult indeed!" [see LSOC, 218]

The Great Teacher Dengyo says: "Shakyamuni taught that the shallow is easy to embrace, but the profound is difficult. To discard the shallow and seek the profound is the way of a person of courage. The Great Teacher T'ien-t'ai trusted and obeyed Shakyamuni and worked to uphold the Lotus school,[13] spreading its teachings throughout China. We of Mount Hiei [the Tendai school of Japan] inherited the doctrine from T'ien-t'ai and work to uphold the Lotus school and to disseminate its teachings throughout Japan."[14] I, Nichiren of Awa Province,[15] have doubtless inherited the teachings of the Law from these three teachers [Shakyamuni, T'ien-t'ai, and Dengyo], and in this era of the Latter Day I work to uphold the Lotus school and disseminate the Law. Together we should be called the four teachers of the three countries. Nam-myoho-renge-kyo, Nam-myoho-renge-kyo. (WND-1, 402)

"TO DISCARD THE SHALLOW AND SEEK THE PROFOUND IS THE WAY OF A PERSON OF COURAGE"

Here, Nichiren Daishonin discusses the concept of the six difficult and nine easy acts, which is found in the "Emergence of the Treasure Tower" chapter of the Lotus Sutra. Compared to such things as "seizing Mount Sumeru and flinging it far off to the measureless Buddha lands" or "loading dry grass on one's back and entering a great fire without being burned" (see LSOC, 218–19), it is far more difficult to propagate the Lotus Sutra after the Buddha's passing. What was Shakyamuni's purpose in teaching the six difficult and nine easy acts? By emphasizing how difficult it will be to advance *kosen-rufu* in the Latter Day, he sought to drive home to the bodhisattvas at the assembly depicted in the Lotus Sutra the fact that they will need to make a powerful vow to guide all people to enlightenment.

The "heart of the 'Treasure Tower' chapter"—this is the heart of the Buddha's vow to realize the happiness of

humanity. It is also the commitment of the Bodhisattvas of the Earth, who inherit this vow of the Buddha and stand up resolutely to accomplish *kosen-rufu* in the Latter Day, no matter how enormous the hardships they may face.

As he indicates in "The Opening of the Eyes," Nichiren established his teaching with a deep understanding of the significance of the "Treasure Tower" chapter explication of the six difficult and nine easy acts and rose into action to fulfill his vow as a Bodhisattva of the Earth.[16] True to this vow, he triumphed over the relentless succession of persecutions that assailed him.

During the Sado exile, his last great persecution, Nichiren eternally established Nam-myoho-renge-kyo as the supreme Law for the enlightenment of

By maintaining a strong and deep resolve to devote our lives to the vow for *kosen-rufu* and fulfill our mission despite all obstacles, we can forge and develop within ourselves the life-state of Buddhahood.

all people. Moreover, in this writing, he issued his declaration for worldwide *kosen-rufu*, which we can read as his great declaration of victory as the Buddha of the Latter Day of the Law.

Thus, Nichiren writes, "Now, as if in a dream, I understand the heart of the 'Treasure Tower' chapter." In other words, he is saying that because, true to his vow, he has endured great persecution and dedicated his life to propagating the Mystic Law in this latter age, he has attained the "heart of the 'Treasure Tower' chapter"—namely, the "heart of the Buddha." Overcoming all manner of hardships and dedicating our lives to the vow to propagate the Lotus Sutra is the sole way to make the "heart of the Buddha" our own.

By maintaining a strong and deep resolve to devote our lives to the vow for *kosen-rufu* and fulfill our mission despite all obstacles, we can forge and develop within ourselves the life-state of Buddhahood. Nichiren makes this point by citing the words of the Great Teacher Dengyo, "To discard the shallow and seek the profound is the way of a person of courage." Here, "a person of courage" means a person of intrepid spirit who stands up confidently with faith that is dedicated to *kosen-rufu*, in accord with the "heart of the Buddha" described in the Lotus Sutra.

When we devote ourselves courageously and tirelessly to the struggle for *kosen-rufu*, the "heart of the Buddha" must well forth in our lives.

THE LOTUS SCHOOL IS CHARACTERIZED BY HUMANISM AND VALUE CREATION

At the end of this writing, Nichiren Daishonin states that he has been undertaking the propagation of the Mystic Law in the Latter Day, having inherited the legacy of the so-called three teachers of the three countries of the "Lotus school"—Shakyamuni in India, T'ien-t'ai in China and Dengyo in Japan. He thus declares that his name will be added to theirs, so that together they will be called the "four teachers of the three countries."

The "four teachers of the three countries" expresses the lineage of the votaries of the Lotus Sutra. It is the true line of succession in the effort to actualize Buddhism's ultimate ideal of universal enlightenment. And votaries of the Lotus Sutra are the creative pioneers who open up the path to this goal.

The teachings of the "Lotus school" bring forth the infinite power of the Mystic Law in our lives as well as those of others. These teachings also enable all people to realize their fullest potential, creating boundless value in their lives in the midst of an evil and defiled age— like lotus blossoms growing in the muddy water. They enable people everywhere to lead victorious lives as brilliant flowers of humanity—allowing the lotus blossoms of our individual lives and those of others to come into full glorious bloom. In other words, the "Lotus school" is characterized by humanism and value creation, seeking to guide all people to the highest state of life.

Nichiren, here, refers to himself not as "Nichiren of Japan," but as "Nichiren of Awa Province," identifying himself as an ordinary human being concerned with his immediate locality. While this way of referring to himself could be interpreted as merely an expression of modesty, it also conveys that the teaching he has established has universal relevance for people everywhere based on their common humanity, transcending national boundaries.

Established in the lineage of the "four teachers of the three countries," the Soka Gakkai is the sole organization dedicated to accomplishing the Buddha's decree and actually spreading the teachings of the true "Lotus school"

throughout the world. It is a noble community of practitioners that continues to call forth countless Bodhisattvas of the Earth around the globe and advances dauntlessly toward peace, into the eternal future.

Mr. Toda cried out, "Let us lead the way to *kosen-rufu*!" And he proclaimed, "The Soka Gakkai is the king of the religious world!"

Together with all of you who have joined me in this struggle, I declare with great pride, "We are the ones who are fulfilling the prophecy of the Buddha of the Latter Day of the Law."

With exhilaration and bright hope, let us lead brilliant lives aiming toward the distant future, so that we can proclaim resounding victory for our lives and the SGI movement.

This lecture was published in the January 2008 issue of The Daibyakurenge, *the Soka Gakkai study journal.*

NOTES:

1. *The Lotus Sutra and Its Opening and Closing Sutras*, p. 330.

2. Four ranks of sages: Buddhist teachers to be relied upon after Shakyamuni Buddha's death. They are explained in the Nirvana and other sutras, which classify them into four ranks according to their level of understanding. In this writing, the four ranks of sages specifically refer to people such as the Buddha's voice-hearer disciples Mahakashyapa and Ananda, and the Buddhist scholars Nagarjuna and Vasubandhu.

3. The periods after Shakyamuni's death are divided into three periods—the Former, Middle and Latter Days of the Law—the first two are, according to various sources, thought to have lasted approximately 500 or 1,000 years each. In the Former Day, the teaching, practice and proof of Shakyamuni's teachings are all present, and those who practice Buddhism and attain enlightenment are more numerous than in the ages that follow. During the Middle Day, the Buddha's teachings gradually become formalities, the people's connection to them weakens and progressively fewer people can gain enlightenment through their practice. The Latter Day, meanwhile, is described as a time when the Buddha's teachings fall into confusion and lose the power to lead people to enlightenment. Said to last for 10,000 years and more—indicating the eternal future—the Latter Day begins in the fifth of the 500-year periods following Shakyamuni's death.

4. Four flavors: Also, the first four flavors. A reference to the first four of the five flavors—fresh milk, cream, curdled milk, butter and ghee (the finest clarified butter). The four flavors is a term used to indicate the pre-Lotus Sutra teachings of the Buddha. T'ien-t'ai used the five flavors as a metaphor for the teachings of the five periods—the Flower Garland, Agama, Correct and Equal, Wisdom, and Lotus and Nirvana periods. Thus he compared the process by which Shakyamuni instructed his disciples and gradually developed their capacity to that of converting milk into ghee.

5. Three schools of the south and seven schools of the north: Also, three schools of southern China and seven schools of northern China. Though generally referred to as "schools," they are actually the 10 principal systems of classification of the Buddhist sutras set forth by various Buddhist teachers in China, during the Northern and Southern Dynasties period (439–589). Hence there are no specific names for the respective schools.

6. *The Words and Phrases of the Lotus Sutra.*

7. *An Essay on the Protection of the Nation.*

8. Nichiren writes: "In the Latter Day of the Law…Hinayana retains nothing but its teaching; it has neither practice nor proof. [Provisional] Mahayana still has its teaching and practice, but no longer provides any proof of benefit, either conspicuous or inconspicuous" (WND-1, 399).

9. In "The Opening of the Eyes," composed in February 1272 and addressed to all of his followers, Nichiren reveals that he is the Buddha of the Latter Day who, embodying the three virtues of sovereign, teacher and parent, guides the people of this evil age to enlightenment. In "The Object of Devotion for Observing the Mind," composed in April 1273, Nichiren clarifies the object of devotion as Nam-myoho-renge-kyo, the fundamental Law by which all people in the Latter Day can attain enlightenment.

10. Westward transmission of Buddhism: Nichiren predicted that his Buddhism of the sun would flow from Japan toward the west, returning to the countries through which Buddhism had originally been transmitted and spreading throughout the entire world.

11. "The moon appears in the west and sheds its light eastward." According to one explanation, this refers to how the location where the moon first becomes visible from the start of the new month shifts gradually eastward with each passing day. According to another explanation, the new moon at the start of the month is very narrow and dim, and appears low in the western sky shortly after dusk, only to quickly vanish below the horizon. It is thought that Shakyamuni's Buddhism is being compared to this phenomenon.

12. Mount Sumeru: In ancient Indian cosmology, the mountain that stands at the center of the world.

13. The Lotus school refers to T'ien-t'ai's teachings, which are based on the Lotus Sutra. It also means Nichiren's teachings.

14. *The Outstanding Principles of the Lotus Sutra.*

15. Present-day southern Chiba Prefecture, Japan.

16. Nichiren writes: "If I were to falter in my determination in the face of persecutions by the sovereign, however, it would be better not to speak out. While thinking this over, I recalled the teachings of the 'Treasure Tower' chapter on the six difficult and nine easy acts. . . . But such acts are not difficult, we are told, when compared to the difficulty of embracing even one phrase or verse of the Lotus Sutra in the Latter Day of the Law. Nevertheless, I vowed to summon up a powerful and unconquerable desire for the salvation of all beings and never to falter in my efforts" ("The Opening of the Eyes," WND-1, 239–40).

STUDY GUIDE
The following is a summary of points from SGI President Ikeda's lecture.

- "On the Buddha's Prophecy" is concerned with the fulfillment of the prophecies of both Shakyamuni and Nichiren Daishonin.

- Shakyamuni's prophecy urges his followers in the evil age after his passing to battle devilish forces and to ensure the widespread propagation of the Lotus Sutra. Nichiren states that he alone has actualized Shakyamuni's prophecy. He predicts that the great Law of Nam-myoho-renge-kyo, the essence of the Lotus Sutra, will spread throughout the world.

- No recipient is specified in this letter, possibly indicating that it is meant for all his followers in the present and future.

THE JOY OF BEING BORN IN THE LATTER DAY OF THE LAW

- The Latter Day, long after Shakyamuni's time, is an age in which his influence as a teacher declines and Buddhist practice has become mere formality, having lost its power to lead people to enlightenment.

  People of Nichiren's time considered the Latter Day to be a time of decline for Buddhism and for life in general.

- Nichiren considered living in the Latter Day to be a cause for rejoicing, as it coincides with the time Shakyamuni predicted for the propagation of the Mystic Law throughout the world.

THE ULTIMATE MYSTIC PRINCIPLE AND THE INFINITELY NOBLE LIFE OF THE BUDDHA

- The teaching that should be spread in the Latter Day of the Law is "the object of devotion of the essential teaching, or the five characters of Myoho-renge-kyo." The person who will spread it is "the votary of the Lotus Sutra." When these two requirements are met, the Latter Day is transformed from a defiled age in which the Buddha's teaching has all but perished into a joyous age of widespread propagation of the Lotus Sutra.

- Myoho-renge-kyo constitutes the ultimate mystic principle for the enlightenment of all people. It is also the infinitely noble life of the Buddha and the supreme Law by which all Buddhas gain enlightenment. It can also be called "the seed of Buddhahood," in the sense that it is the cause for attaining this highest state of life.

- All people inherently possess the seed of Buddhahood, but the ignorance that shrouds their lives prevents that seed from readily functioning. Hence the need for a teacher who shows the way to conquer that darkness and for a teaching that clearly elucidates the existence of this seed within each person's life.

THE VOTARY OF THE LOTUS SUTRA WHO BATTLES DEVILISH FORCES IS THE TEACHER OF THE LATTER DAY

- Nichiren's identification of the votary of the Lotus Sutra as the teacher who will propagate the Mystic Law in the Latter Day is a point of enormous importance in his teaching of Buddhism.

- The person who qualifies as the teacher of the Latter Day of the Law must be someone who can demonstrate through personal example that all individuals can over-come the fundamental darkness and manifest the seed of Buddhahood.

- The votary of the Lotus Sutra puts the sutra's teachings into practice. One who studies, reads or recites the sutra out of formality cannot be considered a votary. The votary must have powerful conviction to defeat the devilish functions that arise in the course of this challenge.

- The "Treasure Tower" chapter of the Lotus Sutra states that it is far more difficult to teach the Lotus Sutra after the Buddha's passing than to fulfill tasks such as "seizing Mount Sumeru and flinging it far off to the measure-less Buddha lands" (see LSOC, 218).

- Shakyamuni's purpose in stressing the difficult nature of propagation is to show his disciples the depth of the vow they must make in order to spread the sutra.

- Nichiren established his teaching with a deep understanding of the significance of the "Treasure Tower" chapter and took action to fulfill his vow as a Bodhisattva of the Earth.

- Nichiren writes: "Now, as if in a dream, I understand the heart of the 'Treasure Tower' chapter." True to his vow, he endured persecution and dedicated his life to propagating the Mystic Law in this latter age.

- By maintaining a deep resolve to devote our lives to the vow for *kosen-rufu* despite all obstacles, we develop the life-state of Buddhahood.

THE LOTUS SCHOOL IS CHARACTERIZED BY HUMANISM AND VALUE CREATION

- Nichiren propagated the Mystic Law in the Latter Day, having inherited the legacy of the three teachers of the three countries of the "Lotus school"— Shakyamuni in India, T'ien-t'ai in China and Dengyo in Japan. He declares that his name will be added and together they will be called the "four teachers of the three countries."

   Established in this lineage, the Soka Gakkai is the sole organization dedicated to accomplishing the Bud-dha's decree to spread the teachings of the true "Lotus school" through-out the world.

(6)

"Winter Always Turns to Spring"

Bringing Forth the Great Power of Faith—The Inspirational
Force of Nichiren Daishonin's Towering Conviction

The Passage for Study in This Lecture

Your late husband had an ailing son and a daughter. I cannot help thinking that he may have grieved that, if he were to abandon them and leave this world, his aged wife, as feeble as a withered tree, would be left alone, and would probably feel very sorry for these children. In addition, he may also have worried about Nichiren. Since the Buddha's words are in no way false, the Lotus Sutra is sure to spread widely. In that regard, perhaps your husband felt that certainly something would happen and this priest would become highly respected. When I was exiled contrary to his expectations, he must have wondered how the Lotus Sutra and the ten demon daughters[1] could possibly have allowed it to happen. Were he still living, how delighted he would be to see Nichiren pardoned! How glad he would be to see that my prediction has been fulfilled, now that the Mongol empire has attacked Japan and the country is in a crisis. These are the feelings of ordinary people.

Those who believe in the Lotus Sutra are as if in winter, but winter always turns to spring. Never, from ancient times on, has anyone heard or seen of winter turning back to autumn. Nor have we ever heard of a believer in the Lotus Sutra who turned into an ordinary [unenlightened] person. The sutra reads, "If there are those who hear the Law, then not a one will fail to attain Buddhahood" [see *The Lotus Sutra and Its Opening and Closing Sutras*, p. 75].

Your husband gave his life for the Lotus Sutra. His entire livelihood depended on a small fief, and that was confiscated because of his faith in the Lotus Sutra. Surely that equals giving his life for the Lotus Sutra. The boy Snow Mountains[2] was able to give his body for half a verse of a Buddhist teaching, and Bodhisattva Medicine King[3] was able to burn his arms as an offering to the Buddha because both were sages, and it was like pouring water on fire. But your husband was an ordinary person, so it was like putting paper in fire. Therefore, he must certainly have received blessings as great as theirs.

He is probably watching his wife and children in the heavenly mirrors of the sun and moon every moment of the day and night. Since you and your children are ordinary persons, you cannot see or hear him; neither can the deaf hear thunder nor the blind see the sun. But never doubt that he is protecting you. Moreover, he may be close at hand.

Just when I was thinking that, if at all possible, I must somehow come and see you, you had a robe sent here to me. This was a totally unexpected circumstance. Since the Lotus Sutra is the noblest of all sutras, I may yet gain influence in this lifetime. If so, rest assured that I will look after your children whether you are still living or are watching from under the sod. While I was in the province of Sado and during my stay here [at Minobu], you sent your servant to help me. In what lifetime could I ever forget what you have done for me? I will repay this debt of gratitude by serving you in the next lifetime. (*The Writings of Nichiren Daishonin*, vol. 1, pp. 535–36)

LECTURE

"I have heard of a marvelous Buddhist expression," said a smiling Jutta Unkart-Seifert, former undersecretary of Austria's Federal Ministry of Education, the Arts and Sport with whom my wife and I have enjoyed a long friendship. She then cited the passage from Nichiren Daishonin's writings, "Winter Always Turns to Spring" (WND-1, 536). Dr. Unkart-Seifert explained that Austria has similar sayings such as "After the rain comes sunshine." She also shared that she had learned to live with a sunny, positive spirit to give hope and inspiration to others from her parents, who were both blind.

The Daishonin's words continue to encourage people throughout the world. Untold people have made a fresh start and forged ahead in their lives with vigor and determination, inspired by his overflowing compassion and unshakable conviction.

In his lectures on the Lotus Sutra, second Soka Gakkai president Josei Toda often told us that if we put into practice even a single line or passage of the Lotus Sutra's 28 chapters, we will become able to understand the sutra in its entirety. In the same way, those who put into practice, show proof of and have deep conviction in even a single line or passage of Nichiren's writings will be strong.

Of course, it is also important to become familiar with the Daishonin's key treatises and letters, specifically his five major writings, and to study his teachings and doctrines in depth. I especially hope that the youth will rouse their seeking spirit and challenge themselves to study his writings.

That said, taking inspiration from any passage of the writings is fine. What we should then do is engrave those words in our hearts, chant about them and strive to put them into practice, as we grapple with life's problems and battle various hardships. This is the quintessence of Buddhist study in the Soka Gakkai, study that has practical relevance to our daily lives.

The Daishonin's golden words are a source of endless encouragement and inspiration for SGI members around the globe, spurring them to transform their lives and gain solid victory. One famous passage is found in the writing we are studying here, namely, "Those who believe in the Lotus Sutra are as if in winter, but winter always turns to spring" (WND-1, 536). It would be no exaggeration to say that these words sum up the philosophy of hope that is the essence of Nichiren Buddhism.

Together let us study this writing, titled "Winter Always Turns to Spring," with the aim of gaining a deeper understanding of the Daishonin's heart.

BUDDHISM IS THE FOREMOST ALLY OF THOSE WHO ARE SUFFERING

Highlights

Letter written: May 1275

Written to: lay nun Myoichi

- Myoichi and her husband upheld Nichiren's teachings despite harsh persecutions.
- Those suffering the greatest hardships can gain the greatest happiness.

Nichiren Daishonin composed this letter at Mount Minobu in May 1275, about a year after he had returned from exile on Sado. It is addressed to the lay nun Myoichi who lived in Kamakura.

Less than four years earlier (in 1271), Nichiren had been subjected to the Tatsunokuchi Persecution and exiled to Sado (where he remained for a period of two-and-a-half years until March 1274). These events led to a severe crackdown against his followers in Kamakura. Among them were Myoichi and her husband, who suffered various persecutions, culminating in the confiscation of their estate. Nevertheless, they maintained steadfast faith in the Lotus Sutra. They were genuine disciples who fought throughout their lives to show solidarity with the Daishonin.

Unfortunately, the husband passed away before Nichiren was pardoned from exile. The bereaved Myoichi, meanwhile, was left alone to raise their two children, one of whom was sickly, while struggling with her own weak physical condition. Yet even in the midst of these trying circumstances, Myoichi continued to sincerely support the Daishonin—for instance, sending a servant to aid and assist him while he was in Sado and also later at Mount Minobu. He wrote this particular letter in response to the additional gift of a robe he had received from the lay nun.

Buddhism is the foremost ally of those who are suffering. It exists to help those suffering the greatest hardships gain the greatest happiness. And it is the responsibility of Buddhist leaders to offer their utmost support in this endeavor.

"Winter Always Turns to Spring" is a letter of wholehearted encouragement. There can be no doubt that Myoichi was persevering valiantly in her Buddhist practice at the time. While many of Nichiren's followers and society in general had been thrown into turmoil in the wake of his exile to Sado (in 1271) and the Mongol invasion (of the previous year, in October 1274), respectively, this letter would seem to indicate that the lay nun did not waver in the slightest, continuing to practice with a pure heart together with the Daishonin.

All the same, Myoichi was facing adverse circumstances that could be likened to winter. We can well imagine that he wrote this letter of heartfelt encouragement to her out of his profound

SGI President Ikeda encourages SGI-Brazil Youth Leader Ricardo Miyamoto at the 21st Soka Gakkai Headquarters Leaders Meeting, Tokyo, September 3, 2008.

wish that she become happy and attain Buddhahood without fail, seeking to fully dispel any lingering feelings of sorrow and anxiety that remained in her heart.

As he says, "It is the heart that is important" ("The Strategy of the Lotus Sutra," WND-1, 1000). Having upheld faith until now, it was important that Myoichi continued on with a fresh, forward-looking spirit. Nichiren wanted to light an inextinguishable flame of hope fueled by faith in the depths of her life, so that no matter what might happen, she could break through all illusions and press ahead confidently without the slightest doubt or hesitation.

"Winter Always Turns to Spring" is a writing of immense compassion in which each word and phrase is imbued with the Daishonin's ardent desire to encourage his disciple.

SHAKYAMUNI'S FINAL WISH: LEADING AJATASHATRU TOWARD ENLIGHTENMENT

Highlights

- People often swing from joy to sorrow depending on circumstances.
- Regret, complaint and discontent can lead to stagnation. Maintain pure, courageous faith to keep moving forward.
- Human revolution is about creating lives of absolute freedom, to expand one's life-state to embrace all hardships and sorrows.

At the beginning of this letter, Nichiren Daishonin considers how Myoichi's husband, as he approached death, was no doubt deeply concerned about the family he was leaving behind. The husband's thoughts, he imagines, were surely turned to his young daughter and ailing son and the difficulties his wife would have to face bringing up their children alone without him. By pondering the thoughts of the husband in this way, the Daishonin also perhaps seeks to articulate the feelings and worries of Myoichi herself.

However, there is no sentimentality or pessimism in Buddhism. His musings about her husband are sure to have

KING AJATASHATRU

King Ajatashatru was a king of Magadha in India in the time of Shakyamuni Buddha. Incited by Devadatta, he gained the throne by killing his father, King Bimbisara, a follower of Shakyamuni. He also made attempts on the lives of the Buddha and his disciples by releasing a drunken elephant upon them. Under Ajatashatru's reign, Magadha became the most powerful kingdom in India.

After killing his father, Ajatashatru came to regret his actions and he broke out in virulent sores. At the advice of his physician and minister Jivaka (who was a Buddhist), he sought out Shakyamuni, who responded by teaching him the doctrines of the Nirvana Sutra. The king converted to Buddhism out of remorse for his evil acts and supported the First Buddhist Council in its compilation of Shakyamuni's teachings undertaken the year following Shakyamuni's death.

filled Myoichi with the assurance and peace of mind that Nichiren understood what she was going through and that he was warmly watching over her and her family.

In the first half of this letter, he relates how Shakyamuni's heart was also troubled as he approached death, specifically preoccupied with the fate of King Ajatashatru (see WND-1, 535). The Buddha was very worried about the king [who had been led astray by Devadatta and was suffering in agony because of his grave offenses against the Law]. Of course, the Buddha's concern for all living beings is impartial and without discrimination. However, like parents who love their children equally yet still worry most about the child who is ill, the Buddha cannot help but worry about living beings who are destined to fall into evil paths. In this letter, the Daishonin uses the example of Shakyamuni to illustrate how the husband, in his own way, must have been concerned about his family before his death.

In the course of this, Nichiren refers to Myoichi as being "aged" and "as feeble as a withered tree," but this should not be taken literally to mean that she was frail or advanced in years. He probably only uses these expressions as a way of conveying the dying husband's concern about how his wife would fare without him, or again as an expression of Myoichi's own feelings arising from anxiety and lack of confidence in herself.

Next, with respect to the fact that the

husband died before the Daishonin was pardoned from exile, he writes: "Since the Buddha's words are in no way false, the Lotus Sutra is sure to spread widely. In that regard, perhaps your husband felt that certainly something would happen and this priest would become highly respected. When I was exiled contrary to his expectations, he must have wondered how the Lotus Sutra and the ten demon daughters could possibly have allowed it to happen. Were he still living, how delighted he would be to see Nichiren pardoned! How glad he would be to see that my prediction has been fulfilled, now that the Mongol empire has attacked Japan" (WND-1, 536).

The Daishonin offers a steady stream of encouragement, determined to deeply touch Myoichi's heart. This conveys his earnest and compassionate struggle to rouse her spirit from its very depths and break through her inner darkness and illusion without leaving a single cloud of doubt.

Here, he speaks of the "feelings of ordinary people" (WND-1, 536). He notes that Myoichi's husband would

have surely lamented over his exile and rejoiced at the fulfillment of his prophecy of the Mongol invasion. This is only natural, he says, since the hearts and feelings of ordinary people tend to swing from joy to sorrow depending on the circumstances. But we must remember here that the feelings of the husband were pervaded by faith in the Mystic Law. They were imbued with the heart of *kosen-rufu* to rejoice at the spread of the Lotus Sutra, as well as the heart of a loyal disciple sharing the same commitment as the Daishonin, the votary of the Lotus Sutra.

When the "feelings of ordinary people"—that is, their rejoicing and sorrowing for their mentor—are viewed with the "eyes of the Buddha," it can be said that Myoichi's husband fought valiantly alongside his mentor to the very end and brought his life to a victorious close, free of all regret.

Therefore, in the following passage, he writes, "Winter always turns to spring," clarifying that Myoichi's husband has most certainly attained Buddhahood.

From his comments on the "feelings of ordinary people," we can see that he

"Winter Always Turns to Spring" is a writing of immense compassion in which each word and phrase is imbued with Nichiren Daishonin's ardent desire to encourage his disciple.

was seeking to praise the husband's faith that permeated such feelings, and also give Myoichi confidence that her husband has definitely gained enlightenment.

The human heart is ever-changing. For example, Myoichi may have felt sad that her husband had not lived to see the Daishonin pardoned. It is only natural that ordinary people would cherish such wistful sentiments. But such feelings can give rise to doubt and illusion that can cloud one's faith. Nichiren therefore reassured Myoichi about the enlightenment of her husband, who had upheld faith right to the end of his life. He wanted to make sure that Myoichi would not lose the vibrant spirit of faith necessary to continue living with hope.

Feelings of regret, complaint and discontent can very well lead to stagnation in faith. It is essential that we maintain a pure and courageous spirit to keep moving forward. As Nichiren states, "The mighty sword of the Lotus Sutra must be wielded by one courageous in faith" ("Reply to Kyo'o," WND-1, 412).

If we challenge ourselves to transform our lives from within—what we call human revolution—with the confidence that we will gain final victory in life, we will be able to greatly expand our state of being. We will be able to attain a life-state of boundless freedom that will allow us to embrace all hardships and sorrows like a great ocean. The time will definitely come when the

significance of all our experiences will become clear.

For that reason, it is vital that we keep forging ahead based on chanting Nam-myoho-renge-kyo in both times of suffering and times of joy. Then, in times of suffering, we will find the wisdom to change poison to medicine, and in times of joy, we will be able to proceed in even higher spirits. We will be great "ordinary people" with lofty states of life who embody the Daishonin's words, "Suffer what there is to suffer and enjoy what there is to enjoy" ("Happiness in This World," WND-1, 681).

WINTER ALWAYS TURNS TO SPRING: OUR ATTAINMENT OF BUDDHAHOOD IS ASSURED

Highlights

- Those who uphold the Mystic Law never fail to become Buddhas.
- Those who chant Nam-myoho-renge-kyo have an important mission to also help others actualize true happiness.

"Those who believe in the Lotus Sutra are as if in winter," Nichiren Daishonin says. Before we can welcome spring, we must go through winter. Attaining Buddhahood in this lifetime entails a fierce struggle to change our karma, as well as to overcome the various challenges posed to our practice by the three obstacles and four devils, and the three powerful enemies. The trials of winter are unavoidable if we wish to soar into a brilliant springtime based on faith.

"Those who believe in the Lotus Sutra are as if in winter"—these are the compassionate words of a strict father advising us to follow the sure path to attaining Buddhahood by battling and triumphing over all karmic impediments. The way we attain Buddhahood is summed up in the words, "Winter always turns to spring."

Winter turns into spring; it does not become autumn. This is an unchanging principle of nature. In the same way, the Daishonin says, those who uphold the Mystic Law, the great teaching for gaining enlightenment, will never fail to become Buddhas or remain in the deluded state of an ordinary, unenlightened person. As the Buddha promises in the Lotus Sutra, those who hear and embrace the Mystic Law will all attain Buddhahood without a single exception (see LSOC, 75). This is a universal principle of life.

From the Buddha's perspective, everyone has a right to happiness. Everyone has the

NICHIREN DAISHONIN'S FIVE MAJOR WRITINGS

These writings are considered among Nichiren's most important writings by his successor, Nikko Shonin.

"On Establishing the Correct Teaching for the Peace of the Land" (July 16, 1260)
This treatise clearly states Nichiren's belief that embracing the supremacy of the Lotus Sutra and discarding other Buddhist practices will establish peace and security.

"The Opening of the Eyes" (February 1272)
Written while Nichiren was exiled on Sado Island, this treatise discusses the virtues of parent, teacher and sovereign. It concludes that Nichiren is endowed with these three virtues and defines the object of devotion, the Gohonzon, in terms of the Person (in contrast with the Law).

"The Object of Devotion for Observing the Mind" (April 25, 1273)
Also written on Sado, this sets forth the theoretical basis for the Gohonzon and defines the Gohonzon in terms of the Law. It teaches that embracing the Gohonzon is in itself observing one's mind, or attaining enlightenment.

"The Selection of the Time" (1275)
This writing explains that there is a correct teaching for each of the three periods of the Former Day, Middle Day and Latter Day of the Law, and that in the Latter Day, the great pure Law implicit in the "Life Span" chapter of the Lotus Sutra should and will be propagated.

"On Repaying Debts of Gratitude" (July 21, 1276)
In appreciation for his former teacher, Dozen-bo, Nichiren wrote of the importance in Buddhism of repaying debts of gratitude to one's teacher, specifically stating that propagating the Law is the greatest means to repay these debts.

potential to lead a life brimming with joy. We who uphold Nichiren Buddhism, moreover, know how to tap the Mystic Law in our lives. That is why we not only have a right to happiness but also have an important mission to help others actualize true happiness in their lives as well.

"Winter always turns to spring" means that ordinary people who triumph over all challenges they encounter in the course of their Buddhist practice will definitely become Buddhas. His words are a mighty lion's roar, proclaiming that his disciples—whose lives are dedicated to enabling others to awaken to and manifest the Buddhahood that inherently exists within them—cannot fail to attain enlightenment.

THE TRIALS OF WINTER BRING FORTH FLOWERS OF VICTORY

Highlights

- Only by overcoming trials can we savor victory in life.
- When striving in faith, the three obstacles and four devils will arise. Buddhahood is achieved through struggle against such obstacles.
- Winning comes from challenging ourselves most during the hardest times, confident of victory and the achievement of *kosen-rufu.*

The important point here is that the joy of spring is made real by the winter that precedes it. Only by overcoming the trials of winter with the power of faith can we come to savor a springtime of victory.

Let us take the example of cherry trees that bloom in spring. The flower buds first form in the summer, and then enter a period of dormancy in autumn. These buds must go through the cold of winter before they can begin their full-fledged growth toward blossoming—a period known as "breaking dormancy." The chill of winter is necessary for the buds' development. The buds, once awakened from their slumber, begin to swell further with the rising temperatures of spring and eventually flower.

Winter can function to awaken inherent power and latent potential—this principle applies to both life and Buddhist practice. All living beings possess the seed of Buddhahood, otherwise known as the Buddha nature. This seed contains potential as vast and boundless as the universe itself. It is awakened from dormancy and brought to fruition by faith in the Lotus Sutra, which enables us to surmount the trials of winter. In other words, it is achieved through our struggles against the obstacles that arise in the course of our Buddhist practice—namely, against the three obstacles and four devils, and the three powerful enemies. We can bring brilliant flowers of victory to bloom in our lives when we weather the hardships of winter and emerge triumphant based on our practice of the Mystic Law.

If, however, in the midst of life's winters, we refrain from the struggle of progressing in faith, if we doubt the power of faith and slacken in our Buddhist practice, we will end up with incomplete results at best. Even for cherry trees, it is said, if the period of winter chill required for breaking dormancy is insufficient, the flowering of the buds will be delayed and the blossoms will be irregular. The key to victory in our lives lies in how hard we struggle when we are in winter, how wisely we use that time, and how meaningfully we live each day confident that spring will definitely come.

Faith in the Lotus Sutra means bravely making our way through the winters of adversity. By taking on the arduous task of changing our karma, we are able to greet the spring and build happiness and good fortune in our lives. Therefore, we must not avoid the trials of winter. If we have the courage to face winter's challenges, then we can advance boundlessly toward the wonderful springtime of attaining Buddhahood and achieving *kosen-rufu*.

The Lotus Sutra teaches the importance of surmounting life's winters. And the Daishonin assures us: "Winter always turns to spring." Our continuous effort to transform winter into spring is the fundamental path for achieving unsurpassed fulfillment and growth in our lives. By advancing with all our might on

TATSUNOKUCHI PERSECUTION

Nichiren Daishonin earned the enmity of the influential priest Ryokan after publicly shaming him for failing to end a drought through prayer. Humiliated, Ryokan used his influence to make treasonous accusations against Nichiren. As a result, Nichiren was interrogated and later arrested by Hei no Saemon, a government official in collaboration with Ryokan. Around midnight, Nichiren was arrested without due process and taken by Hei no Saemon's men to the execution site at the beach at Tatsunokuchi.

After Nichiren and his disciple Shijo Kingo had arrived at the site, just before dawn, at the very moment Nichiren was about to be beheaded, a luminous object shot across the sky, brightly illuminating the area. The terrified soldiers called off the execution.

Nichiren was then sent into exile on Sado Island.

He later wrote, "As for my teachings, regard those before my exile to the province of Sado as equivalent to the Buddha's pre-Lotus Sutra teachings" ("Letter to Misawa," WND-1, 896). Hence, Nichiren asserts, the teachings he had expounded before his exile to Sado should be regarded as incomplete or provisional. This persecution is described as the time when Nichiren "cast off the transient and revealed the true," or revealed his true identity as a Buddha.

this path, we can open the way to attaining Buddhahood in this lifetime and enjoy a glorious, spring-like state of being that will shine with immeasurable good fortune and benefit across the three existences of past, present and future.

GREAT "ORDINARY PEOPLE" DEDICATED TO THE MYSTIC LAW

Highlights

- Despite loss of their fief, Myoichi and her husband remained steadfast in faith.
- Ordinary people who always base themselves on faith in the Mystic Law can enter the eternally abiding state of Buddhahood.

Those who always base themselves on faith and practice with the spirit of "not begrudging one's life" are great "ordinary people."

In this section, Nichiren Daishonin contrasts the efforts of the boy Snow Mountains with those of an ordinary person. He notes that while it may not be all that difficult for a sage-like figure such as Snow Mountains to give his life in pursuit of the eternal truth, it is extremely difficult for an ordinary person to carry out a selfless practice and sacrifice something extremely valuable—as Myoichi's husband did in giving up the fief[4] that was equivalent to his life. Accordingly, the Daishonin says there is no difference between the benefit gained by Snow Mountains in offering his life for the Law and the benefit of Myoichi's husband in persevering in faith without begrudging his life.

Mr. Toda used the phrase "an ordinary person enlightened since time without beginning." In other words, ordinary people who dedicate their lives to the Mystic Law are able to enter "the realm of time without beginning"—that is, the eternally abiding state of Buddhahood.

Myoichi's husband remained steadfast in faith despite losing the fief that

The joy of spring is made real by the winter that precedes it. Only by overcoming the trials of winter with the power of faith can we come to savor a springtime of victory.

he and his family depended on for their livelihood. The infinite benefit he attained as a result of such selfless faith surely meant that on death his life merged into the realm of Buddhahood in the universe—a realm often expressed in the Daishonin's writings as "the pure land of Eagle Peak"—dwelling freely in a vast and boundless state of life. This is clear in light of his writings. Nichiren also says that from this eternal realm, the husband is always watching over his wife and children and protecting them, like the sun and the moon in the heavens.

It is unmistakable that the husband has attained Buddhahood. So Nichiren's concern is directed instead toward the wife left behind. He warmly tells Myoichi, who is nursing a sick child and struggling amid challenging circumstances, that she has nothing to worry about and that her husband is definitely watching over her from the pure land of Eagle Peak. From these words, we can feel the Daishonin's sincere consideration, embracing Myoichi and her children like a gentle spring breeze. He also assures the lay nun that she need have no doubt whatsoever.

I am certain that I am not alone in being deeply moved by the profound compassion of the Daishonin that is evident in these words of encouragement. It is obvious that he ardently wished to bring happiness to mothers and children everywhere, and indeed to all people who were suffering. The warmth of his compassion is truly like

THE THREE POWERFUL ENEMIES

Three types of arrogant people who persecute those who propagate the Lotus Sutra after Shakyamuni's death (see LSOC, 232–34).

- **Arrogant Lay People.** Those ignorant of Buddhism who curse and speak ill of the practitioners of the Lotus Sutra and attack them with swords and staves.

- **Arrogant Priests.** Those with perverse wisdom and hearts that are fawning and crooked who, though failing to understand Buddhism, boast they have attained the Buddhist truth and slander the sutra's practitioners.

- **Arrogant False Sages.** Priests who pretend to be sages and who are revered as such, but when encountering the practitioners of the Lotus Sutra become fearful of losing fame or profit and induce secular authorities to persecute them.

The Great Teacher Miao-lo states: "Of these three, the first can be endured. The second exceeds the first, and the third is the most formidable of all. This is because the second and third ones are increasingly harder to recognize for what they really are" ("The Opening of the Eyes," WND-1, 270).

Nichiren called them the "three powerful enemies" and identified himself as the votary, or true practitioner, of the Lotus Sutra because he was subjected to attacks from all three types of arrogant people, just as prophesied in the sutra (see WND-1, 243).

the spring sunshine that melts the winter snow.

Nichiren sought to praise the staunch faith of both husband and wife, and to support the bereaved Myoichi and her family. He wanted these followers who had shared in his travails to advance with hope and pride to the very end and to attain a life-state of great victory and appreciation for their Buddhist practice. In that spirit, the Daishonin continues to offer encouragement filled with conviction and compassion.

THE BOND OF MENTOR AND DISCIPLE ARE ETERNAL

Highlights

- The mentor and disciple bond endures throughout the three existences.

- This bond is forged by striving together to overcome great obstacles to realize *kosen-rufu*.

- The Soka Gakkai is experiencing a springtime of benefit because of all efforts made based on the joint struggle of mentor and disciple.

True disciples strive to repay their debt of gratitude to their mentor throughout their lives. I have spent my entire life doing so to Mr. Toda.

Myoichi, for her part, sent a servant to be of assistance to Nichiren Daishonin,

as well as the offering of the robe mentioned in this writing. In response, the Daishonin says to this mother, who was dedicated to *kosen-rufu* and had withstood great hardships together with him, that he will devote himself to repaying his debt of gratitude to her not only in this lifetime but also in the next, and that he will watch over her young children in the event something should happen to her. His words embrace the entire family with their warmth.

Nothing is more fortunate than having a teacher or mentor in Buddhism. No communication is more heartfelt than that shared within the beautiful realm of mentor and disciple and of fellow practitioners who dedicate their lives to the Mystic Law. The mentor-disciple bond endures across the three existences. This eternal bond is forged by disciples striving together with the mentor to overcome great obstacles and working to realize *kosen-rufu*—that is, by waging a struggle to overcome the trials of winter.

In February 1951, Mr. Toda's businesses were in a dire situation. Gazing at some fresh shoots that had sprung up from the earth in a corner of the tiny garden outside his frugal office, my mentor remarked: "Spring is here at last. When spring comes, fresh life force like this issues forth. Winter always turns to spring. Faith in the Lotus Sutra is like winter in that respect."

Around that time, I wrote in my diary:

Spring—spring will soon arrive, a season aglow with hope. My passion and great conviction will grow like the trees and grass. . . .

Youth, arise!
Youth, advance!
Youth, move!
Onward, ever onward!
Unafraid of towering
   precipices or raging
   waves. . . .

Now Mr. Toda and the Gakkai are being slandered and maliciously spoken ill of. But a profound emotion wells up from deep within my heart—just let them see us after 10 or 20 years, after we have grown![5]

With that spirit, I have built the Soka Gakkai into the organization it is today. Because I have lived my life based on the spirit of the oneness of mentor and disciple, I can now welcome, along with Mr. Toda who lives on in my heart, the spring of worldwide *kosen-rufu*. Today, people everywhere have high praise and expectations for our efforts. We have triumphed through all. And the SGI is enjoying a glorious springtime of benefit, with

THE THREE OBSTACLES AND FOUR DEVILS

These are negative functions that arise when we practice Buddhism correctly.

The three obstacles are:
- the obstacle of earthly desires, arising from the three poisons of greed, anger and foolishness;
- the obstacle of karma due to negative causes created by committing various destructive acts;
- the obstacle of retribution resulting from negative actions in the three evil paths.

The four devils are:
- the hindrance of the five components: obstructions caused by one's physical and mental functions;
- the hindrance of earthly desires: obstructions arising from the three poisons;
- the hindrance of death: one's own untimely death obstructing one's practice of Buddhism, or the premature death of another practitioner causing one to doubt;
- the hindrance of the devil king: the devil king assumes various forms or takes possession of others to cause one to discard one's Buddhist practice; the hindrance most difficult to overcome.

Borrowing the words of the Great Teacher T'ien-t'ai, Nichiren reminds us: "As practice progresses and understanding grows, the three obstacles and four devils emerge in confusing form, vying with one another to interfere. . . . One should be neither influenced nor frightened by them. If one falls under their influence, one will be led into the paths of evil. If one is frightened by them, one will be prevented from practicing the correct teaching" ("Letter to the Brothers," WND-1, 501).

innumerable capable people proudly blooming in communities around the globe.

Now, as we embark on the second act of *kosen-rufu*, leading figures in all spheres of endeavor are keenly watching our movement, which heralds the start of a new springtime for humanity. They are placing great hopes on our efforts as a bright force for change, moving humanity away from a winter of war and misery toward a springtime of peace and happiness for all.

With confidence and good cheer, with joy and vitality, let us tell others about this great philosophy of hope that is summed up in the words, "Winter always turns to spring." Let us illuminate humanity with the light of compassion and wisdom of Nichiren Buddhism, and thereby usher in the spring of peace, the spring of culture and the spring of an age of humanity.

Around the world,
the sun rises
brightly—
the Mystic Law
the key to radiant happiness.

This lecture was published in the December 2007 issue of The Daibyakurenge, *the Soka Gakkai study journal.*

NOTES:

1. Ten demon daughters: The ten demon daughters who appear in the "Dharani" chapter of the Lotus Sutra. They vow to shield and guard the sutra's votaries. Speaking to the Buddha in unison, they proclaim: "If there are those who . . . / trouble and disrupt the preachers of the Law, / their heads will split into seven pieces / like the branches of the arjaka tree" (LSOC, 351).

2. The boy Snow Mountains: The name of Shakyamuni Buddha in a previous lifetime when he was practicing austerities in the Snow Mountains in pursuit of enlightenment. The boy Snow Mountains had mastered all the non-Buddhist teachings, but had yet to hear of Buddhism. The god Shakra decided to test the boy's resolve. Disguised as a demon, he recited half a verse from a Buddhist teaching. Hearing this, the boy begged the demon to teach him the second half of the verse, but the demon demanded flesh and blood in payment. After the boy received the latter half of the verse, he scrawled this teaching on rocks and trees for the sake of those who might pass by. He then jumped from a tree into the demon's mouth. In that moment, the demon changed back into Shakra and caught him. Shakra praises Snow Mountains' willingness to give his life for the Law and predicts that he will certainly attain Buddhahood.

3. Bodhisattva Medicine King: A bodhisattva said to possess the power to cure physical and mental diseases. The "Medicine King" chapter of the Lotus Sutra describes the austerities he performed in a previous lifetime as a bodhisattva named Gladly Seen by All Living Beings, emphasizing his selfless dedication to the Law.

4. Under feudalism, a fief is an estate of land entrusted from a lord in return for loyalty and service.

5. Daisaku Ikeda, *A Youthful Diary: One Man's Journey from the Beginning of Faith to Worldwide Leadership for Peace* (Santa Monica, California: World Tribune Press, 2006), pp. 91–92.

(7)

"The Dragon Gate"

"My Wish Is That All My Disciples Make a Great Vow"—
Carrying On the Great Vow for the Happiness of All Humanity

The Passage for Study in This Lecture

A waterfall called the Dragon Gate exists in China. Its waters plunge a hundred feet, swifter than an arrow shot by a strong warrior. It is said that a great many carp gather in the basin below, hoping to climb the falls, and that any that succeeds will turn into a dragon. Not a single carp, however, out of a hundred, a thousand, or even ten thousand, can climb the falls, not even after ten or twenty years. Some are swept away by the strong currents, some fall prey to eagles, hawks, kites, and owls, and others are netted, scooped up, or even shot with arrows by fishermen who line both banks of the falls ten *cho* wide. Such is the difficulty a carp faces in becoming a dragon. . . .

Attaining Buddhahood is no easier than for men of low status to enter court circles, or for carp to climb the Dragon Gate. Shariputra, for example, practiced bodhisattva austerities for sixty kalpas in order to attain Buddhahood, but finally could persevere no longer and slipped back into the paths of the two vehicles.[1] Even some of those who formed ties with the Lotus Sutra in the days of the Buddha Great Universal Wisdom Excellence sank into the sufferings of birth and death for the duration of major world system dust particle kalpas. Some others who

113

received the seeds of Buddhahood in the even more remote past suffered for the length of numberless major world system dust particle kalpas. All these people practiced the Lotus Sutra, but when harassed in one way or another by the devil king of the sixth heaven, who had taken possession of their rulers and other authorities, they backslid and forsook their faith, and thus wandered among the six paths for countless kalpas.

Until recently these events seemed to have had no bearing on us, but now we find ourselves facing the same kind of ordeal. My wish is that all my disciples make a great vow. We are very fortunate to be alive after the widespread epidemics that occurred last year and the year before. But now with the impending Mongol invasion it appears that few will survive. In the end, no one can escape death. The sufferings at that time will be exactly like what we are experiencing now. Since death is the same in either case, you should be willing to offer your life for the Lotus Sutra. Think of this offering as a drop of dew rejoining the ocean, or a speck of dust returning to the earth. A passage from the third volume of the Lotus Sutra reads, "We beg that the merit gained through these gifts may be spread far and wide to everyone, so that we and other living beings all together may attain the Buddha way" [see *The Lotus Sutra and Its Opening and Closing Sutras*, p. 168].

With my deep respect,
Nichiren

The sixth day of the eleventh month
Reply to Ueno the Worthy

I write this letter in deep gratitude for your dedication throughout the events at Atsuhara. (*The Writings of Nichiren Daishonin*, vol. 1, pp. 1002–03)

LECTURE

The youth are the "pillar" that will shoulder world peace. The youth are the "eyes" that will open the future of humanity. The youth are the "great ship" that will lead all people to happiness.[2] Now more than ever, the times call for an alliance of courageous youth who will stand up for truth and justice. Young people are the hope of tomorrow. A society's future is bright when its youth are filled with passion and enthusiasm and cherish lofty ideals. Young people shape the times. That is why it is our mission and responsibility as Buddhists to foster youth who are able to take on that task.

It is also especially crucial for us in the SGI to ensure a steady flow of youthful successors who can keenly perceive the pain and suffering of the times and pioneer a new age. This is the only way we will be able to accomplish the noble endeavor of *kosen-rufu*. Consequently, genuine leaders of *kosen-rufu* foster young people and entrust everything to them.

We need to maintain a youthful spirit ourselves and strive together with the youth; we need to nurture young people and confidently bequeath the future to them. Those who consistently work together with the youth to realize noble shared goals are victors who possess a lofty spirit. In contrast, those who use or exploit young people demonstrate the behavior of arrogant, high-handed dictators or lazy, incompetent cowards.

The main theme of the Lotus Sutra centers around Shakyamuni transmitting the Law to his true successors and entrusting them with the mission to widely propagate it after his passing. Similarly, in Nichiren Daishonin's writings, we see him praying unceasingly for "[those] who can inherit the soul of the Lotus Sutra" ("The Hero of the World," WND-1, 839), earnestly wishing for his followers' health and victory, safety and longevity, and success and growth. His letters abound with instructive and encouraging words for the disciples who will succeed him.

In this profoundly significant month [March 2008] in which we celebrate the 50th anniversary of March 16, Kosen-rufu Day[3]—a day of passing the baton from mentor to disciples—I would like to study the Daishonin's writing "The Dragon Gate" to delve into the deep meaning of this life-to-life transmission. This is a fervent letter sent to Nanjo Tokimitsu, who was then a 21-year-old struggling to protect his fellow believers amid the intense pressures of the Atsuhara Persecution.[4]

In this letter, the Daishonin proclaims: "My wish is that all my disciples make a great vow" (WND-1, 1003).

This great vow is the great vow of the Buddha—which is ultimately the great vow for *kosen-rufu*, as Nichiren indicates when he says: "The 'great vow' refers to the propagation of the Lotus Sutra" (*The Record of the Orally Transmitted Teachings*, p. 82). And it is the noble vow reflected in the Daishonin's own declaration in "The Opening of the Eyes": "Here I will make a great vow.... I will be the pillar of Japan. I will be the eyes of Japan. I will be the great ship of Japan. This is my vow, and I will never forsake it!" (WND-1, 280–81).

In his personal copy of Nichiren's writings, first Soka Gakkai president Tsunesaburo Makiguchi double-underlined the passage, "Here I will make a great vow," and also wrote "great vow" in large characters in the margin next to it. He lived out his life true to this great vow, never succumbing to the persecution of Japan's militaristic authorities. A letter that Mr. Makiguchi sent to his family from prison just a month before he passed away conveys the serene state of mind of one who has truly dedicated his life to spreading the Mystic Law. He wrote: "It is only natural that the three obstacles and four devils should have assailed me; it is just as the sutra states."[5]

Josei Toda, his disciple and future second Soka Gakkai president, accompanied Mr. Makiguchi to prison, carrying out a two-year struggle behind bars before standing alone in the ravaged landscape of postwar Japan to rebuild the Soka Gakkai. His deep resolve is expressed in the Soka Gakkai song he wrote, titled "Song of Comrades":

I now receive the Buddha's decree
and stand up alone,
proudly upholding the great vow
to spread the Mystic Law.
Allies are few, enemies many.

NANJO TOKIMITSU

Nanjo Tokimitsu, whose parents were devout disciples of Nichiren Daishonin, assumed the duties of the steward of Ueno Village while still in his teens, following the deaths of his father and older brother.

In 1274, immediately after Nichiren took up residence at his hermitage at Mount Minobu, Tokimitsu went to see him. This encounter seems to have deepened his faith in Nichiren's teachings. In 1275, Nikko, later Nichiren's designated successor, visited the grave of the late Nanjo Hyoe Shichiro (Tokimitsu's father) on Nichiren's behalf; from that time on, Tokimitsu looked up to Nikko as his teacher in the practice of Nichiren's teachings and aided him in his propagation efforts. Tokimitsu offered his residence for use as a center of propagation activities.

During what came to be known as the Atsuhara Persecution, Tokimitsu used his influence to protect other believers, sheltering some in his home. Nichiren honored him for his courage and tireless efforts by calling him "Ueno the Worthy."

Nichiren's extant letters to Tokimitsu number more than 30.

Mr. Toda also declared: "No matter what enormous hardships might arise, I will never forsake the great vow for *kosen-rufu*. . . . I will do what I have to do—that is, strive to save the poor and the sick and those who are suffering. For that purpose, I will keep speaking out with all my might."[6]

In my youth, I stood up alone as Mr. Toda's loyal disciple and did everything I could to support and assist him. In the course of those struggles, I inherited this great vow from my mentor. The great vow for *kosen-rufu* is inherited only through the joint struggle of mentor and disciple.

My spirit of waging a shared struggle with my mentor has continued to this very day. There has never been a day when Mr. Toda was absent from my heart. I have lived my life these past 50 years with a vow and commitment as if each day were March 16.

My keenest wish now, the area where I am challenging myself most, is to enable all people, particularly the youth, to savor and shine with the deep and abiding joy that comes from dedicating one's life to the great vow for *kosen-rufu*. I wish this especially for the youth, since it is to them we must entrust the future.

In "The Dragon Gate," which we will study this time, the Daishonin is making an ardent appeal for his young disciple to arouse a great vow for *kosen-rufu* and carry on his struggle. Let us learn from this writing, which can be taken as a source of inspiration for the spirit of March 16, Kosen-rufu Day.

BUDDHAHOOD IS ATTAINED THROUGH SURMOUNTING DIFFICULTIES

Highlights

Letter written: November 6, 1279; at the height of the Atsuhara Persecution.

Written to: 21-year-old Nanjo Tokimitsu, who risked his life to protect fellow practitioners.

- Nichiren praises his successors' selfless efforts; teaching that the great vow of mentor and disciple pulses in such actions.

Nanjo Tokimitsu stood up valiantly to confront the harsh oppression directed toward Nichiren Daishonin's followers during the Atsuhara Persecution. "The Dragon Gate" is the title of a letter that Nichiren, then 58, wrote to his disciple on November 6, 1279.

Tokimitsu was a youthful successor who had started practicing Nichiren Buddhism as a child. From his teens, he looked up to the Daishonin's leading disciple, Nikko Shonin, as an elder brother, seeking him out for guidance and instruction. Throughout his life, Tokimitsu continued to work tirelessly to propagate the Mystic Law.

This letter was written at the very height of the Atsuhara Persecution. At great personal risk, the 21-year-old Tokimitsu bravely protected his fellow practitioners, offering a number of them shelter in his own home. This led to his being targeted by the authorities in various ways. A short time later, they unjustly levied heavy taxes against him. Eventually, he found himself in a situation where he could not even afford a horse for himself, and had difficulty adequately clothing his wife and children. In this letter, Nichiren refers to Tokimitsu [who was also known as Ueno after the village where he lived]— as "Ueno the Worthy" in praise of his dauntless struggle for justice in the face of all obstacles.

In the postscript to this letter, Nichiren speaks of his gratitude or wonderment. The original Japanese is vague, and it thus is difficult to interpret the true meaning. One way the sentence can be read is, "I write this letter in deep gratitude for your dedication throughout the events at Atsuhara" (WND-1, 1003). That is, as words praising Tokimitsu for his efforts during the Atsuhara Persecution and thanking him for his devotion. However, it can also be read as, "I write this letter in profound wonderment at the events at Atsuhara." That would be an expression of awe and wonder at the fact that ordinary farmer believers in Atsuhara were now actually demonstrating their willingness to lay down their lives for their faith in the same selfless spirit that he himself possessed. In that sense, this letter could be regarded as the Daishonin's response to all the Atsuhara followers who had aroused such deep faith, and that he addressed it to Tokimitsu as their representative.

In either case, this writing praises the selfless efforts of successors and teaches that the great vow or shared commitment of mentor and disciple pulses in this way of practice.

My keenest wish now, the area where I am challenging myself most, is to enable all people, particularly the youth, to savor and shine with the deep and abiding joy that comes from dedicating one's life to the great vow for *kosen-rufu.*

THE TALE OF THE DRAGON GATE

Highlights

- The story of the Dragon Gate illustrates the difficulty of attaining Buddhahood.

- Remaining steadfast in faith in the Latter Day entails facing the insidious obstacles that hinder our attainment of Buddhahood.

- In uniting with fellow members based on the solid bond of mentor and disciple, we can lead lives of profound dignity and confidence.

In this letter, Nichiren Daishonin emphasizes that attaining Buddhahood entails overcoming many hurdles and difficulties. To make his point, he draws analogies from the ancient Chinese tale of the Dragon Gate waterfall and the history of the Taira clan in Japan. He also gives an example from the Buddhist scriptures on the difficulty of attaining Buddhahood, citing the story of how Shariputra, one of Shakyamuni's 10 major disciples, regressed in his Buddhist practice in a past existence.

Some sources place the legendary Dragon Gate on the upper or middle reaches of the Yellow River. It was held that carp that managed to climb the falls would become dragons. In this letter, the Daishonin describes the Dragon

Gate as 100 feet high and ten *cho* (0.6 miles) wide. In some of his other writings [see "Letter to Akimoto" (WND-1, 1021) and "Climbing Up Dragon Gate" (WND-2, 673)], he describes it as being 1,000 feet high and located on Mount T'ien-t'ai.[7] Given these divergences, it is difficult for us to come up with a definitive picture of the falls. Be that as it may, however, the story goes that the force of the current is so intense that most of the carp are unsuccessful in their attempts to climb the falls, no matter how many times they try. Moreover, birds of prey and fishermen lie in wait to catch them. Only a carp that can overcome all these challenges and reach the top of the waterfall can become a dragon with the power to control the rain and thunderclouds. This story is related in the Chinese historical text *The Book of the Later Han*. In many countries in the East to this day, the expression "climbing the Dragon Gate" is used to indicate surmounting difficult hurdles or high barriers to gain success in society or one's profession.

Through this example, Nichiren highlights for Tokimitsu that remaining steadfast in one's Buddhist practice to the very end is an undertaking fraught with as many difficulties as a carp faces in climbing the Dragon Gate and turning into a dragon. The strong currents of the waterfall that drive the fish back can be likened to the conditions of an evil age defiled by the five impurities as described in the Lotus Sutra; while the prey and fishermen can be likened to the three obstacles and four devils and the three powerful enemies that hinder one's efforts to attain Buddhahood.

Persevering in faith in the evil age of the Latter Day of the Law is like swimming upstream against a powerful current. It is hard enough just to resist the insidious forces exerted by our own earthly desires and fundamental darkness.[8] Shakyamuni compared these forces to a strong current or flood.[9] Nichiren explains that this is even more true in the Latter Day, when even seemingly remarkable human wisdom and ingenuity can be inundated by an inexorable tide of deluded impulses fueled by the three poisons of greed, anger and foolishness—an ever-growing tide that wreaks havoc as a force of evil (see "The Kalpa of Decrease," WND-1, 1121).[10]

Precisely because it is so difficult to carry out faith in the Mystic Law in such an age, the bond of mentor and disciple in Buddhism takes on decisive importance. Likewise, a harmonious community of fellow practitioners solidly united in purpose—in what Nichiren terms "the spirit of many in body, one in mind"—is also indispensable. The Soka Gakkai possesses the bond of mentor and disciple that is strong enough to withstand any adversity. And its members—noble ordinary people who are polishing their lives by striving in faith with the same commitment as their mentor—are allied

together in solid unity. Moreover, countless members, like magnificent dragons born through the triumphant ascent of the waterfall, are leading lives of profound dignity and confidence forged through continually challenging themselves in their faith and self-development.

PRESIDENT MAKIGUCHI'S EFFORTS TO PROVIDE PERSONAL ENCOURAGEMENT

Highlights

- The great vow of Buddhism is actualized by way of seeking to inspire and encourage each person we meet through dialogue and conveying the greatness of the Mystic Law.

In 1939, Mr. Makiguchi made his first visit to the city of Yame in Fukuoka Prefecture, Kyushu (the southernmost of Japan's four main islands), for the purpose of sharing Nichiren Buddhism with others. During that trip, he also spoke about the writing "Climbing Up Dragon Gate" (WND-2, 673). Talking to a woman who had just decided to follow her husband in becoming a Soka Gakkai member, Mr. Makiguchi said: "You must overcome various hardships and become a splendidly capable person. No matter what might happen, never abandon your faith." And the next day, saying, "Let's not waste any time putting this into practice," he took the couple with him to visit an acquaintance who lived in the Unzen area of neighboring Nagasaki Prefecture, personally showing them how to introduce others to Buddhism. Mr. Makiguchi used to say: "Propagation is the essence of religion. A life devoted to benefiting others represents great good."

Back in those days, just the train journey from Tokyo to Yame took more than 24 hours. Nevertheless, Mr. Makiguchi traveled to Yame again the following year, and again the year after that, holding discussion meetings there. He would go anywhere if it would help even one person.

Mr. Makiguchi also once traveled alone to Koriyama in Fukushima Prefecture (in the northeastern region of Japan's main island of Honshu) to introduce Nichiren Buddhism to the parents of a young man in Tokyo who had taken faith. And he pursued this course even as he faced increasing pressure from the militaristic authorities.

When Mr. Makiguchi set out for one destination, he would never just stop there. Instead, he would eagerly make his way from there to a new area, seeking to enable people to form a connection with Buddhism and to find new capable people for *kosen-rufu*.

The great vow of Buddhism can only be actualized through the persistent challenge of going out into society and earnestly seeking to do whatever we

THE FIVE IMPURITIES

The "Expedient Means" chapter of the Lotus Sutra states: "The buddhas appear in evil worlds of five impurities. . . . In an evil world of the five impurities those who merely delight in and are attached to the desires, living beings such as this in the end will never seek the buddha way" (LSOC, 66 and 80).

The five impurities are:

impurity of the age: includes repeated disruptions of the social or natural environment;

impurity of desire: the tendency to be ruled by the five delusive inclinations of greed, anger, foolishness, arrogance and doubt;

impurity of living beings: the physical and spiritual decline of human beings;

impurity of thought or view: the prevalence of wrong views such as five false views, which include the belief that life ends with death or that after death life persists in some eternal, unchanging form; denial of cause and effect; and viewing erroneous practices as the correct way to attain enlightenment;

impurity of life span: the shortening of the life spans of living beings.

According to *The Words and Phrases of the Lotus Sutra*, the most fundamental of these five are the impurities of thought and desire, which result in the impurity of living beings and the impurity of life span. These in turn give rise to the impurity of the age.

can to inspire and encourage each person we encounter, leaving no stone unturned, so to speak. That is why both Mr. Makiguchi and Mr. Toda placed such great importance on one-to-one dialogue and discussion meetings. The way to truly fulfill the great vow for *kosen-rufu* is to continue reaching out in dialogue to the person right in front of us and conveying through our spirit and lives the greatness of the Mystic Law, the key to genuine happiness.

DESTRUCTION TAKES BUT AN INSTANT; CONSTRUCTION REQUIRES AN ALL-OUT STRUGGLE

Highlights

- When the tireless and dedicated spirit of construction is forgotten, collapse begins, quickly leading to ruin.

- Arrogance, ingratitude and bureaucratism bring about decline.

- Disciples who make their mentor's heart their own and throw themselves into the challenge of construction can break through such tendencies.

There are a great many obstacles to successfully carrying out one's Buddhist practice.

Following his description of the Dragon Gate, Nichiren Daishonin offers another example, this time relating to the history of the Taira, or Heike, clan in Japan. The clan's members started out as lowly gatekeepers of the imperial palace, and it took generations of devoted service before they eventually gained the status to enter court circles. A period of 250 years passed before the clan at last achieved its zenith during the time of Taira no Kiyomori [the first samurai to hold the highest office in the imperial government].[11] But as suggested by the famous line in Japanese literature, "Unless a man is a Heike [a member of the Taira clan], he is not a human being,"[12] the despotic conduct of the Taira stood out. They also lacked people of outstanding character and ability. As a result, within several years of Kiyomori's death, the Taira were completely destroyed.

Destruction takes but an instant, while construction requires an all-out struggle. This applies equally to any organization or individual. When the tireless and dedicated spirit of construction is forgotten, collapse begins, quickly leading to ruin. It only takes a moment.

The Soka Gakkai must never forget the spirit of construction. We must never lose the fundamental spirit to strive for people's happiness and to open the way for the youth. Following the Soka path of mentor and disciple means engraving this spirit deep in our lives and making it shine into the eternal future.

Decline is brought about by arrogance, ingratitude and bureaucratism. The only way to vanquish these obstacles is for disciples to make the mentor's heart their own and throw themselves into the challenge.

After relating the two examples of the waterfall and the Taira clan, Nichiren concludes: "Attaining Buddhahood is no easier than for men of low status to enter court circles, or for carp to climb the Dragon Gate" (WND-1, 1002).

Precisely because his followers were undergoing a period of intense, life-threatening persecution by the ruling authorities, the Daishonin taught Tokimitsu the unflinching attitude in faith that the times demanded. He explains in stark terms just how exacting the path to attaining Buddhahood is. The fact that he does so is perhaps also an indication of his profound trust and high aspirations for his young disciple.

BE WARY OF NEGATIVE INFLUENCES, OR "EVIL FRIENDS"

Highlights

- Evil friends cause practitioners of the Lotus Sutra to regress in or abandon their faith.
- Whether we are defeated by evil friends or not depends on how we take on the Buddha's great vow to save all people from misery. Is it a burden or a mission?
- Truly embracing this vow means eagerly and joyfully taking on the sufferings of still more and more people and challenging even greater difficulties for the sake of peace and happiness.

Next, citing examples from the sutras, Nichiren Daishonin mentions the difficulty of continuing one's Buddhist

Decline is brought about by arrogance, ingratitude and bureaucratism. The only way to vanquish these obstacles is for disciples to make the mentor's heart their own and throw themselves into the challenge.

EARTHLY DESIRES

Earthly desires is a generic term for all the workings of life that cause one psychological and physical suffering and impede the quest for enlightenment, including desires and illusions in the general sense. Earthly desires are also referred to as fetters or bonds, because they bind people to the realm of delusion and suffering. Buddhism regards them as the fundamental cause for affliction and suffering.

According to Hinayana teachings, earthly desires and enlightenment are two independent and opposing factors, and the two cannot coexist. Mahayana teachings, on the other hand, reveal that earthly desires are one with and inseparable from enlightenment. This is because all things, even earthly desires and enlightenment, are manifestations of the unchanging reality or truth—and thus are non-dual at their source. Nichiren states: "[Again, when Nichiren and his followers recite the words Nam-myoho-renge-kyo], they are burning the firewood of earthly desires, summoning up the wisdom fire of bodhi or enlightenment" (*The Record of the Orally Transmitted Teachings*, p. 11).

In *The Wisdom of the Lotus Sutra*, President Ikeda writes: "The Buddha's enlightenment lies not in 'eradicating' earthly desires but rather in infusing them with compassion and wisdom. It is a matter of changing the turbid river of earthly desires, karma and suffering into a pure stream of compassion and wisdom, of turning the negative waves of life into waves of goodness" (vol. 2, pp. 131–32).

practice. The point stressed here is the fearful nature of negative influences, or what Buddhism refers to as "evil friends."[13]

In a past existence, Shariputra, despite being an advanced practitioner who had endured countless austerities, regressed in faith because he allowed himself to be swayed by such an external influence. In his case, he was influenced by a Brahman who begged for his eye and then trampled on it. As a result, Shariputra decided that such people were too difficult to save and gave up his desire to follow the bodhisattva way.

Such negative influences, or evil friends, are essentially the workings of the devil king of the sixth heaven.[14] The reality of the devil king is the fundamental darkness that is inherent in our lives and those of others.

Here, the devil king, manifesting in the form of the eye-begging Brahman, succeeded in swaying Shariputra's mind. Nichiren also spoke of the devil king taking possession of rulers and other authorities and causing various practitioners of the Lotus Sutra to regress and abandon their faith. Even those who had formed direct ties to the Lotus Sutra and Shakyamuni in the remote past sank into the sufferings of birth and death for the staggeringly long duration of major world system dust particle *kalpas* or numberless major world system dust particle *kalpas* due to having been led astray by this devil (see WND-1, 1003).

He had long warned Tokimitsu about the fearfulness of negative influences, or evil friends. Explaining, for example, that evil friends may approach in the form of allies, he instructed his young disciple to summon strong faith when they appeared in his environment. By doing so, he says, the heavenly deities, or the positive functions in the universe, would surely lend their protection.[15]

Incidentally, the Tang dynasty poet Bai Juyi[16] wrote a well-known poem related to the Dragon Gate. It tells the story of a carp that attempted to climb the waterfall but fell back and, having cut its forehead on the rocks below, decided to abandon the endeavor. Bai Juyi asks what the carp must be feeling, and provides an answer to the effect: "Apparently, if you become a dragon, you have the hard work of ascending into the heavens and making the rain fall. Rather than taking on such hardship, it's probably better to remain a carp and swim about freely."[17] Having observed the vicissitudes of the political realm, Bai Juyi no doubt held the sentiment that one might be happier where one is now, living just as one pleases, rather than shouldering onerous responsibilities that often come with success.

Dragons have the job of making the rain fall—this same work can be regarded as a burden or as a mission, depending on how one looks at it. This difference in outlook or attitude is also what determines whether we will be defeated by negative influences, or evil friends, or successfully attain Buddhahood. Truly, as Nichiren says, "It is the heart that is important" ("The Strategy of the Lotus Sutra," WND-1, 1000). And this difference in heart or spirit comes down to whether or not we embrace the great vow that is mentioned in this letter.

To bring our practice of the Lotus Sutra, or the Mystic Law, to successful completion means that we must eagerly and joyfully embrace the mission of taking on the sufferings of still more and more people and of challenging even greater difficulties in our cause for peace and happiness. Nichiren urges us to actively seek this way of life, to valiantly climb the Dragon Gate of faith as successors of *kosen-rufu*, and attain Buddhahood without fail. As practitioners of the Mystic Law, this is what it means for us to "live based on a great vow."

THE GREAT VOW: OUR FOUNDATION IN AN AGE OF CONFUSION

Highlights

- The way to bring forth the great strength to withstand all hardships is found in: (1) striving to attain Buddhahood in this lifetime; and (2) dedicating our lives to the great vow of the Buddha.

- During the Atsuhara Persecution, three of Nichiren's disciples gave their lives to protect his teachings.

125

- When we base our lives on the Mystic Law and carry out the great vow to accomplish *kosen-rufu,* our lives fuse with the eternal cycle of birth and death in the indestructible realm of Buddhahood.

Nichiren Daishonin writes, "Until recently these events seemed to have had no bearing on us, but now we find ourselves facing the same kind of ordeal" (WND-1, 1003). "These events" refers to how Shariputra and those who received the seeds of Buddhahood in the remote past regressed in their practice for an incredibly long period of time. He is pointing out that his disciples at that present moment were facing a similar danger. Needless to say, he is alluding to the Atsuhara Persecution.

The only way to repel this fierce attack of the devil king is to base one's life on "a great vow" (WND-1, 1003). We cannot bring forth the strength to withstand great hardships or persecution for the sake of the Lotus Sutra unless we make our ultimate goal the attainment of Buddhahood in this lifetime and dedicate our lives to the great vow of the Buddha for the realization of *kosen-rufu.* Therefore, he calls out from the depths of his being, "My wish is that all my disciples make a great vow" (WND-1, 1003). A life based on a great vow is truly profound and unshakable.

Next, he states, "No one can escape death" (WND-1, 1003). Epidemics had raged throughout the land during 1277 and 1278—the two years prior to when this letter was written. In an effort to halt these epidemics, the era name had been changed from Kenji to Koan (in 1278), but it had no effect.[18] In another writing, the Daishonin describes the terrible toll these epidemics had taken: "People die like trees toppling before a great wind or plants flattened by a severe snowfall" ("On the Three Calamities," WND-2, 802).

In addition, the people of Japan were assailed by the fear and anxiety that the Mongols might attempt another invasion. The first Mongol invasion occurred in October 1274, five years before this letter was written. The second Mongol invasion happened in April 1281, two years after this writing. The ferocity of the first invasion left the entire populace filled with a sense of dread. They were terrified that Japan might be utterly destroyed if it failed to ward off another attack.

The inexorable reality of death must have been deeply impressed on the minds of the people of the day. Therefore, he writes: "In the end, no one can escape death. The sufferings at that time will be exactly like what we are experiencing now. Since death is the same in either case, you should be willing to offer your life for the Lotus Sutra" (WND-1, 1003).

The Atsuhara Persecution led to the execution of three farmer disciples who are known as the "three martyrs of Atsuhara." There are two theories about when their execution happened. One states that it occurred on October 15,

1279, just before this letter was written (in November 1279). Another holds that it took place in April 1280, the following year. If we take the former view as being correct, then the words, "Since death is the same in either case, you should be willing to offer your life for the Lotus Sutra," can be read as an indication that their deaths had profound significance in terms of Buddhism and as praise of their just and courageous struggles. Of course, it is not the Daishonin's intention to glorify death. He is praising strong faith that does not waver even in the face of death.

Why, then, should there be no cause for regret in laying down one's life for the Lotus Sutra? Regarding this, he says: "Think of this offering as a drop of dew rejoining the ocean, or a speck of dust returning to the earth" (WND-1, 1003). From the standpoint of eternity, our present existence is as fleeting as dew. And, compared to the colossal scale of the universe, our lives are as tiny as specks of dust. However, by solidly basing our lives on the Mystic Law—which is as vast as the ocean and as firm as the earth—we can establish an unshakable and boundless state of life that is at one with that all-encompassing Law. This is his message.

In another writing, he also states: "Like the dew merging with the great ocean or soil added to the great earth, [the benefit of this offering] will remain in lifetime after lifetime, and never abate for existence after existence" ("A Mother's Gift of a Robe," WND-2, 532). Dew, by merging with the ocean, and

THE FOUR UNIVERSAL VOWS OF BODHISATTVAS

The following are the four universal vows bodhisattvas make when embarking on Buddhist practice:

- **to save innumerable living beings;**

- **to eradicate countless earthly desires;**

- **to master immeasurable Buddhist teachings;**

- **to attain supreme enlightenment.**

Nichiren Daishonin, in revealing his great vow to save all human beings through spreading the teachings of the Lotus Sutra, modeled the way to attaining Buddhahood in this lifetime. In making this same great vow, one can uncover the strength and commitment to overcome weaknesses, challenge any and all difficulties, and joyfully take on the sufferings of others.

SGI President Ikeda says: "To live with a vow is the essence of our humanity. When we live out our lives based on the great vow of the Buddha, then no matter what vicissitudes we may encounter, we will be protected and our lives will come to shine with splendid brilliance. The power that emerges from living in accord with that vow is crucial to enabling all people to lead lives of true dignity in the evil age of the Latter Day of the Law that is polluted by the five impurities" (*The World of Nichiren Daishonin's Writings*, vol. 1, p. 15).

dust, by returning to the earth, continue and live on eternally, in a manner of speaking. In the same way, our lives, as people dedicated to realizing *kosen-rufu*, will merge into the Buddhahood in the universe, and eternally repeat the cycle of birth and death in that indestructible realm. Moreover, we will always be reborn to fulfill the supreme mission of *kosen-rufu* in the place and circumstances of our choosing. In that sense, we can interpret Nichiren's call to "make a great vow" to mean "enter an eternal and unsurpassed way of being."

LIVING FOR THE HAPPINESS OF ONESELF AND OTHERS

Highlights

- The great vow means dedicating our lives to the happiness of all people as well as our own.
- A teacher or mentor sets forth and demonstrates this noble way of life, while genuine disciples emulate that example.

In closing, Nichiren writes: "A passage from the third volume of the Lotus Sutra reads, 'We beg that the merit gained through these gifts may be spread far and wide to everyone, so that we and other living beings all together may attain the Buddha way' [LSOC, 168]" (WND-1, 1003). This passage is found in "The Parable of the Phantom City" chapter of the sutra, which is contained in the third volume. It appears in the section where the Brahma kings offer their palaces to the Buddha with the wish that the benefit arising from doing so will spread widely to many people, so that both they and others can attain the Buddha way.

As indicated by the phrase "all together," it is important to wish for the happiness of all people as well as one's own. This great vow to strive for and realize the happiness of ourselves and others—both in this lifetime and eternally throughout all future existences—is the essence of Mahayana Buddhism.

From our standpoint as practitioners of Nichiren Buddhism, the great vow means dedicating our lives to *kosen-rufu*. A teacher or mentor sets forth and demonstrates this noble way of life, while genuine disciples emulate that example.

We have now entered an age when Bodhisattvas of the Earth awakened to Nichiren Buddhism are standing up all over the world and striving for *kosen-rufu* with solid unity of purpose. Our movement constitutes an alliance of Bodhisattvas of the Earth who share the same great vow. The young people who will shoulder the second act of *kosen-rufu* have stood up in communities everywhere. I entrust everything to you! The future is in your hands!

This installment was published in the March 2008 issue of The Daibyakurenge, *the Soka Gakkai study journal.*

NOTES:

1. This story is found in *The Treatise on the Great Perfection of Wisdom*. Once, when Shariputra was engaged in offering alms as part of his bodhisattva practice in a previous existence, a Brahman begged him for his eye. Shariputra gave it to him, but the Brahman was so revolted by its smell that he dropped it on the ground and trampled on it. Seeing this, Shariputra discontinued his bodhisattva practice, retreating into the Hinayana teachings, or the way of voice-hearers, and failed to attain Buddhahood (see WND-1, 1004).

2. Here, SGI President Ikeda is echoing Nichiren Daishonin's declaration: "I will be the pillar of Japan. I will be the eyes of Japan. I will be the great ship of Japan. This is my vow, and I will never forsake it!" (WND-1, 280–81).

3. On March 16, 1958, second Soka Gakkai president Josei Toda entrusted the future of *kosen-rufu* to President Ikeda and the members of the youth division. This date is commemorated annually in the Soka Gakkai as Kosen-rufu Day.

4. Atsuhara Persecution: A series of threats and acts of violence against followers of Nichiren Daishonin in Atsuhara Village, beginning around 1275 and continuing until around 1283. On September 21, 1279, 20 of the Daishonin's farmer believers were arrested on false charges and sent for trial to Kamakura. There, the deputy chief of the Office of Military and Police Affairs, Hei no Saemon, tried to force them to recant their faith. They refused, and three of them were subsequently beheaded.

5. Translated from Japanese. Tsunesaburo Makiguchi, *Makiguchi Tsunesaburo zenshu* (Collected Writings of Tsunesaburo Makiguchi) (Tokyo: Daisanbunmei-sha, 1987), vol. 10, p. 301.

6. Translated from Japanese. Josei Toda, *Toda Josei zenshu* (Collected Writings of Josei Toda) (Tokyo: Seikyo Shimbunsha, 1989), vol. 4, pp. 61–62.

7. Mount T'ien-t'ai: A mountain in Zhejiang Province in China where the Great Teacher T'ien-t'ai lived and where the T'ien-t'ai school was based. Mount T'ien-t'ai prospered as a center of Chinese Buddhism, and a number of temples were built there.

8. Fundamental darkness: The most deeply rooted illusion inherent in life, said to give rise to all other illusions. Darkness in this sense means inability to see or recognize the truth, particularly, that the Buddha nature is inherent in one's life.

9. The Buddha states to the effect that people who give up craving, people whose hearts are free of taints, can be called people who have crossed the strong current or flood of earthly desires. [See *The Group of Discourses (Suttanipata)*, translated by K. R. Norman (Oxford: The Pali Text Society, 1995), vol. 2, p. 122 (No. 1082)].

10. Nichiren writes: "Thus, the extremity of greed, anger, and foolishness in people's hearts in the impure world of the latter age makes it difficult for any worthy or sage to control. This is because, though the Buddha cured greed with the medicine of the meditation on the vileness of the body, healed anger with the meditation on compassion for all, and treated foolishness with the meditation on the twelve-linked chain of causation, teaching these doctrines now makes people worse and compounds their greed, anger, and foolishness. For example, fire is extinguished by water, and evil is defeated by good. In contrast, however, if water is poured on fire that has emerged from water, it would be as if one had poured oil, producing an even greater conflagration" ("The Kalpa of Decrease," WND-1, 1121).

11. Taira no Kiyomori (1118–81): Leader of the Taira, or Heike, clan. After achieving political preeminence, he dominated the imperial court. He married his daughter to the emperor and eventually installed his grandson as emperor.

12. This is a quote attributed to Tokitada no Taira (1130–89), Kiyomori's brother-in-law. From *The Tale of the Heike*, translated by Hiroshi Kitagawa and Bruce T. Tsuchida (Tokyo: University of Tokyo Press, 1975), vol. 1, p. 16.

13. Evil friends: Also, evil companions or evil teachers. People who cause others to fall into the evil paths by misleading them in connection with Buddhism. Evil friends refer to those who influence or approach other people with the intention of leading them away from correct Buddhist practice and to an erroneous teaching.

14. Devil king of the sixth heaven: The king of devils, who dwells in the highest or the sixth heaven of the world of desire. He is also named Freely Enjoying Things Conjured by Others, the king who makes free use of the fruits of others' efforts for his own pleasure. He obstructs Buddhist practice and delights in sapping the life force of other beings.

15. In "The Source of Aniruddha's Good Fortune," the Daishonin writes: "When those who are vital to your interests [that is, people who are important to you] try to prevent you from upholding your faith, or you are faced with great obstacles, you must believe that [Buddhist gods such as] king Brahma and the others will without fail fulfill their vow [to protect the practitioners of the Lotus Sutra], and strengthen your faith more than ever. . . . If people try to hinder your faith, I urge you strongly to feel joy" (WND-2, 566). And in "The Workings of Brahma and Shakra," he says: "Both those who are close to you and those who are not will unexpectedly admonish you as if they were your true friends, saying, 'If you believe in the priest Nichiren, you will surely be misled. You will also be in disfavor with your lord.' Then, because the plots that people devise are fearsome even to worthy persons, you will certainly abandon your faith in the Lotus Sutra" (WND-1, 800).

16. Bai Juyi (also Po Chü-i; 772–846): A poet and a government official who was one of the great writers of the Tang dynasty in China. He composed poems describing the sorrows of the people and censuring the abuses of officials, and at one time suffered banishment because of his forceful remonstrations to the emperor.

17. Translated from the Japanese. Bai Juyi, *Haku Rakuten zenshishu* (Collected Poems of Bai Juyi), translated and annotated by Misao Saku (Tokyo: Nihon Tosho Center, 1989), vol. 2, p. 691.

18. Era names were usually changed on the accession of a new emperor, or when some natural disaster of severe proportions occurred—the intention in the latter case being that a more auspicious name would change the fortunes of the particular era for the better.

(8)

"The Strategy of the Lotus Sutra"

Faith for Absolute Victory—The Legacy
Passed from Mentor to Disciple

The Passage for Study in This Lecture

I have carefully read your letter, in which you described the recent skirmish with powerful enemies. So they have finally attacked you. It is a matter of rejoicing that your usual prudence and courage, as well as your firm faith in the Lotus Sutra, enabled you to survive unharmed.

When one comes to the end of one's good fortune, no strategy whatsoever avails. When one's karmic rewards are exhausted, even one's retainers no longer follow one. You survived because you still have both good fortune and rewards. Moreover, in the "Entrustment" chapter,[1] the heavenly gods and benevolent deities pledged to protect the votaries of the Lotus Sutra.[2] Of all the guardian deities in heaven, it is the gods of the sun and moon who visibly protect us. How can we doubt their protection? The heavenly deity Marichi in particular stands in service before the god of the sun. When the god of the sun protects the votaries of the Lotus Sutra, how could the honorable one of heaven Marichi, who is his vassal, possibly abandon them? The "Introduction" chapter of the sutra reads, "[At that time Shakra with his followers, twenty thousand sons of gods, also attended.] There were also the sons of gods Rare Moon, Pervading Fragrance, Jeweled Glow,[3] and the four heavenly kings, along with their followers, ten thousand sons of gods."[4] Marichi must be among the thirty thousand sons of gods[5] who were present at the ceremony.[6] Otherwise, this deity could only abide in hell.

You must have escaped death because of this deity's protection. Marichi gave you skill in swordsmanship, while I, Nichiren, have bestowed on you the five characters of the title of the Lotus Sutra. There can be no doubt that Marichi protects those who embrace the Lotus Sutra. Marichi also upholds the Lotus Sutra and helps all living beings. Even the words "Those who join the battle are all in the front lines"[7] derive from the Lotus Sutra. This is what is meant by the passage "If they should expound some text of the secular world or speak on matters of government or occupations that sustain life, they will in all cases conform to the correct Law."[8] Therefore, you must summon up the great power of faith more than ever. Do not blame the heavenly gods if you exhaust your good fortune and lose their protection.

Masakado was renowned as a brave general who had mastered the art of war, yet he was defeated by the armies under the emperor's command. Even Fan K'uai and Chang Liang had their failures. It is the heart that is important. No matter how earnestly Nichiren prays for you, if you lack faith, it will be like trying to set fire to wet tinder. Spur yourself to muster the power of faith. Regard your survival as wondrous. Employ the strategy of the Lotus Sutra before any other. "All others who bear you enmity or malice will likewise be wiped out."[9] These golden words will never prove false. The heart of strategy and swordsmanship derives from the Mystic Law. Have profound faith. A coward cannot have any of his prayers answered.

With my deep respect,
Nichiren

(*The Writings of Nichiren Daishonin*,
vol. 1, pp. 1000–01)

LECTURE

Fifty-five years ago, in 1953, when I was 25, I strove in the vanguard of our efforts to foster capable people and develop our movement as the leader of the young men's division First Corps. Devoting my energies to fostering one person at a time, I built a solid network of youth directly connected to our mentor, second Soka Gakkai president Josei Toda, and committed to realizing his goal of a membership of 750,000 households. When I started out as its leader, the First Corps only had about 300 members, but within a year I had expanded it into a united force of 1,000 young men dedicated to *kosen-rufu*.

The young men's division general meeting held at the end of that year was attended by many eager new young successors. On that occasion, a smiling Mr. Toda remarked: "I'm so charged by your high energy that I feel like I'm in my 20s again! I'm sure that, if Mr. Makiguchi [the Soka Gakkai's founding president] were here to see you all, he would also be very happy."[10] He then continued as if speaking personally to each of us: "Incidentally, there's something I'd like your advice on. How do we go about achieving *kosen-rufu*? I'd like you to come up with ways we can do this."[11] He always trusted and

respected the youth and was prepared to do anything he could to contribute to their growth and development.

He would often say, "When you are young, it is very important to believe in yourself."[12] And: "It is essential for young people to have something they can truly believe in. They need to trust their own hearts."[13] The purpose of faith is to make our hearts strong and steadfast, to develop inner strength and conviction. Everything depends on our minds and our hearts. The ultimate conclusion of Nichiren Buddhism is summed up in the words: "It is the heart that is important" (WND-1, 1000).

Buddhism is primarily concerned with victory and defeat. It is a struggle between enlightenment[14] and ignorance.[15] *Kosen-rufu* is a battle between the Buddha and devilish functions. The heart is what decides our victory or defeat in all things. Spiritual victors can lead lives undefeated by anything. The secret to adorning our lives with brilliant victory is the "strategy of the Lotus Sutra."

In this installment, we will study "The Strategy of the Lotus Sutra," in which Nichiren Daishonin teaches the key ingredients for faith that is the source of absolute victory. Let us strive to learn from these lessons and engrave them in our lives.

PRUDENCE, COURAGE AND FIRM FAITH

Highlights

Written: October 1279

Recipient: Nichiren's trusted disciple Shijo Kingo

- Kingo's efforts to urge Lord Ema to embrace faith in the Lotus Sutra resulted in Kingo falling out of favor with his lord and being persecuted and threatened by his peers.

- Nichiren says Kingo's survival was due to his prudence, courage and steadfast faith in the Mystic Law.

- Faith is a struggle between the Buddha and devilish functions. It's crucial to have strong faith and keep working at strengthening it without cease.

After Nichiren Daishonin was pardoned and returned from exile on Sado[16] (in 1274), Shijo Kingo, one of his leading disciples, felt inspired to urge his feudal lord Ema to embrace faith in the Lotus Sutra. Ema, however, was a follower of Ryokan, the chief priest of Gokuraku-ji, the temple of the True Word Precepts school. Kingo thus gradually fell out of favor with Ema. Taking advantage of this, fellow retainers circulated malicious rumors to discredit Kingo to his lord. This is how the persecutions against him started.

Eventually, Ema delivered an ultimatum demanding that Kingo either give up his faith or leave his service with the clan. But throughout this difficult period, Kingo continued to persevere with strong faith and devoted himself earnestly to serving his lord, based on Nichiren's guidance and encouragement. Consequently, in 1278, having succeeded in regaining Ema's trust, he was granted landholdings three times the size of those previously in his possession.[17]

Despite this upturn in fortunes, hostile elements driven by jealousy and resentment sought to kill Kingo. Anticipating such a development, Nichiren had long warned his disciple to stay alert and take various precautions. This was one reason Kingo could prevail over his enemies and emerge unharmed from an attack they had made on him. Evidently, he had reported the incident to his mentor, and "The Strategy of the Lotus Sutra" is the letter the Daishonin wrote in reply.

October 1279, when this letter is dated, coincides with the height of the Atsuhara Persecution.[18] The entire community of Nichiren's believers was engaged in a struggle against formidable obstacles.

In his letter, Nichiren lists three reasons why Kingo triumphed in his recent skirmish. The first was "usual prudence"—in other words, staying alert, taking careful precautions, paying close attention to what was happening and never slackening for a moment in

SGI President Ikeda with Sir Rogelio M. Quiambao (center) and Sir Virgilio Esguerra (right), the former and current supreme commanders, respectively, of the Order of the Knights of Rizal, Hachioji, Tokyo, October 11, 2008.

any of those efforts. The second was "courage"—namely, the courage to deal calmly with any crisis, along with the wisdom that derives from such courage. And third was "firm faith in the Lotus Sutra"—the strong resolve to maintain steadfast faith in the Mystic Law, no matter what happened. The latter provides the foundation for everything else because, ultimately, prudence and courage derive from faith.

Of course, it is a mistake to think that everything will somehow work out OK just because we're practicing Nichiren Buddhism. Indeed, precisely because we are practicing Nichiren Buddhism, it is vital that we be strongly determined to prevent all accidents and keep devilish forces from taking advantage.

When Shijo Kingo was in the midst of adversity, Nichiren gave him detailed advice, ranging from how to behave toward his lord to how to turn down invitations to go drinking at night with his colleagues.[19] Even after Kingo showed actual proof of victory in the form of receiving new landholdings from his lord, the Daishonin cautioned him to be all the more careful. This is an important point.

Nichiren writes: "An enemy will try to make you forget the danger so that he can attack" ("General Stone Tiger," WND-1, 952), and "The protection of the gods depends on the strength of one's faith" (WND-1, 953). Precisely when we are moving forward vigorously, we must be careful not to grow negligent or complacent. Arrogance and recklessness put us off guard. The Daishonin urges: "Be millions of times more careful than ever"

("The Hero of the World," WND-1, 839). That is his solemn advice.

Faith is a struggle between the Buddha and devilish functions. If we let down our guard or are the least bit careless, we risk being overrun and defeated by negative forces. That's why it's crucial for us to have strong faith and keep working at strengthening it without cease. Acting with wisdom based on such faith is the key to victory.

Nichiren constantly emphasizes to his followers the importance of waging a faith-based struggle against the "three obstacles and four devils."[20] It is essential that we also remember to cultivate the kind of faith with which to combat all obstacles and devilish functions. Such faith is an indispensable requirement for victory.

FAITH THAT ACTIVATES THE HEAVENLY DEITIES

Highlights

- We are responsible for improving our good fortune and increasing our karmic rewards.
- The workings of the heavenly deities: When we chant Nam-myoho-renge-kyo, we reveal our innate Buddha nature and in turn activate the Buddha nature in all life, which then functions to protect us.

Nichiren Daishonin asserts that Shijo Kingo survived the attack on him because he "still had both good fortune

"From the profound view of Buddhism, fortune is not just a matter of chance or coincidence; it is actually the result of the benefits we have accumulated in our lives. We're the ones responsible for improving our fortune and increasing our good karmic rewards."

and rewards" (WND-1, 1000). "Good fortune" here means lucky or fortuitous circumstances, while "rewards" refers to benefits that have been received in return for virtuous acts. From the profound view of Buddhism, fortune is not just a matter of chance or coincidence; it is actually the result of the benefits we have accumulated in our lives. We're the ones responsible for improving our fortune and increasing our good karmic rewards.

The Daishonin then goes on to discuss the principle of protection by the heavenly deities—the benevolent functions of the universe—in order to clarify that Shijo Kingo's own faith in the Lotus Sutra was the source of the "good fortune and rewards" that saved him from danger.

In the Lotus Sutra, the heavenly deities are described as having pledged to protect the sutra's votaries. Here, Nichiren says that among all these innumerable guardian deities, it is the gods of the sun and the moon who carry out the function of protecting the *saha* world[21] in a form clearly discernible to us who inhabit it. He further states that specifically in the case of Shijo Kingo's recent skirmish, protection was no doubt lent by the heavenly deity Marichi, a vassal of the god of the sun.

Marichi, a deification of light, was said to proceed before the sun as it crossed the sky and that because of this, no one could see his true form, restrain him or cause him harm. Marichi

HEART AND MIND

In Chinese and Japanese, the same characters can be translated into English as either "heart" or "mind." That is because they contain elements of both intellect and emotion. For example, being "of the same mind as Nichiren" does not mean having undergone the same education or possessing the same degree of intelligence. Rather, *mind* here indicates determination and faith. Similarly, "it is the heart that is important" should not be read as referring to emotion alone, exclusive of thought or wisdom. *Heart*, in this case, indicates intent, similar to a sincere desire or vow.

appears to have been worshipped as a guardian deity by warriors during Nichiren's day.

Nichiren counts Marichi among the followers of the gods of the sun, the moon and the stars—collectively known as the three heavenly gods of light—who gathered at the assembly where Shakyamuni preached the Lotus Sutra, and regards him as a heavenly deity who protects those who believe in the sutra.

The Daishonin states that it was Marichi who gave Shijo Kingo his skill in swordsmanship when he succeeded in driving off his attackers, and that this function of Marichi was produced by the power of the five characters of Myoho-renge-kyo that Nichiren had bestowed on Kingo.

The protection of the heavenly deities functions in accord with the principle of "the Buddha nature manifesting itself from within resulting in protection from without" (see "The Three Kinds of Treasure," WND-1, 848). In other words, when we believe in the Lotus Sutra and chant Nam-myoho-renge-kyo, we reveal our innate Buddha nature, and this in turn activates the Buddha nature of all living beings, which then function to protect us from without. This is what is meant by the workings of the heavenly deities. Hence, Nichiren declares that those who uphold faith in Nam-myoho-renge-kyo, the essence of the Lotus Sutra, will definitely be safeguarded by these protective forces.

THE MYSTIC LAW IS THE SOURCE OF ALL WISDOM

Highlights

- The purification of the six senses means that through the power of the Mystic Law, we can overcome all hindrances and create the greatest possible value.
- Belief in the Mystic Law brings true wisdom regarding all affairs of society.
- Faith should spur us to do our very best, to apply ourselves with wisdom, dedication and energy.

Nichiren Daishonin then goes on to explain the principle that "the affairs of this world are Buddhism,"[22] in order to show that faith in the Lotus Sutra can serve as a source of value creation in all spheres of endeavor. He offers as an example the famous nine-character mantra of the day recited by warriors as an incantation to protect them from harm in battle: "Those who join the battle are all in the front lines." These words are thought to have originated from Chinese Taoist teachings, but in the Kamakura era of Nichiren's day, they were widely recited among members of the warrior class.

Nichiren asserts that this phrase also derives from the Lotus Sutra, citing as evidence the following passage from the sutra's "Benefits of the Teacher of the Law" chapter: "If [those who uphold the Lotus Sutra] should expound some text of the secular world or speak on matters of government or occupations that sustain life, they will in all cases conform to the correct Law" [see LSOC, 304] (WND-1, 1000).

The "Benefits of the Teacher of the Law" chapter clarifies the benefit of the "purification of the six senses"[23] that accrues to practitioners who uphold and preach the correct teaching after the Buddha's passing. In other words, we can purify our six sense organs—the eyes, ears, nose, tongue, body (skin) as well as the mind—and bring forth our rich potential for value creation. Through the power of the Mystic Law, we can overcome all hindrances, such as ignorance and delusion, and create the greatest possible value in our lives. This is what is meant by the benefit of the "purification of the six sense organs."

The sutra passage cited by Nichiren specifically corresponds to one benefit that accrues from purifying the mind. It tells us that when the functions of the mind are purified through upholding the Lotus Sutra, then when we speak on any matter of worldly affairs, our words will be correct and will conform with Buddhism.

When recited by a practitioner of the Mystic Law, even the warrior mantra "Those who join the battle are all in the front lines" will manifest the value it was originally believed to possess—namely, that of protecting those who recite it. This is because its protective power is ultimately a function of the Mystic Law.

Of all the best wisdom and cultural traditions that have developed with the aim of promoting happiness, security and prosperity, none of them, in essence, run counter to the Mystic Law.

Nichiren writes: "When the skies are clear, the ground is illuminated. Similarly, when one knows the Lotus Sutra, one understands the meaning of all worldly affairs" ("The Object of Devotion for Observing the Mind," WND-1, 376). If we "know the Lotus Sutra"—in other words, if we believe in the Mystic Law—we will "understand the meaning of all worldly affairs"—that is, we can bring forth true wisdom regarding all affairs of society, such as those of work or daily life, and live correctly. At the same time, it means that we must make every effort to develop this ability. Faith

shouldn't make us complacent. Rather, it should spur us to do our very best, to apply ourselves with wisdom, dedication and energy to all areas of our lives—be it work, study, raising children or fostering friendships in the local community.

THE ESSENCE OF BUDDHISM: THE HEART IS MOST IMPORTANT

Highlights
- Happiness is not determined by external conditions; it comes down to one's heart or mind.
- A deluded mind is trapped in a descending cycle of negativity and misery while an enlightened mind carves out a path of optimism and hope.
- The potential for ignorance and enlightenment exists within us.
- A mind free of the fetters of ignorance is filled with the Buddha wisdom that enables one to rise above and overcome all ills and misfortunes.

"Masakado" is a reference to Taira no Masakado, a great Japanese warrior of the Heian period (794–1185) who possessed outstanding military skill and achieved dominion over the Kanto region in eastern Japan. Nevertheless, he and his forces were destroyed on the orders of the imperial court, which felt threatened by his growing power.

139

THE LIFE OF SHIJO KINGO

Shijo Kingo lived in Kamakura with his wife, Nichigen-nyo, and daughters Tsuki-maro and Kyo'o. As a samurai retainer, he served the Ema family, a branch of the ruling Hojo clan. Kingo was well versed in both medicine and the martial arts. In temperament, he was straightforward, loyal and passionate.

He is said to have converted to Nichiren Daishonin's teachings around 1256. When Nichiren was taken to Tatsunokuchi to be beheaded in 1271, Kingo accompanied him, resolved to die by his side.

After Nichiren was exiled to Sado Island, Kingo sent a messenger to him with various offerings. Through this messenger, Nichiren entrusted Shijo Kingo with his treatise "The Opening of the Eyes." A few months later, Kingo himself journeyed to Sado to visit Nichiren.

Kingo's lord, Ema, was a benefactor of Ryokan, a True Word Precepts school priest who bitterly opposed Nichiren and worked to have him and his followers persecuted or killed. Despite years of tension between Kingo and Lord Ema, Kingo never abandoned his faith in Nichiren's teachings, even when Ema threatened to confiscate Kingo's fief. Later, when Ema grew ill, he turned to Kingo for medical assistance. Ema recovered fully and, out of gratitude and renewed trust in his retainer, granted Kingo an estate three times larger than his original one.

When Nichiren was on his deathbed, Shijo Kingo attended to him and, later, participated in his funeral.

Fan K'uai (Fan Kuai), who excelled in valor, and Chang Liang (Zhang Liang), a brilliant strategist, were famous generals of ancient China. They lent their support to Liu Pang (Liu Bang), who later became the first emperor of the Han dynasty; both made important contributions to the dynasty's founding. Their quick-witted and decisive action also saved Liu from assassination during his meeting with another noted warlord, Hsiang Yu (Xiang Yu). This is the well-known "Hongmen Banquet" incident. The activities of Fan K'uai and Chang Liang are described in such Chinese classics as the *Compendium of Eighteen Histories*, a work Mr. Toda read and studied until the end of his life.

No matter how skilled Fan K'uai and Chang Liang may have been in the art of war, had they not shared Liu Pang's commitment to fight for a noble cause, they could not have made the great contributions they did to the founding of the Han dynasty; all their strategies would have been to no avail. Power, military prowess, wealth, fame and other external trappings do not automatically translate into victory. Nor do they guarantee happiness.

"It is the heart that is important" (WND-1, 1000). This is Nichiren Daishonin's ultimate conclusion. Happiness is not determined by educational background, titles, social status, organizational position or age. It all comes down to one's heart and mind. A heart can be clouded by darkness, or ignorance; or it can shine brightly as an entity of the Mystic Law, free of all such ignorance. A deluded mind is trapped in a descending cycle of negativity and misery, with the sufferings of birth and death only intensifying. In contrast, an enlightened mind—one that shines as an entity of the Mystic Law—carves out a solid, ascending path of optimism and hope, having the power to transform that which is negative into something positive. The potential for both these states of mind exists within us. Ignorance and enlightenment are one in essence (see "The Entity of the Mystic Law," WND-1, 418). Therefore, the entity of "a mind clouded by the illusions of the innate darkness of life" can come to shine as a sparkling jewel of "the essential nature of phenomena, the true aspect of reality" (see "On Attaining Buddhahood in This Lifetime, WND-1, 4).[24] We can transform ignorance into enlightenment, thereby "changing poison into medicine." That is why the Law is described as mystic or wonderful.

A mind that has broken free of the fetters of ignorance is as vast as the sky and as free as a soaring eagle. Further, it is as dignified and majestic as the colossal Treasure Tower[25] in the Lotus Sutra, freely delighting in the Law and abounding with absolute peace of mind. It is filled with the Buddha wisdom that enables us to rise above and overcome all ills and misfortunes.

The power of the mind is truly unfathomable. A subtle change in one's heart can change everything. The practice that lets us draw forth this power is chanting Nam-myoho-renge-kyo for ourselves and others. Nichiren writes: "This mind that is beyond comprehension constitutes the core teaching of the sutras and treatises. And one who is awake to and understands this mind is called a Thus Come One [i.e., a Buddha]" ("The Unanimous Declaration," WND-2, 844).

Making full use of this power of the mind is the key to victory in terms of both our daily lives and our eternal existence. This is none other than the "strategy of the Lotus Sutra."

SHARING THE SAME COMMITMENT AS THE MENTOR

Highlights

- When we single-mindedly chant Nam-myoho-renge-kyo with faith in the Gohonzon, it is like facing a mirror and seeing our towering life-state of Buddhahood clearly reflected back at us.

- "It is the heart that is important" means having: the heart of faith to actively propagate the Mystic Law; the heart of a disciple to actively support the mentor; and the heart of a lion to actively speak out for truth and justice.

Nichiren Daishonin actualized this ultimate true potential of the heart and

141

mind, and he inscribed the Gohonzon—the object of devotion—as a direct expression of the vast and boundless state of life he achieved. Consequently, when we single-mindedly chant Nam-myoho-renge-kyo with faith in the Gohonzon, it is like facing a mirror and seeing our inner universe—the towering life-state of Buddhahood—clearly reflected back at us. We can manifest in our own lives the same courageous life-state of the lion king, just as the Daishonin did.

Nichikan Shonin,[26] the 26th high priest, who is known as a great restorer of Nichiren Buddhism, writes, "Through the power of the Mystic Law, we manifest the life of Nichiren within ourselves."[27] He also says: "When we believe in the object of devotion with our whole heart, the object of devotion itself becomes our heart. Therefore, the world of Buddhahood is itself the nine worlds. When we single-mindedly chant Nam-myoho-renge-kyo, our lives in their entirety become the object of devotion."[28]

The Daishonin declares, "This Gohonzon also is found only in the two characters for faith"[29] ("The Real Aspect of the Gohonzon," WND-1, 832). In the passage "It is the heart that is important," *heart* can be interpreted as "faith." A heart of true and genuine faith is an unsurpassed treasure; it contains within it all the treasures of the universe.

In "The Strategy of the Lotus Sutra," as in other writings, the Daishonin emphasizes one important point regarding our attitude in faith—that we approach our Buddhist prayer and all

our efforts with the same spirit as the mentor. We can discern this message in the following passage: "No matter how earnestly Nichiren prays for you, if you lack faith, it will be like trying to set fire to wet tinder" (WND-1, 1000–01). In another letter to Shijo Kingo, the Daishonin also warns, "If lay believers and their teacher pray with differing minds, their prayers will be as futile as trying to kindle a fire on water" ("The Eight Winds," WND-1, 795).

Further, in a letter he sent from Minobu to the lay nun Sennichi on Sado Island, Nichiren praises her ongoing seeking spirit toward his teachings despite the distance separating them: "Though you remain in Sado, your heart has come to this province. . . . It is the heart that is important" ("The Drum at the Gate of Thunder," WND-1, 949). He warmly encourages her, telling her that even though she is far away, her heart has reached him, and that they share a profound connection. One's sincerity of heart is the most important thing, he assures her.

In the passage, "It is the heart that is important," *heart* can also be interpreted as "the spirit of sharing the same heart as the mentor." The Daishonin writes, "Those with the heart of a lion king are sure to attain Buddhahood. Like Nichiren, for example" ("Letter from Sado," WND-1, 302).

The heart of faith to actively propagate the Mystic Law, the heart of a disciple to actively support the mentor, and the heart of a lion to actively speak out for truth and justice—these are the most powerful weapons and strategies we have for achieving peace and securing happiness throughout the three existences of past, present and future. This, Nichiren says, is the "strategy of the Lotus Sutra" (WND-1, 1001).

THE STRATEGY OF THE LOTUS SUTRA: FAITH THAT BRINGS ABSOLUTE VICTORY

Highlights
- The "strategy of the Lotus Sutra" refers to faith in the Gohonzon.
- Basing ourselves on the Gohonzon, we can overcome all that hinders us on the path to attaining Buddhahood.
- Cowardice prevents us from seeing the truth and can cause minor hardships to seem like huge, immovable obstacles.
- Courage indicates the most robust, healthy spirit deriving from our inherent Buddha nature, which allows us to vanquish our fundamental darkness.

In its original sense, the term *strategy* refers to battle tactics, the science of warfare or martial arts. Considered more broadly, it can be taken to mean a method for achieving better results in all areas, for leading a victorious life of value creation.

The "strategy of the Lotus Sutra"

refers to faith in the Gohonzon. It is faith that battles ignorance and delusion, breaks through negative karma, and wins without fail through confident prayer and the boundless wisdom and courage that flow forth as a result.

No matter what the situation, when we base ourselves on the Mystic Law, the ultimate Law of the universe, we will never be deadlocked. The unparalleled power of the Mystic Law enables us to overcome all obstacles or enemies that hinder us on the path to attaining Buddhahood. Nichiren Daishonin cites the passage from the "Medicine King" chapter of the Lotus Sutra: "All others who bear you enmity or malice will likewise be wiped out" [see LSOC, 329] (WND-1, 1001). These words indicate one example of the immense good fortune that comes from embracing and propagating the Lotus Sutra. Having the ability to defeat all obstacles and negative forces through faith in the Mystic Law is the power of the "strategy of the Lotus Sutra."

Hence, Nichiren indicates that the "strategy of the Lotus Sutra" is in fact the essence of the "strategy and swordsmanship" that allowed Shijo Kingo to emerge unscathed and victorious from his encounter with enemies (see WND-1, 1001).

The foundation of all of our efforts, endeavors and challenges—whether in the realm of staying healthy, leading a fulfilling life or showing actual proof of winning trust in the community and in society—is the strategy of the Lotus Sutra, or, in other words, strong faith.

At the end of his letter to Shijo Kingo, the Daishonin writes: "Have profound faith. A coward cannot have any of his prayers answered" (WND-1, 1001).

"Cowardice shuts the eyes"[30]—this was the insight of the 19th-century American Renaissance philosopher Ralph Waldo Emerson. Cowardice prevents us from seeing the truth, from seeing things as they are. It can cause even a minor hardship to seem like a huge, immovable obstacle and make even the door to a solution appear instead like a thick wall. Courage is, therefore, crucial.

Emerson says something very interesting: "It is plain that there is no separate essence called courage, no cup or cell in the brain, no vessel in the heart containing drops or atoms that make or give this virtue; but [courage] is the right or healthy state of every man, when he is free to do that which is constitutional to him to do. It is directness—the instant performing of that which he ought."[31] In terms of Buddhism, courage indicates the soundest and most robust spirit that derives from our inherent Buddha nature, which could be described as our most "healthy state"; it means the fighting spirit to vanquish our fundamental darkness and instantly reveal our enlightened Dharma nature.

For us, courage means challenging the real-life issues confronting us right where we are with the belief that we ourselves are entities of the Mystic Law. This is the way to employ the strategy of the Lotus Sutra and construct an indestructible history of victory and glory.

As a young man working under Mr. Toda, I battled various hardships. Whenever I reached an impasse, I would chant Nam-myoho-renge-kyo to break through. I would chant and challenge myself afresh. Determined to win victory for my mentor and for *kosen-rufu*, I fiercely pitted myself each day against one obstacle after another. And in the end, I triumphed over all adversity.

"For my mentor!" "For *kosen-rufu*!"— when youth strive with this strong resolve to reply to their mentor and contribute to *kosen-rufu*, they can bring forth their true full potential and ability. This, from my personal experience, is the "strategy of the Lotus Sutra."

In order to realize Mr. Toda's vision, I exerted myself on the front lines of countless hard-fought battles, and as a result, I came to understand the true meaning of faith that brings absolute victory. During the 11 years that I served my mentor, I showed unequivocal actual proof of victory based on the "strategy of the Lotus Sutra." This brought Mr. Toda great joy.

The time has now come for me to entrust this practical philosophy for certain victory to my genuine disciples.

Just as Mr. Toda called out 55 years ago, I call out to all the youth who are my true successors: "My young friends, how will you accomplish *kosen-rufu*? What are the challenges that lie before you? Where and how will you fight and win?"

This installment was published in the April 2008 issue of The Daibyakurenge, *the Soka Gakkai study journal.*

NOTES:

1. "Entrustment," the 22nd chapter of the Lotus Sutra (*The Lotus Sutra and Its Opening and Closing Sutras*, p. 319).
2. Possibly a reference to the passage that reads: "We will respectfully carry out all these things just as the world-honored one has commanded" (LSOC, 320).
3. Rare Moon, the god of the moon; Pervading Fragrance, the god of the stars; Jeweled Glow, the god of the sun.
4. See LSOC, 36.
5. The thirty thousand sons of gods were followers of the gods of the moon, stars and sun.
6. The assembly where Shakyamuni preached the Lotus Sutra.
7. A quote from the fourth-century Taoist work *Pao-p'u Tzu* (*Baopuzi*). Chinese soldiers believed that reciting this phrase while drawing four vertical and five horizontal lines in the air with their fingers would protect them from harm.
8. See LSOC, 304.
9. See LSOC, 329. In the sutra, the sentence reads in the past tense. It was changed here to fit the context of the letter.
10. Translated from Japanese. Josei Toda, *Toda Josei zenshu* (Collected Writings of Josei Toda) (Tokyo: Seikyo Shimbunsha, 1989), vol. 4, p. 106.
11. *Toda Josei zenshu*, p. 107.
12. *Toda Josei zenshu*, p. 541.
13. *Toda Josei zenshu*, p. 543.
14. *Enlightenment* here refers to the Dharma nature, the unchanging nature inherent in all things and phenomena. Dharma nature is a concept equal to the "true aspect" (Jpn *jisso*) of all phenomena, or "the true aspect of reality" (*shinnyo*). In Buddhism, the term *dharma* means both phenomena and the truth underlying them. A Buddha is defined as one who is enlightened to the essential nature of phenomena, and an ordinary person as one who is ignorant of this nature. Hence both enlightenment and ignorance, or darkness, originate from one source, the essential nature of phenomena.
15. Ignorance: Also, illusion or darkness. In Buddhism, ignorance about the true nature of existence. Ignorance is the first of the twelve-linked chain of causation, the sequence of causal relationships connecting ignorance with suffering. In the concept of the twelve-linked chain of causation, ignorance is the fundamental cause of delusion, suffering and transmigration in the realm of delusion and suffering.
16. Sado exile: When the authorities failed in their attempt to execute Nichiren at Tatsunokuchi in September 1271, they sentenced him to exile on Sado Island the following month. He was eventually pardoned after two-and-a-half years and returned to Kamakura in November 1274.
17. In 1277, Ema fell ill and had to seek treatment from Shijo Kingo, who was also a skilled physician. He recovered under Kingo's care and thereafter placed renewed trust in him. In 1278, Kingo received from Ema an estate three times larger than his former one.
18. Atsuhara Persecution: A series of threats and acts of violence against followers of Nichiren in Atsuhara Village, in Fuji District of Suruga Province, beginning around 1275 and continuing until around 1283. In 1279, 20 farmers were unjustly arrested and sent to Kamakura, where they were interrogated by Hei no Saemon, the deputy chief of the Office of Military and Police Affairs, who demanded that they renounce their faith; however, not one of them yielded. Eventually, three of these peasant followers were executed—the brothers Jinshiro, Yagoro and Yarokuro. They are known as the three martyrs of Atsuhara.
19. In a writing titled "Nine Thoughts to One Word," Nichiren advises Shijo Kingo: "Even if summoned by your lord, you should first send an aide to your lord's residence to make certain that it is in fact your lord who has sent the summons. Then fasten your breastplate, don a headband, and provide yourself with men to attend you front and back and to your left and right, and only then venture forth. When you reach the residence of someone who lives near your lord and is friendly toward you, or the room assigned to you in your lord's mansion, you should remove your armor there before presenting yourself to your lord. When you come back to your own home, before you enter, send someone in ahead of you to inspect the doorways, the area under any bridges, the area behind the stables, the upper apartments, and any other dark places before you venture in yourself" (WND-2, 730–31).
20. Three obstacles and four devils: Various obstacles and hindrances to the practice of Buddhism. The three obstacles are: (1) the obstacle of earthly desires; (2) the obstacle of karma; and (3) the obstacle of retribution. The four devils are: (1) the hindrance of the five components; (2) the hindrance of earthly desires; (3) the hindrance of death; and (4) the hindrance of the devil king.
21. *Saha* world: This world, which is filled with suffering. Often translated as the world of endurance. *Saha* means the earth; it derives from a root meaning "to bear" or "to endure." In this context, the *saha* world indicates a world in which people must endure suffering.
22. Nichiren cites the Great Teacher T'ien-t'ai as saying: "In the Golden Light Sutra it is recorded that 'all the good teachings that exist in the world derive from this sutra. To have a profound knowledge of this world is itself Buddhism'" ("The Opening of the Eyes," WND-1, 221).
23. Purification of the six sense organs: Also, purification of the six senses. This refers to the five sense organs—eyes, ears, nose, tongue, body (skin)—plus the mind becoming pure, making it possible to apprehend all things correctly. The "Benefits of the Teacher of the Law" chapter of the Lotus Sutra explains that those who uphold and practice the Lotus Sutra acquire 800 benefits of the eyes, nose and body, and 1,200 benefits of the ears, tongue and mind, and that through these benefits the six sense organs become refined and pure.
24. Nichiren writes: "A mind now clouded by the illusions of the innate darkness of life is like a tarnished mirror, but when polished, it is sure to become like a clear mirror, reflecting the essential nature of phenomena and the true aspect of reality. Arouse deep faith, and diligently polish your mirror day and night. How should you polish it? Only by chanting Nam-myoho-renge-kyo" ("On Attaining Buddhahood in This Lifetime," WND-1, 4).
25. According to the Lotus Sutra, this massive tower emerges from below the earth and measures 250 *yojanas* wide and 500 *yojanas* high. It is adorned with the seven kinds of treasures: gold, silver, lapis lazuli, seashell, agate, pearl and carnelian. Seated inside the tower is Many Treasures Buddha.
26. Nichikan Shonin (1665–1726).
27. "Totaigi sho mondan" (Commentary on "The Entity of the Mystic Law").
28. "Kanjin no Honzon sho mondan" (Commentary on "The Object of Devotion for Observing the Mind").
29. The Japanese word for *faith* consists of two Chinese characters.
30. Ralph Waldo Emerson, *Society and Solitude* (Boston: Houghton, Mifflin and Company, 1870), p. 244.
31. *Society and Solitude*, p. 251.

"Lessening One's Karmic Retribution"

Action Is the Soul of Genuine Practitioners of
Nichiren Buddhism—Transforming One's Destiny
and Helping Others Do the Same

The Passage for Study in This Lecture

The Nirvana Sutra teaches the principle of lessening one's karmic retribution. If one's heavy karma from the past is not expiated within this lifetime, one must undergo the sufferings of hell in the future, but if one experiences extreme hardship in this life [because of the Lotus Sutra], the sufferings of hell will vanish instantly. And when one dies, one will obtain the blessings of the human and heavenly worlds, as well as those of the three vehicles and the one vehicle.[1] Bodhisattva Never Disparaging was not abused and vilified, stoned and beaten with staves without reason. He had probably slandered the correct teaching in the past. The phrase "when his offenses had been wiped out"[2] indicates that, because Bodhisattva Never Disparaging met persecution, he was able to eradicate his offenses from previous lifetimes. (This concludes my first point.) (*The Writings of Nichiren Daishonin*, vol. 1, p. 199)

One may be letter-perfect in reciting the Lotus Sutra, but it is far more difficult to act as it teaches. The "Simile and Parable" chapter states, "If this person . . . on seeing those who read, recite, copy, and uphold this sutra, should despise, hate, envy, or bear grudges against them …" The "Teacher of the Law" chapter reads, "Since hatred and jealousy toward this sutra abound even when the Thus Come One is in the world, how much more will this be so after his passing?" The "Encouraging Devotion" chapter reads, "Many ignorant people will attack us with swords and staves … again and again we will be banished." The "Peaceful Practices" chapter states, "It [the Lotus Sutra] will face much hostility in the world and be difficult to believe." Although these quotations from the sutra are the Buddha's prophecies, there is no reference to when these persecutions will occur. In the past, Bodhisattva Never Disparaging and the monk Realization of Virtue read and lived these passages. But setting aside the two thousand years of the Former and Middle Days of the Law, now, in the Latter Day, in all Japan only Nichiren seems to be doing so. From the present situation, I can well imagine how followers, relatives, disciples, and lay supporters must have grieved in the past when during the reigns of evil kings so many of their sage monks met persecution.

Nichiren has now read [and lived] the entirety of the Lotus Sutra. Even a single phrase or verse assures one's enlightenment; since I have read the entire sutra, how much more certain is my enlightenment. I am more confident than ever. Though I may sound presumptuous, my most fervent wish is to realize the security and peace of the entire land. In an age when none will heed me, however, it is beyond my power. I will close now to keep this brief. (WND-1, 200)

LECTURE

This year [2008] marks the 200th anniversary of the first performance of Beethoven's[3] famous Fifth Symphony, "Fate," in Vienna. This symphony's first movement opens with the well-known, four-note "fate" motif. According to some, the German composer described the intention behind this motif as "Fate knocking at the door!"[4]

Beethoven was 38 when he debuted this work. Faced with encroaching deafness since his late 20s, he was plunged into such depths of loneliness and despair that he contemplated taking his life. This symphony is the fruit of his ultimate triumph over adversity, and it continues to inspire people around the world to stand up and confront their destiny.

The power of the human spirit is infinite. No matter what fate might have in store for us, we can definitely overcome it. We can break through our sufferings and find joy.

In my youth, I would often play Beethoven records in my small apartment. I used to listen to the Fifth Symphony during that most trying period in 1950, when I took on the business crisis facing my mentor and strove to support him in every way possible. I'll never forget how each time I heard the opening strains, I was stirred and encouraged by the vigor of life that abounds in the music.

THE BODHISATTVA WAY OF LIFE

Beethoven declared, "My art shall be exhibited only in the service of the poor."[5] To struggle with one's own destiny while at the same time striving to impart courage to others so that they can challenge and triumph over their own destinies—this calls to mind the bodhisattva way of life. A bodhisattva firmly believes that there is no hardship or suffering that cannot be surmounted.

The doctrine of changing karma taught in Nichiren Buddhism is an unrivaled principle of victory in life, bringing hope, courage and confidence to all people. It embodies a philosophy of supreme humanism, which holds that each individual inherently possesses the power to weather any destiny. It also constitutes a tenet of unsurpassed respect for the sanctity of life, revealing the fundamental causality of life by which we can actually tap and manifest this power. In short, it represents a hope-filled teaching for all humanity, illuminating as it does the latent power innate in each person's life.

In this installment, we will study "Lessening One's Karmic Retribution," a letter Nichiren Daishonin composed in October 1271, amid the tumultuous period following the Tatsunokuchi Persecution and leading up to the Sado

Exile.[6] Why was he destined to encounter such great persecutions? This letter clarifies the significance of hardships and obstacles faced by practitioners of the Lotus Sutra and, in the process, explains the principle of changing one's karma or destiny that is the foundation of Nichiren Buddhism.

Let us study this important writing with the intent of learning from the Daishonin's lofty spirit.

GREAT HARDSHIPS LEAD TO THE ATTAINMENT OF BUDDHAHOOD

Highlights

Written: October 5, 1271—one month following Nichiren's near execution at Tatsunokuchi and a few days before his exile to Sado Island

Recipients: Three of Nichiren's leading disciples: Ota Jomyo, Soya Kyoshin and Dharma Bridge Kimbara

- Hardships are a part of life; encountering hardships for the sake of the Lotus Sutra is the path that leads directly to attaining enlightenment.

- Nichiren urges his followers to be united as they advance *kosen-rufu* during this critical period.

In this writing, we can discern Nichiren Daishonin's towering state of life through

which he views great hardships as an opportunity to attain Buddhahood. He clarifies the common truth of Buddhism and human existence that hardships are a part of life, saying that we should not be perturbed by them. His spirit is expressed in the words: "Difficulties will arise, and these are to be looked on as [peace and comfort]" (see *The Record of the Orally Transmitted Teachings*, p. 115).

In another writing, Nichiren states that if one were to give his or her life for the Lotus Sutra or suffer persecution on account of the *daimoku* [Nam-myoho-renge-kyo], then the life discarded and the adversities encountered will all serve to enable that person to attain Buddhahood (see "The Persecution at Tatsunokuchi," WND-1, 196). And elsewhere, he says, "It seems to me that on the path to attain Buddhahood it may invariably be when one has done something like lay down one's life that one becomes a Buddha" ("Banishment to Sado," WND-1, 202).

Encountering great hardships for the sake of the Lotus Sutra is the path that leads directly to attaining Buddhahood. Therefore, there is nothing to fear. There is no greater cause for joy. This was no doubt Nichiren's state of mind following the Tatsunokuchi Persecution.

For approximately one month after his near execution at Tatsunokuchi on September 12, 1271, until his departure for Sado Island on October 10 of the same year, Nichiren was held in custody at the residence of the deputy constable of Sado, Homma Rokuro Saemon,[7] in

Echi, Sagami Province (the present-day city of Atsugi in Kanagawa Prefecture, a short distance from Kamakura).

As reflected in his statement "I survived even the Tatsunokuchi Persecution" (*Gosho zenshu*, p. 843),[8] Nichiren manifested the life-state of a lion king who defeats all devilish forces and dedicates his life to the vow to lead all people to enlightenment. And he wrote many impassioned letters to his followers in such places as Kamakura and Shimosa Province (present-day Chiba Prefecture), encouraging them to stand up with the same spirit as he.

At that time, one or more followers in the Shimosa area rushed to see Nichiren out of concern for his safety. This letter was composed in response to their sincere actions. Dated October 5, 1271, it is addressed to Ota Jomyo, Soya Kyoshin and Dharma Bridge Kimbara.[9]

At the outset, Nichiren refers to an episode involving two brothers, followers of Shakyamuni Buddha, who—depending on the source used—were both individually named Chudapanthaka or were together referred to as Chudapanthaka.[10] Either way, when one was called, both would answer. Nichiren says that whenever one of his three followers—Ota, Soya and Kimbara—came to visit, he felt as if he were in the company of all three.

It is not clear whether the trio actually went to Echi together, or whether just one of them went as a representative. From the way the letter opens, however, it seems likely that only one of them traveled there. This probably also

makes sense given that it wouldn't have been easy to meet Nichiren while he was in custody. Even supposing that all three had in fact gone to visit him, he could not have spoken to them freely or for any length. This may also be a reason why the letter is addressed to all three.

In any event, as we can see from the content of this letter, Nichiren seeks to urge his followers to unite together solidly at this critical time, to advance together in the spirit of "many in body, one in mind."

THE SIGNIFICANCE OF HARDSHIPS

Highlights

- Nichiren offers three perspectives on the significance of hardships:
  1. Persecutions represent excellent opportunities for Nichiren's disciples to transform their destinies.
  2. Those who spread Buddhism will inevitably experience persecution.
  3. Coming under harsh attack for propagating the Lotus Sutra signifies that Nichiren is a votary of the Lotus Sutra.
- We experience adversity as a means to realize our great inner strength, thereby achieving true peace in life.

In "Lessening One's Karmic Retribution," Nichiren Daishonin explains from

PURIFYING THE SIX SENSE ORGANS

The six sense organs are faculties of sensory discernment: the five known sense organs—eyes, ears, nose, tongue and body (or skin)—as well as the mind. These give rise to the "six consciousnesses"—sight, hearing, smell, taste, touch and the mind that integrates sensory input.

In pre-Lotus Sutra teachings, the six sense organs are regarded as the source of earthly desires. However, the "Benefits of the Teacher of the Law" chapter of the Lotus Sutra says that one can purify the functions of the six sense organs by carrying out the five practices of embracing, reading, reciting, teaching and transcribing the Lotus Sutra. With the six sense organs purified, one is freed of attachment to and delusion about their corresponding objects—color and form, sound, odor, taste, texture and phenomena.

Nichiren equates "benefits" or "blessings" with purifying our six sense organs. The way to gain benefits and purify our senses is through chanting Nam-myoho-renge-kyo (see *The Record of the Orally Transmitted Teachings*, p. 148).

three perspectives the significance of the great hardships he and his followers encountered.

First, he presents the principle of "lessening one's karmic retribution," pointing out that the current momentous persecutions they are undergoing represent an excellent opportunity to transform their destiny.

Second, he cites examples from the past to clarify that those who spread the correct teaching of Buddhism will inevitably experience persecution (see WND-1, 199).[11] Referring to Shakyamuni and several of his 24 successors,[12] Nichiren explains that even practitioners in the Former Day of the Law in India, who carried out *shakubuku* (namely, refuting others' erroneous views and awakening them to the truth of Buddhism) when it was necessitated by the times and locality they found themselves in, were beset with persecution. He then anticipates that the difficulties he will have to face will be all the greater, for he is propagating the Lotus Sutra—the Buddha's highest teaching—in Japan, a land far removed from the birthplace of Buddhism in India and where people disregard the correct teaching. Moreover, he is doing so at the start of the evil age of the Latter Day of the Law, a time when *shakubuku* would be the only effective method of propagation.[13] Therefore, the Daishonin states that he has long been prepared to meet great hardships and has in fact been waiting for them to arrive.

Third, he cites various sutra passages to indicate that his having come under harsh attack for propagating the Law signifies that he has read and lived the Lotus Sutra, suggesting that he himself is the votary of the Lotus Sutra in the Latter Day.

As this shows, throughout this writing, Nichiren seeks above all to shed light on the significance of a practitioner of the Mystic Law meeting with persecution. He also endeavors to answer the questions posed by his followers, who were wondering why they should face difficulties in the course of their practice. He would later discuss this point more thoroughly in his treatise "The Opening of the Eyes."

In the writing we are presently studying, Nichiren refers to the principle of lessening one's karmic retribution and highlights the significance of hardships in terms of karma, a subject relevant to all people. In other words, he uses his own example of overcoming persecution to explain the meaning of difficulties, which are universal. This letter can be seen as a reply to the fundamental question of why hardships are an inevitable part of human life.

Nichiren's point, simply put, boils down to this: "Difficulties will arise, and these are to be looked on as [peace and comfort]" (see OTT, 115). It is when we have broken through an obstacle that we can savor a true sense of peace and ease. By contrast, such a state of being will forever elude those who shun difficulties and try to run away from challenges.

There is no such thing as a life free of hardships. We experience adversity precisely so that we can achieve true peace in life. But unless we are aware of our inner strength to withstand hardships, we will find one difficulty giving rise to another, and we will ultimately be crushed by their weight. The Latter Day is a time when people's lives are shrouded in darkness or ignorance[14] and destructive influences prevail. People are drawn into a downward spiral of negative causes and misery. Therefore, if we hope to guide people to happiness in the Latter Day of the Law, it is of utmost importance to teach them about their innate power to triumph over suffering. This is the teaching of Nichiren Buddhism.

The principle of lessening one's karmic retribution set forth in this writing explains the quintessential power that resides within us and enables us to withstand hardships. Nichiren demonstrated this power by weathering intense persecutions himself.

LESSENING ONE'S KARMIC RETRIBUTION EQUALS ATTAINING BUDDHAHOOD IN THIS LIFETIME

Highlights

- Regarding lessening karmic retribution, Nichiren cites two points:

1 Even heavy karma that gives rise to hellish retribution can be expiated immediately by manifesting our innate Buddhahood.

2 Lessening karmic retribution is the gateway to attaining Buddhahood in this lifetime; it implies a fundamental transformation in our lives.

- How we change our attitude or inner resolve at this moment is crucial. We can freely create our future through our determination and action right now.

153

The principle of lessening one's karmic retribution appears in the Nirvana Sutra.[15] The Chinese characters for this term literally mean "transforming the heavy and receiving it lightly." The prevailing view of karma in Nichiren Daishonin's time was that if people had accumulated such heavy offenses in past lifetimes it would be impossible to expiate all of their evil karma in the course of their present existence; they would have to undergo hellish sufferings in future lifetimes before their retribution could end. But Nichiren's teaching of the principle of lessening karmic retribution held that a person could expiate even the heaviest negative karma from past lifetimes through receiving retribution in a lighter form in this present existence.

The theory of karma in Nichiren Buddhism is an empowering teaching that can revitalize people's lives. It teaches that, no matter how heavy, there is no negative karma that cannot be transformed for the better. In this writing, Nichiren's doctrine of changing karma or destiny is discussed in terms of the principle of lessening one's karmic retribution.

Two major points concerning lessening karmic retribution are highlighted in this writing:

The first point is in regard to Nichiren's declaration that "the sufferings of hell will vanish instantly" (WND-1, 199). What he is saying is that even the heavy karma that gives rise to hellish retribution can be expiated immediately, right now; not gradually at some distant future time. This is made possible by the principle of the "mutual possession of the Ten Worlds."

Generally, karma is taught as being formed by past causes and manifested as present effects. In other words, there is a time lag between cause and effect; they are not simultaneous. Nichiren Buddhism, however, teaches that karma can

"Transforming our karma is nothing other than changing those inner life tendencies that keep us trapped in negativity and unhappiness and solidly putting ourselves on a positive path."

be transformed as a result of manifesting the Buddhahood existing inherently within us. Just as the myriad stars in the sky disappear when the sun rises, the unfathomable store of negative karma in our lives can be erased when we bring forth the life-state of Buddhahood.

Accordingly, the second point—one that is very important—is that lessening karmic retribution is also the gateway to attaining Buddhahood in this lifetime. In this writing, Nichiren states: "The sufferings of hell will vanish instantly. And when one dies, one will obtain the blessings of the human and heavenly worlds [the worlds of humanity and heaven], as well as those of the three vehicles [the worlds of voice-hearers, cause-awakened ones and bodhisattvas] and the one vehicle [the world of Buddhahood]" (WND-1, 199).

The "blessing of the one vehicle" constitutes the benefit of attaining Buddhahood.

Lessening karmic retribution is not a simple settling of our karmic accounts; it implies a fundamental transformation of our lives, whereby we put a stop to the negative cycle of suffering and delusion and enter a new positive trajectory of happiness. When we do so, we can savor in lifetime after lifetime the blessings of the worlds of humanity, heaven, voice-hearers, cause-awakened ones, bodhisattvas and Buddhahood.

In other words, lessening karmic retribution leads directly to the great path of attaining Buddhahood. In that sense, when we lessen our karmic retribution,

it doesn't mean merely zeroing out a minus balance but rather that we effect a momentous change in the direction of our very lives, shifting from a downward descent toward an infinite upward ascent, from a negative path to a positive one of genuine good. This is the power of the Mystic Law, which has the ability to transform the negative into the beneficial—to turn poison into medicine.

The doctrine of lessening one's karmic retribution in Nichiren Buddhism is nothing other than the principle for redirecting our lives toward happiness right at this very moment—here, now, just as we are. Similarly, transforming our karma is nothing other than changing those inner life tendencies that keep us trapped in negativity and unhappiness and solidly putting ourselves on a positive path.

Therefore, the present moment in which we wage this struggle is vitally important. In "The Opening of the Eyes," Nichiren cites a passage from the Contemplation on the Mind-Ground Sutra, which states: "If you want to understand the causes that existed in the past, look at the results as they are manifested in the present. And if you want to understand what results will be manifested in the future, look at the causes that exist in the present" (WND-1, 279). Our present is the result or effect of our past causes. At the same time, the present itself becomes the cause that will shape our future. The three existences—past, present and future—are all contained in the present, in this instant. The important thing is how we change our attitude or inner resolve at this moment. This is because we can freely create our future through our determination and action right at this very instant.

Nichiren's teaching of changing karma opens the way for a brilliant revolution of hope, freeing people from the predominant dark, fatalistic view of karma or destiny.

THE BENEFIT OF THE PURIFICATION OF THE SIX SENSE ORGANS

Highlights

- Despite being abused and vilified, Bodhisattva Never Disparaging ceaselessly tried to convey the fundamental tenet of the Lotus Sutra—that all living beings possess the Buddha nature.

- As a result, he received the benefit of purifying his senses, achieving the indestructible and eternal life-state of Buddhahood.

- Through his struggle to triumph over adversity and protect the Law, he defeated ignorance, the source of negative karma.

Next, Nichiren Daishonin cites the example of Bodhisattva Never Disparaging, who appears in the Lotus

Sutra's "Never Disparaging" chapter, which is named after him. Nichiren asserts that the passage "when his offenses had been wiped out" (*The Lotus Sutra and Its Opening and Closing Sutras*, p. 312) indicates the principle of lessening karmic retribution and changing one's destiny.

Bodhisattva Never Disparaging showed unwavering respect toward everyone he met, bowing to them in veneration while ceaselessly trying to communicate the fundamental tenet of the Lotus Sutra that all living beings possess the Buddha nature. For his efforts, however, he was abused and vilified, stoned and beaten with staves by arrogant monks, nuns and lay believers. Yet he remained undaunted by such persecution and continued to treat all people with respect. He ultimately gained the benefit of the "purification of the six sense organs"—a grouping that includes the eyes, ears, nose, tongue, body (skin) as well as the mind—and attained Buddhahood.

Though Bodhisattva Never Disparaging encountered hardships as a result of practicing the correct teaching, by triumphing over those difficulties and continuing in his practice, he obtained the benefit of eradicating the slander of the Law he had committed in past lifetimes. This, Nichiren states, is the meaning of "when his offenses had been wiped out."

What kind of benefits, then, did Bodhisattva Never Disparaging receive "when his offenses had been wiped out"?

As one benefit in his present lifetime, he attained the vibrant life force that is the hallmark of the purification of the six sense organs. This is said to have enabled him to perfectly understand the essence of the Lotus Sutra, and he was later reborn as Shakyamuni Buddha. In other words, he did not merely transform his life in his current existence, but he achieved the indestructible life-state of Buddhahood that would endure into the eternal future.

The "Benefits of the Teacher of the Law" chapter of the Lotus Sutra outlines in detail the benefit of the purification for each of the six sense organs.

For example, "eye benefits" are described as follows. As a result of upholding and practicing the Lotus Sutra, our eyes, just as they are, gain the ability to view all that exists in the thousand-millionfold world,[16] including the great seas and Mount Sumeru.[17] And even though we do not possess heavenly or divine eyes, we can see all living beings down as far as the world of hell and up to the summit of the world of heavenly beings and also apprehend all their karmic causes and conditions and the

CAUSALITY

Buddhism expounds the law of cause and effect that operates in life, ranging over past, present and future existences. This causality underlies the idea of karma.

Causality is viewed from two perspectives: simultaneous and non-simultaneous. From the non-simultaneous viewpoint, causes formed in the past are manifested as effects in the present. Causes formed in the present will be manifested as effects in the future. Buddhism emphasizes the causes we create and accumulate in the present, because these determine our future.

From the viewpoint of Buddhist practice, *cause* represents the bodhisattva practice for attaining Buddhahood and *effect* represents the benefit of Buddhahood. Based on the principle that the ordinary person and the Buddha are essentially the same, it is taught that cause (the nine worlds, or practice) and effect (Buddhahood, or the result of practice) are non-dual and simultaneous.

Nichiren Daishonin writes: "Shakyamuni's practices and the virtues he consequently attained are all contained within the five characters of Myoho-renge-kyo. If we believe in these five characters, we will naturally be granted the same benefits as he was" ("The Object of Devotion for Observing the Mind," WND-1, 365).

Nichiren refers to two kinds of Buddhist teachings, those that view things from the standpoint of "cause to effect" and those that approach things from "effect to cause." The former corresponds to Shakyamuni's teachings by which ordinary persons carry out Buddhist practice (cause) aiming at the goal of Buddhahood (effect). In contrast, the latter indicates Nichiren's teaching, in which ordinary persons while manifesting their innate Buddhahood (effect) through faith and practice, go out among the people of the nine worlds (cause) in order to also lead them to Buddhahood.

results or effects that await them (see LSOC, 292–93).

In other words, we can understand the thousand-millionfold world and clearly see the essence of our lives and those of others as if they were reflected in a clear mirror. When our eyes are purified—when we see with the undistorted vision of the enlightened Dharma nature from which the impurities of ignorance have been cleansed—we can understand which causes lead to happiness and which lead to suffering and misery. This enables us to turn any state of life within the Ten Worlds[18]—from hell to Buddhahood—into a wellspring of value creation.

The benefit of the purification of the six sense organs attained by Bodhisattva Never Disparaging is the vigorous life force with which to withstand painful hardships. Bodhisattva Never Disparaging was persecuted because he lived in an evil age, but throughout his ordeals he never wavered in his belief in the Lotus Sutra and its teaching that all living beings possess the Buddha nature. Through his struggle to triumph over adversity and protect the Law, he defeated the ignorance or darkness that is the fundamental source of negative karma—the inability to believe in the Buddha nature of all people—and gained the benefit of purifying his senses, which brought forth his innate life force as an entity of the Mystic Law.

This is the benefit of transforming one's karma through dedicated efforts to uphold the Lotus Sutra.

THE BENEFIT OF PROTECTING THE LAW

Highlights

- *Shakubuku*—the practice of clarifying the correct teaching of Buddhism and refuting slander of the Law—is the driving force for lessening karmic retribution.
- Efforts to defend the Law and protect the Lotus Sutra necessitate battling the destructive influence of slandering the Law.
- In defeating disbelief and slander, we conquer the ignorance or darkness in our own lives, manifest our innate life force as entities of the Mystic Law and erase sufferings that stem from accumulated negative karma.

Allow me here, in connection with lessening one's karmic retribution, to reaffirm the great significance of *shakubuku*—the practice of clarifying the correct teaching of Buddhism and refuting slander of the Law.

In this writing, Nichiren Daishonin says it is only natural that he should encounter great persecution as a result of carrying out *shakubuku* in the remote land of Japan during the Latter Day of the Law. As I mentioned earlier, he says that he has been prepared for such an eventuality and has been waiting for it to arise. In an evil age rampant with negative influences, the practice of *shakubuku* serves to protect the Law and as such becomes the driving force for lessening karmic retribution and transforming karma.

Nichiren clearly states that by conducting *shakubuku* in the Latter Day, one can receive the benefit that accrues from protecting the Law—namely, that of lessening karmic retribution.[19] For example, in "The Opening of the Eyes," he writes: "When I vigorously berate those throughout the country who slander the Law, I meet with great difficulties. It must be that my actions in defending the Law in this present life are calling forth retributions for the grave offenses of my past. If iron does not come into contact with fire, it remains black, but if it contacts fire, it turns red. If you place a log across a swift stream, waves will pile up like hills. If you disturb a sleeping lion, it will roar loudly" (WND-1, 282).

The Latter Day of the Law is an age that abounds with negative influences and evil companions[20] as well as widespread slander of the Lotus Sutra. These all combine to exacerbate people's fundamental ignorance and cause them to lose sight of the Buddha nature. Efforts to defend the Law, to protect the teachings of the Lotus Sutra, are therefore crucial and ultimately necessitate our battling the destructive influence of slander of the Law pervading society.

In other words, even the countless negative causes from past lives that have brought us painful retribution in the present are all in essence the result of

"As SGI members, we dedicate ourselves to *kosen-rufu* and strive wholeheartedly to help others change their karma, while grappling head-on with our own karma. Nichiren's spirit lives in such noble actions, and such actions themselves enable us to live as lion kings overflowing with unsurpassed happiness and fulfillment."

159

nd disbelief in the Mystic
...orance and disbelief also
lie at the root of all slander of the Law.
Therefore, through the benefit we
obtain from our efforts to protect the
Law by defeating disbelief and slander,
we can conquer the ignorance or darkness in our own lives. And when we do
so, our innate vibrant life force as an
entity of the Mystic Law—the dynamic
life force of Buddhahood—manifests,
and we can erase sufferings that stem
from accumulated negative karma.

The concept of the non-simultaneity
of cause and effect explains the general
idea of causality in which karma from
past lives manifests in our present existence. In contrast, the concept of the
"simultaneity of cause and effect" indicates the causality by which we can
reveal our Buddhahood—that is, vanquishing our ignorance in this present
lifetime and immediately tapping the
life force of Buddhahood inherent
within us. The former constitutes a
sequential change, while the latter is an
instantaneous change.

While the foregoing is an explanation of the principle of transforming
one's karma, this same principle is
expressed as lessening one's karmic retribution when the focus is on the degree
of hardships one experiences.

Efforts to protect the Law—which
bring us the benefit of changing our
karma—are invariably accompanied by
hardships. If we persevere in such
efforts, sternly rebuking slander of the
Law, it is natural that we will face attack

from forces hostile to the Lotus Sutra,
and that great persecution will arise.
Even Bodhisattva Never Disparaging,
who propagated the guiding tenet of
the Lotus Sutra, underwent persecution
in the form of being stoned and beaten
with staves. But even this can be
regarded as no more than light suffering, compared with the heavy suffering
he might otherwise have had to
undergo as retribution for unfathomable offenses committed in past
lifetimes. This principle is called lessening one's karmic retribution because,
by experiencing minor suffering, we can
expiate negative karma that ought to
have brought far greater suffering.

ACTION IS THE DIRECT PATH TO CHANGING OUR KARMA

Highlights

- In Buddhist practice, the important thing is that one's words and
  actions are in harmony.
- Nichiren selflessly strove to open
  the path to Buddhahood for all
  people.

This passage reveals that Nichiren Daishonin's practice of *shakubuku* is what it
means to read and live the Lotus Sutra.

In Buddhist practice, the important
thing is that one's words and actions are
in harmony. In terms of the six stages of

practice[21] set forth by the Great Teacher T'ien-t'ai of China, genuine practice only begins at the stage of perception and action,[22] when one's words and actions are in sync.

Likewise, in Nichiren Buddhism, action is of key importance. In this writing, he points out that, while it is relatively easy to recite the Lotus Sutra with letter-perfect accuracy—a form of Buddhist practice that many in Japanese society of the day prided themselves on—it is very difficult to conduct oneself exactly as the sutra teaches.

In particular, Nichiren cites four passages of the Lotus Sutra that he has read with his life. Each passage asserts that those who propagate the Lotus Sutra after the Buddha's passing in the evil age of the Latter Day of the Law are certain to incur enmity and hardship in society. Because he has encountered just such obstacles, Nichiren declares that he alone in the Latter Day has practiced in a way that completely accords with the sutra's predictions.

Further, he says he can imagine how followers in the past must have grieved when Buddhist teachers who spread the correct teaching during the reigns of evil rulers met persecution. These words echo his concern for how his own disciples must have felt as they continued to fight valiantly alongside him despite the punishing onslaught by the authorities, culminating in the Tatsunokuchi Persecution and the ensuing Sado Exile.

But, as if to dispel these dark clouds, Nichiren serenely declares that since he has lived the entirety of the Lotus Sutra, the wonderful benefit of enlightenment awaits him, and that he is more confident than ever. He also states that he is propagating the correct teaching not only for his own attainment of Buddhahood but out of his wish to realize the security and peace of the entire land.

Nichiren was waging a momentous struggle to open the path to Buddhahood for all people of the Latter Day of the Law. It was also an unprecedented struggle to transform the destiny of the land and, further, to transform the destiny of all humankind. This is the Daishonin's spirit. From this, it becomes clear that only Nichiren can be considered as the true votary of the Lotus Sutra and the fundamental teacher who, with profound insight into the underlying nature of life, selflessly strove to open the path for transforming destiny in order to actualize happiness for all people and secure a peaceful world.

To reassure his followers, he seeks to convey to them his profound state of mind by describing his tangible efforts to read and live the Lotus Sutra. He calls out to them in effect, "Follow me with confidence!"

It goes without saying that, in the present defiled age of the Latter Day, only the Soka Gakkai—the organization carrying out the Buddha's decree—has inherited Nichiren's spirit and undergone persecution for the sake of *kosen-rufu* exactly as described in his writings and in the Lotus Sutra.

The Soka Gakkai's first and second

presidents, Tsunesaburo Makiguchi and Josei Toda, were modern-day teachers who, recognizing this noble mission of the Soka Gakkai, boldly embarked on the widespread propagation of Nichiren Buddhism.

A woman once asked Mr. Toda why he was ill. He answered: "My being sick like this is an enormous case of lessening karmic retribution. Because of this illness, the immense difficulties that the Soka Gakkai would have had to face are being reduced."

I can never forget Mr. Toda's profound spirit. Day in and day out, he really threw himself into the turbulent maelstrom of obstacles and devilish functions pervading the universe and exercised the leadership of a lion king.

As President Toda's true disciple, I have made steadfast efforts to protect the Law, thereby opening the eternal path through which our members can transform their karma.

At the time of the Osaka Incident,[23] when I rose up to bear the full brunt of attacks on our organization, Mr. Toda told me, "When you take the lead and challenge great hardships, then, in accord with the principle of consistency from beginning to end,[24] you will open the way to the attainment of Buddhahood in this lifetime not only for yourself but for all your fellow members."

Today, countless members around the globe, in 192 countries and territories, are advancing with confidence, pride and joy along the supreme path of transforming karma into mission, and have shown victorious actual proof of "changing poison into medicine" through faith. I believe there is no greater testament to the principle of lessening karmic retribution.

In this writing, Nichiren describes with irrepressible vigor his unshakable confidence and his immense struggles as the votary of the Lotus Sutra. To me, each word and phrase seems to pulse with his passionate spirit, calling out to us: "Become strong like Nichiren!" "Win together with Nichiren!"

As SGI members, we dedicate ourselves to *kosen-rufu* and strive wholeheartedly to help others change their karma, while grappling head-on with our own karma. Nichiren's spirit lives in such noble actions, and such actions themselves enable us to live as lion kings overflowing with unsurpassed happiness and fulfillment.

"Together, let's press onward to *kosen-rufu*"—so goes a line from the refrain of a well-loved Soka Gakkai song.[25] All of you, the infinitely precious members of the SGI, are challenging yourselves earnestly day in and day out to transform your own destiny and guide others to do the same. The heavenly deities cannot fail to rejoice and to protect you. Nichiren Daishonin would surely applaud you. And Mr. Makiguchi and Mr. Toda would also smilingly commend you.

This lecture was published in the June 2008 issue of The Daibyakurenge, *the Soka Gakkai study journal.*

NOTES:

1. Human and heavenly worlds or the worlds of humanity and heaven. The worlds of the three vehicles or the worlds of the voice-hearers, cause-awakened ones and bodhisattvas. The world of the one vehicle or the world of Buddhahood.
2. *The Lotus Sutra and Its Opening and Closing Sutras*, p. 312.
3. Ludwig van Beethoven (1770–1827): German composer. Active in Vienna during the transitional period between Classical and Romantic eras in Western classical music. Despite suffering from hearing loss, Beethoven composed many masterpieces, including nine symphonies.
4. Anton Felix Schindler, *Beethoven as I Knew Him*, edited by Donald MacArdle and translated by Constance S. Jolly (London: Faber and Faber, 1996), n.p.
5. Ludwig van Beethoven, *Beethoven: Letters, Journals and Conversations*, edited and translated by Michael Hamburger (London: Thames and Hudson, 1951), p. 40.
6. Tatsunokuchi Persecution and Sado Exile: On September 12, 1271, the authorities arrested Nichiren Daishonin and took him to a place called Tatsunokuchi on the outskirts of Kamakura, where they tried to execute him under cover of darkness. When the execution attempt failed, he was held in detention at the residence of the deputy constable of Sado, Homma Rokuro Saemon, in Echi (present-day Kanagawa Prefecture). After about a month, during which the government debated what to do with him, he was exiled to Sado Island, which was tantamount to a death sentence. But when Nichiren's predictions of internal strife and foreign invasion were ultimately fulfilled, the government issued a pardon in March 1274, and Nichiren returned to Kamakura.
7. Homma Rokuro Saemon (n.d.): Deputy constable of Sado Island. He served under Hojo Nobutoki, a powerful figure who was constable of both Musashi Province and Sado Island. Homma had a fief and residence in Echi (present-day Kanagawa Prefecture).
8. "Oko Kikigaki" (The Recorded Lectures); not translated in *The Writings of Nichiren Daishonin*, vols. 1 or 2.
9. Ota Jomyo, Soya Kyoshin and Dharma Bridge Kimbara (also pronounced Kanahara) were all followers of Nichiren Daishonin who resided in Shimosa Province. "Dharma Bridge" was a title established in the mid-ninth century as an official rank for priests, but later it simply became a title of honor.
10. Accounts vary considerably according to the source, which include such Buddhist scriptures as the Increasing by One Agama Sutra and the Stories of the Words of Truth Sutra.
11. Nichiren writes: "The twenty-five teachers who transmitted the Buddhist teachings [i.e., Shakyamuni and his twenty-four successors of the Former Day of the Law], with the exception of Shakyamuni Buddha, were all temporary manifestations of Buddhas or great bodhisattvas whose advent had been predicted by Shakyamuni. Of these, the fourteenth, Bodhisattva Aryadeva, was killed by a non-Buddhist, and the twenty-fifth, the Venerable Aryasimha, was beheaded by King Dammira. Buddhamitra and Bodhisattva Nagarjuna also suffered many persecutions. Yet others propagated Buddhism under the protection of devout kings, without encountering persecution. This would seem to be because good countries and evil countries exist in the world, and shoju and shakubuku exist [to be used respectively in these two types of countries] as ways of propagation. It was like this even during the Former and Middle Days of the Law, as it was in India, the center of Buddhism. This country [Japan] is far away from India, and this is the beginning of [the evil age of] the Latter Day of the Law. I was certain beforehand that such things would happen; I have simply been waiting for the inevitable" ("Lessening One's Karmic Retribution," WND-1, 199).
12. Twenty-four successors: Also, twenty-four patriarchs. Those who, after Shakyamuni's death, successively inherited the lineage of his teachings and propagated them in India.
13. *Shakubuku* is one of two methods of teaching and propagating Buddhism, the other being *shoju*. *Shakubuku* means directly awakening people to the correct teaching by refuting their mistaken views, whereas *shoju* involves gradually leading others to the correct teaching without refuting their mistaken views. In general, *shoju* is to be employed during the Former and Middle Days of the Law, whereas *shakubuku* is to be used in the Latter Day.
14. Ignorance: In Buddhism, this means ignorance about the true nature of existence. It is deemed the fundamental cause of suffering and delusion. It prevents people from recognizing the true nature of their lives and taking faith in the Mystic Law, which enables all to attain enlightenment.
15. Nirvana Sutra, vol. 29.
16. Thousand-millionfold world (also, major world system): One of the world systems described in ancient Indian cosmology. A world consists of a Mount Sumeru, its surrounding seas and mountain ranges, a sun, a moon and other heavenly bodies. This concept might be compared in modern terms to that of a solar system from the standpoint of the planet one inhabits. One major world system comprises one billion worlds, and hence it is referred to as the thousand-millionfold world. The universe was conceived of as containing countless major world systems.
17. Also known as Mount Meru. Indian cosmology describes this mountain as standing at the center of the world. Some sutras describe it as being made of gold, silver, emerald and crystal. The god Shakra resides on the summit, with his 32 retainer gods, while the four heavenly kings live halfway up—one to each of its four sides.
18. The Ten Worlds: Ten potential states or conditions of life that a person can manifest or experience.
19. In "The Opening of the Eyes," Nichiren also cites the Parinirvana Sutra, which states: "It is due to the blessings obtained by protecting the Law that they can diminish in this lifetime their suffering and retribution" (WND-1, 281).
20. Evil companion: Also, evil friend or evil teacher. One who causes others to fall into the evil paths by misleading them in connection with Buddhism. An evil companion deludes others with false teachings in order to obstruct their correct Buddhist practice.
21. Six stages of practice: Six stages in the practice of the Lotus Sutra formulated by T'ien-t'ai (538–97) in his *Great Concentration and Insight*. They are: (1) the stage of being a Buddha in theory, (2) the stage of hearing the name and words of the truth, (3) the stage of perception and action, (4) the stage of resemblance to enlightenment, (5) the stage of progressive awakening and (6) the stage of ultimate enlightenment.
22. Stage of perception and action: This is the third stage of practice where one rejoices upon hearing the teaching of the Mystic Law, and then correctly practices the Lotus Sutra, one's words matching his or her actions. In "Lessening One's Karmic Retribution," Nichiren cites the words of T'ien-t'ai's *Great Concentration and Insight*, saying that this stage means that "one acts as one speaks and speaks as one acts" (WND-1, 199).
23. Osaka Incident: The occasion when SGI President Ikeda, then Soka Gakkai youth division chief of staff, was arrested and wrongfully charged with election law violations in a House of Councilor's by-election in Osaka in 1957. At the end of the court case, which dragged on for almost five years, he was fully exonerated of all charges.
24. Consistency from beginning to end: One of the ten factors of life listed in the "Expedient Means" chapter of the Lotus Sutra. It indicates that all nine factors from "appearance" to "manifest effect" consistently and harmoniously express the same condition of existence at any given moment.
25. From the Soka Gakkai song, "Kofu ni hashire" (Onward to Kosen-rufu).

(1 0)

"Letter to Misawa"

Vanquishing the Devil King With Intrepid Faith—
Inheriting Nichiren Daishonin's Self-reliant Courage

The Passage for Study in This Lecture

When an ordinary person of the latter age is ready to attain Buddhahood, having realized the essence of all the sacred teachings of the Buddha's lifetime and understood the heart of the important teaching set forth in [T'ien-t'ai's] *Great Concentration and Insight,* this devil [the devil king of the sixth heaven¹] is greatly surprised. He says to himself, "This is most vexing. If I allow this person to remain in my domain, he not only will free himself from the sufferings of birth and death, but will lead others to enlightenment as well. Moreover, he will take over my realm [this suffering *saha* world] and change it into a pure land. What shall I do?" The devil king then summons all his underlings from the threefold world of desire, form, and formlessness² and tells them: "Each of you now go and harass that votary, according to your respective skills. If you should fail to make him abandon his Buddhist practice, then enter into the minds of his disciples, lay supporters, and the people of his land and thus try to persuade or threaten him. If these attempts are also unsuccessful, I myself will go down and possess the mind and body of his sovereign to persecute that votary. Together, how can we fail to prevent him from attaining Buddhahood?"

I, Nichiren, have long been aware of all this and therefore know how difficult it is for an ordinary person of the latter age to become a Buddha in this lifetime. (*The Writings of Nichiren Daishonin*, vol. 1, pp. 894–95)

As for my teachings, regard those before my exile to the province of Sado as equivalent to the Buddha's pre-Lotus Sutra teachings....

On the night of the twelfth day of the ninth month in the eighth year of Bun'ei [September 12,] (1271), I was very nearly beheaded at Tatsunokuchi. From that time, I felt pity for my followers because I had not yet revealed this true teaching to any of them. With this in mind, I secretly conveyed my teaching to my disciples from the province of Sado. After the Buddha's passing, great scholars and teachers such as Mahakashyapa, Ananda, Nagarjuna, Vasubandhu [of India], T'ien-t'ai, Miao-lo [of China], Dengyo, and Gishin [of Japan] knew this teaching, but kept it in their hearts and did not express it in words. The reason was that the Buddha had forbidden them to spread it, stating, "After my passing, this great Law should not be revealed until the Latter Day of the Law arrives."[3] I may not be an envoy sent by the Buddha, but my appearance in this world coincides with the age of the Latter Day. Moreover, quite unexpectedly, I came to realize this teaching, which I now expound to prepare the way for a sage.[4]

With the appearance of this teaching, all the teachings advocated by the scholars and teachers of Buddhism during the Former and Middle Days of the Law will be like stars after sunrise, or an awkward apprentice beside a skilled craftsman. It is stated that, once this teaching is revealed in this era, the Buddha images as well as the priests of the temples built in the Former and Middle Days will all lose their power to benefit people, and only this great teaching will spread throughout the entire land of Jambudvipa [the entire world].[5] Since all of you have a bond with this teaching, you should feel reassured. (WND-1, 896)

LECTURE

My mentor, second Soka Gakkai president Josei Toda, often used to remark: "When it comes to battling serious karma and undergoing our human revolution, huge obstacles and hardships can in fact serve as a powerful impetus, propelling us forward. Just ambling along a level road won't help us change our karma." The greater the difficulties and challenges we encounter, the greater the life-state we can develop. Therefore, we mustn't be intimidated by the three obstacles and four devils[6]—that is, the obstacles and hindrances that invariably arise in the course of our Buddhist practice. Our wisdom derived from faith allows us to see through such phenomena, recognizing them for what they are, based on Nichiren Daishonin's teachings, and regarding their occurrence as an opportunity to change our karma. We can then stand up with even deeper conviction and courage, chanting Nam-myoho-renge-kyo with unwavering resolve and forging boldly ahead.

Nichiren writes, "The three obstacles and four devils will invariably appear, and the wise will rejoice while the foolish will retreat" (WND-1, 637). Either we advance or we retreat; there is no middle ground. Either we cringe in fear and surrender to the devilish functions—the negativity in our own lives or in the lives of others—or we challenge this negativity and deepen our conviction in faith. This difference in resolve determines everything. Nichiren himself faced the major ordeals of the Tatsunokuchi Persecution and the Sado Exile with supreme confidence and composure.

Through battling great hardships, individuals can establish an inner state of indestructible happiness. And their example can open the way for countless others to similarly free themselves from suffering.

The essence of devilish functions is to deprive people of their benefit and even their lives (see "Opening the Eyes of Wooden and Painted Images," WND-1, 87). This is achieved through undermining people's resolve. Such functions work to destroy people's desire to seek and continue advancing on the path to attaining Buddhahood. Consequently, people who persevere in faith and stay firmly committed to moving forward on this path will remain impervious to attacks by these negative functions. Developing such inner strength is the true purpose of our Buddhist practice.

In the writing we are studying this time, "Letter to Misawa," Nichiren urges his followers to continue striving together with him, undaunted by any circumstance, for *kosen-rufu*—a struggle between the Buddha nature and the negativity inherent in life.

July [when this lecture was originally published] marks the month in which the first three Soka Gakkai presidents—united by the bonds of mentor and disciple in faith—stood up to the devilish nature of power.[7] Through Nichiren's writing, let us study the intrepid faith that is not only crucial to defeating the devil king of the sixth heaven but is also the essence of the shared commitment of mentor and disciple.

DEFEATING THE DEVIL KING IS THE HALLMARK OF A GENUINE TEACHER OF BUDDHISM

Highlights

Written: February 23, 1278

Recipient: Misawa, a feudal lord in Suruga Province.

- First, Nichiren describes the nature of the devil king of the sixth heaven.

- In this letter, he makes three main points:

  1 He describes the vast life-condition necessary to defeat the devil king, clarifying the significance of obstacles in Buddhism, outlining the qualifications of a genuine teacher and stressing the importance of mustering faith strong enough to withstand impending hardships.

  2 He asserts that the body of his teachings should be classified into two periods—"pre-Sado" and "post-Sado."

  3 To ensure the recipient is not swayed by added pressure from authorities, he points out that the erroneous teachings of the True Word school—on whose prayers the government relied for the defeat of the Mongols—would lead to the country's destruction.

At the start of "Letter to Misawa," Nichiren Daishonin describes in a very simple way the nature of the devil king of the sixth heaven, which he fully understood. He explains that because of this devil's workings he has encountered one great persecution after another, and he indicates that a person qualified to be a genuine teacher of Buddhism in the Latter Day of the Law is one who has thoroughly defeated this devil king.

"Letter to Misawa" [written at Minobu] is dated February 23, 1278, and addressed to a follower of that name, a feudal lord who resided and held a fief in Misawa in Fuji District of Suruga Province (part of present-day Shizuoka Prefecture). According to this letter, Misawa and Nichiren had not been in contact for some time. This could have been either because Misawa's faith had been weak or because of a decision on Nichiren's part to curtail their communications due to various circumstances in Suruga Province.

Suruga was an area of strategic importance for the Kamakura government, both militarily and as a transport route. It was also home to many fiefs that were under direct control of the ruling Hojo clan members. For Nichiren's followers—whose movements were closely monitored by the government at the time—it was necessary to act with great care and prudence in that region.[8] Added to these circumstances was the unfolding persecution in Atsuhara (also in Fuji District of Suruga Province)—which had already begun in 1278, when this letter was written, and would reach its culmination the following year.[9]

As a gift from the Mikhail A. Sholokhov State Museum and Reserve,
Museum Director Alexander Sholokhov (right) gives SGI President Ikeda
a framed photograph of his grandfather, December 13, 2008.

It is evident from this writing that these circumstances and developments in Suruga prompted the Daishonin to use caution and restraint so as not to cause Misawa to be persecuted by the military government. But when a messenger arrived from this follower with whom he had long been out of touch, it seems Nichiren took the opportunity to offer important guidance and encouragement that would help deepen his faith.

Nichiren makes three main points in this letter. First, he explains that his battle against the devil king of the sixth heaven has led him to encounter severe persecution. In doing so, he communicates the imperturbable life-state of someone who has triumphed over the devil king. Here, the Daishonin clarifies the significance of obstacles in Buddhism and outlines the qualifications of a genuine teacher of Buddhism. Also, in

view of the troubling developments in Atsuhara, he conveys the essence of the Mystic Law so that Misawa can muster faith strong enough to withstand the impending hardships.

The compassion of a genuine Buddhist teacher is like the gentle love of a mother, warmly embracing and supportive of those who are suffering. At the same time, it is also like the strict love of a father, fostering a spirit of self-reliance so that people may cultivate their own happiness. Through writing of the fierce struggles he has undergone, Nichiren offers Misawa important lessons in faith. We can read this as an expression of a father's strict love.

Second, Nichiren asserts that the body of his teachings should be classified into two periods—"pre-Sado" and "post-Sado." Just as the teachings of Shakyamuni have been delineated between the expedient or provisional, pre-Lotus Sutra teachings and the true teaching of the Lotus Sutra,[10] a critical distinction must be made, Nichiren emphasizes, between what he taught before his exile to Sado and his teachings from that time onward.[11]

Whereas the first point concerns itself with Nichiren's vast state of life, focusing on the aspect of the Person, this second point concerns itself with the division of Nichiren's teachings into pre-Sado and post-Sado, focusing on the aspect of the Law.[12]

Strictly speaking, what we refer to as the post-Sado period actually begins from the moment Nichiren "cast off the transient and revealed the true"[13] at the time of the Tatsunokuchi Persecution, where he achieved total victory in his struggle with the devil king of the sixth heaven.

Also, the most notable difference between Nichiren's pre-Sado and post-Sado teachings is that the latter explicitly mentions the Gohonzon, the object of devotion.

Nichiren inscribed the Gohonzon as a representation of the supreme enlightenment—the highest and noblest state of being—that he had attained as an ordinary person. By doing so, he provided a clear mirror for the enlightenment of all human beings. The Gohonzon serves as a mirror and guide so that people in the Latter Day of the Law can awaken to the incomparable dignity and nobility of their own lives. The Gohonzon embodies "the great teaching to be spread throughout the world" in the Latter Day (see WND-1, 896).

In this writing, Nichiren informs Misawa of the difference between his pre-Sado and post-Sado teachings and encourages him, saying that he "should feel reassured" (WND-1, 896) at his having formed a connection with this great teaching.

"While many people study Buddhism, few actually attain Buddhahood—first, because it is difficult to encounter a correct teacher and, second, because those who do manage to practice correctly are certain to meet with the three obstacles and four devils."

For his third point, the Daishonin states unequivocally that the erroneous teachings of the True Word school[14]—on whose prayers the government was relying for the defeat of the Mongols[15]—would in fact lead to the country's destruction. He cites examples of past rulers in China and Japan who had misguidedly placed their faith in the True Word teachings and brought ruin upon themselves (WND-1, 897). In this way, he wishes to have Misawa recognize the government's error and calls his attention to the grave peril threatening Japan. We can surmise that Nichiren wanted Misawa to be aware of these things so that Misawa's faith would not be swayed if a public debate[16] were to take place between Nichiren's disciples and the priests of the True Word school.

The Daishonin had already frequently discussed these three points in other writings such as "The Opening of the Eyes" that he had composed during and after his exile on Sado. These points constituted important doctrines that, given the times, could only be passed on with great caution and prudence. This seems to be why Nichiren had refrained from speaking of them in detail to Misawa, a resident of Suruga who ran a high risk of persecution from the authorities.

As the shadow of persecution loomed ever larger over the community of believers in Suruga Province, Nichiren's compassion prompted him to help Misawa forge greater resolve in faith through this concise summary of the most vital points in his Buddhist teaching.

FAITH IS A STRUGGLE WITH THE THREE OBSTACLES AND FOUR DEVILS

Highlights

- Though many study Buddhism, few actually attain Buddhahood because (1) it is difficult to encounter a correct teacher and (2) those who practice correctly are certain to meet with the three obstacles and four devils.

- Even if someone overcomes the three obstacles and the first three of the four devils, he or she will not attain enlightenment if ultimately defeated by the devil king.

- Mr. Toda cautioned us to beware of the insidious workings of the devil king—the representation of the fundamental darkness inherent in our own lives.

In "Letter to Misawa," Nichiren Daishonin embarks on a detailed discussion of the essential nature of the devil king of the sixth heaven.

He begins by noting that while many people study Buddhism, few actually attain Buddhahood—first, because it is difficult to encounter a correct teacher and, second, because those who do manage to practice correctly are certain to meet with the three obstacles and four devils (see WND-1, 894).

When we practice the correct teaching of Buddhism, then the three obstacles and four devils are sure to appear, just as "the shadow follows the body and clouds accompany rain" (WND-1, 894). And among the three obstacles and four devils, the most formidable is the last of the four devils—the devil king of the sixth heaven, or heavenly devil. In this writing, Nichiren states that even if we have managed to overcome the three obstacles (earthly desires, karma and retribution) and the first three of the four devils (the hindrances of earthly desires, the five components and death)[17]—we cannot attain enlightenment if we are ultimately defeated by the devil king.

In a lecture he gave on "Letter to Misawa," Mr. Toda remarked: "If you can practice correct faith, then you can defeat the likes of the hindrance of death. You can even prolong your life. I know of many people who have done this. . . . You can triumph over the hindrance of death. The most fearful is the last [of the four hindrances], the devil king. If you look at those who have abandoned their faith, you'll generally find that they've fallen victim to this devil king."[18]

Mr. Toda always exuded tremendous confidence when he gave guidance. On another occasion, he declared, "So long as you have faith, you can defeat even the hindrance of death and actualize the principle of prolonging one's life through faith."[19] This is something Mr. Toda personally demonstrated, which is precisely why he consistently urged us to beware of the insidious workings of the devil king of the sixth heaven.

Indeed, the devil king is our greatest enemy in the effort to attain Buddhahood, because the devil king represents the fundamental darkness[20] inherent in our own lives.

FUNDAMENTAL DARKNESS MANIFESTS AS THE DEVIL KING

Highlights

- Fundamental darkness is ignorance of the fact that our lives and those of others are entities of the Mystic Law. It can manifest as dark impulses that lead to negative and destructive actions.

- Because this powerful negative force can work in subtle and insidious ways and freely manipulate others, it is referred to as the devil king, or by the name Freely Enjoying Things Conjured by Others.

- Fundamental darkness can be vanquished by the supreme wisdom gained from faith in the correct teaching of the Lotus Sutra and Nam-myoho-renge-kyo.

- The devil king abhors the possibility that the number of those who practice Buddhism correctly will increase and that many will be freed from his influence.

- By remaining on the path of mentor and disciple, we can identify such negative forces at the deepest level and repudiate them.

Nichiren Daishonin writes, "Fundamental darkness manifests itself as the devil king of the sixth heaven" ("The Treatment of Illness," WND-1, 1113). Fundamental darkness means fundamental ignorance of the fact that our lives and those of others—and indeed all things in the universe—are entities of the Mystic Law. This fundamental ignorance is the source of all other illusions that give rise to misery and suffering. It also manifests as dark impulses that lead to negative and destructive actions. Since the ultimate illusion of fundamental ignorance is the most difficult to recognize and identify, it can exert a harmful influence on our lives without our being aware of it. And, because fundamental darkness is inherent in all life, it produces dark impulses not only in our lives but in those of others as well. Because this powerful negative force can work in extremely subtle and insidious ways and freely manipulate others, it is referred to as the "devil king," or Freely Enjoying Things Conjured by Others.

Ultimately, however, for all its negative or destructive influence, fundamental darkness, at essence, is nothing but ignorance. Therefore, it can be vanquished by wisdom. A person who brings forth this kind of wisdom is a Buddha. The supreme wisdom for achieving this goal is found in the correct teaching of Buddhism, which is none other than the Lotus Sutra of Shakyamuni and the teaching of Nam-myoho-renge-kyo of the Three Great Secret Laws[21] expounded by Nichiren Daishonin.

By "substituting faith for wisdom"[22]—bringing forth Buddha wisdom through faith in the correct teaching—we, as ordinary people, can triumph over fundamental darkness just as we are. The power with which we can subdue fundamental darkness is solely the power of faith, our minds and the inherent enlightened wisdom within our own lives.

In this letter, Nichiren clarifies the truly frightening and formidable nature of the devil king of the sixth heaven. And through his own actions, he exemplifies how our inner spiritual strength is the force that can vanquish this devil king.

Nichiren states that the *saha* world in which we dwell is a domain ruled by the devil king. This human world—shaped by the functions of our desires, physical actions and spiritual and intellectual pursuits [reflecting the threefold world of desire, form (matter) and formlessness (spirit)][23]—is subject to an endless cycle of suffering stemming from fundamental darkness, and can therefore be considered as the domain of the devil king.

What does the devil king abhor most of all? It is the possibility that the Buddha's forces could multiply and take over his realm. When a votary of the Mystic Law, the correct teaching of Buddhism, attains enlightenment, it doesn't just stop there; that person invariably leads many others to free themselves from the fetters of the devil king as well. So the devil king summons all his underlings and commands them to do everything in their power to harass that votary.

These devilish minions are sometimes referred to as the "ten kinds of troops" or "ten armies" of the devil king.[24] They represent various earthly desires or delusions that arise from fundamental darkness to obstruct our Buddhist practice—manifesting one after another like great legions of demons. They constitute hindrances in the form of: (1) greed, (2) care and worry, (3) hunger and thirst, (4) love of pleasure (also, craving), (5) drowsiness and languor, (6) fear, (7) doubt and regret, (8) anger, (9) preoccupation with wealth and fame and (10) arrogance and contempt for others.

If the votary of the correct teaching remains impervious to these hindrances, Nichiren asserts, the devil king will then order these forces to enter the lives of the votary's disciples, lay followers and other people of his land and cause them to persecute that votary. This means that the fundamental darkness within these people's lives is stimulated, prompting them to act as devilish functions.

For instance, in India, Devadatta,[25] Sunakshatra[26] and King Ajatashatru[27] harbored enmity toward Shakyamuni; while in Japan, Sammi-bo,[28] the lay nun of Nagoe[29] and other faithless disciples turned against Nichiren. The root cause for their treachery and disloyalty was that they had all allowed themselves to be defeated by the armies of the devil king. Even the five senior priests—who along with Nikko Shonin were designated by Nichiren as the guardians of his teachings—ultimately turned against their teacher. They could not understand Nikko's insistence on practicing with the same spirit as Nichiren.

Nichiren ascribed the reasons for Sammi-bo, the lay nun of Nagoe and others' betrayal and abandonment of faith to their cowardice, arrogance, greed and skepticism.[30] They had succumbed to the influence of such armies of the devil king as "preoccupation with wealth and fame" and "arrogance and contempt for others," as well as "fear," "doubt and regret" and "anger." As a result, they could not remain in the pure

"By 'substituting faith for wisdom'—bringing forth Buddha wisdom through faith in the correct teaching—we, as ordinary people, can triumph over fundamental darkness just as we are. The power with which we can subdue fundamental darkness is solely the power of faith, our minds and the inherent enlightened wisdom within our own lives."

realm of faith; they had allowed their faith to be destroyed. But because they couldn't bear to admit their own defeat, they resented and maligned those practicing correctly.

In more recent times, the base individuals who not only deserted but cruelly defamed our first and second presidents, Tsunesaburo Makiguchi and Josei Toda, were exactly the same.

Around 1950, Mr. Toda's businesses fell into their biggest crisis yet. I witnessed people who had once called Mr. Toda their mentor suddenly do a complete about-face and address him disdainfully and criticize him. How ungrateful some people can be. This experience brought home to me the sad reality of how easily people can be ruled by their fundamental darkness. I vowed to stand up to those who had shown Mr. Toda such ingratitude.

To betray even the profound debt of gratitude one owes a teacher in faith is an indication of the weakness of those who succumb to the workings of the devil king of the sixth heaven. By resolving never to veer from the path of mentor and disciple, we can develop the ability to identify such devilish functions at the deepest level and repudiate them.

I resolved to thoroughly demonstrate what it means to live with gratitude for one's mentor in faith, and I have steadfastly put this into practice. I believe that because I have done so, I could fully experience the true inner strength one derives from breaking through darkness or ignorance. I am also convinced that we of the Soka Gakkai have confidently shared the humanistic teachings of Nichiren Buddhism with others and spread these principles and ideals around the globe by persevering on this path of mentor and disciple and winning in every struggle against devilish functions.

Nichiren Buddhism is a teaching that illuminates what it means to be a human being. It is a people-centered philosophy that points the way toward revealing and establishing our highest humanity through taking on the momentous spiritual struggle against the devil king of the sixth heaven.

Returning to the passage we are studying, Nichiren says that if the underlings of the devil king—the devil's armies—fail to cause the votary of the correct teaching to abandon his faith, then the devil king himself will descend from the heaven in which he resides and take possession of the body of the sovereign, who will then persecute the votary. This represents the activation of the devilish nature of power.

What is the devilish nature of power? It is the ultimate negative function manifested by fundamental darkness, which rejects the belief that all living beings are supremely noble entities of the Mystic Law. More specifically, it refers to the tendency to look down on human life and use others at will toward evil ends. The devilish nature of power is the most potent manifestation of the devilish workings that pervade the human world, which has been shaped by the activation of fundamental darkness or ignorance.

When Nichiren says that the devil king will possess the body of the ruler, he means that negative functions arising from fundamental darkness will dominate the ruler's life. It also indicates that society as a whole—in which the ruler is a key figure—will come to function based on delusion and negativity deriving from this fundamental darkness and ignorance. In short, the society will be run by people whose minds are confused and deluded. [In his treatise "On Establishing the Correct Teaching for the Peace of the Land,"] Nichiren declares this to be what the Lotus Sutra describes as "evil demons taking possession of others"[31] and "the spirits [demons] showing signs of rampancy."[32]

"NOT ONCE HAVE I THOUGHT OF RETREAT"

Highlights

- When we stand up for *kosen-rufu,* the devil king invariably appears.

- Self-reliant faith is essential in defeating the devil king.

- *Kosen-rufu* spreads with the appearance of disciples committed to walking the path of attaining Buddhahood based on the correct teaching with the same spirit as their teacher.

- Nichiren bequeathed the Gohonzon, which embodies the oneness of the Person and the Law, to us so we could subdue fundamental darkness. The establishment of the Gohonzon distinguishes between Nichiren's pre-Sado and post-Sado teachings.

In "Letter to Misawa," after explaining how difficult it is to endure obstacles caused by the devil king of the sixth heaven, Nichiren Daishonin discusses his own challenging struggles. In particular, he mentions that, even before establishing his teaching, he deeply recognized that when one stands up for *kosen-rufu,* this devil king will invariably appear.

He goes on to say that one who expounds the correct teaching of Buddhism in the Latter Day of the Law is certain to meet with great persecutions, and that these will be "a hundred, thousand, ten thousand, million times greater than those in the Buddha's lifetime" (WND-1, 895). Yet, he says, those who are aware of this teaching but fail to spread it are destined to "fall into the great citadel of the hell of incessant suffering"[33] (WND-1, 895).

And so Nichiren, begrudging his life not the slightest, embarked on the great path of leading all people to enlightenment. He made the important resolution, "In this life, I knew that if I were truly resolved to withstand the harshest trials, then I must speak out" (WND-1, 895). Because of his profound pledge to never retreat a single step from any obstacle, he could open the way for his people-centered Buddhist philosophy to spread into the eternal future of the Latter Day of the Law.

In this writing, Nichiren declares that he had indeed met with one great persecution after another, just as he had expected, but that he is filled with immense satisfaction, free of doubt or regret. We can perceive here the essence of faith for defeating the devil king of the sixth heaven—self-reliant faith. The struggle is not up to anyone else; it is up to us. We must pledge to stand alone and take on all hardships. Only then will Nichiren Buddhism spread widely among the people.

Self-reliant faith means nonregressing faith. We must be determined to keep pressing forward, no matter the obstacles. Should we face unexpected trials or hardships, we must grit our teeth, hold our ground and refuse to be defeated. Standing firm until the power of the devil king is exhausted constitutes the first step for our future progress. We must courageously move forward, come what may. We must strengthen our inner fortitude, like waves that grow stronger the greater the obstacles they meet. The key to our surmounting the onslaughts of devilish functions is maintaining a spirit to win through all, to not waver the slightest in our resolve.

Nichiren showed us by example that it is possible to overcome any form of devilish function or negativity. And he taught us that *kosen-rufu* spreads with the appearance of disciples, who, with the same spirit as their teacher, are committed to pursuing the path of Buddhahood based on the correct teaching.

In another writing, Nichiren declares, "Not once have I thought of retreat" ("The Great Battle," WND-2, 465). As this indicates, he never felt inclined to abandon his struggle against the devil king of the sixth heaven. Even during the Tatsunokuchi Persecution—a manifestation of the workings of the devilish nature of power and the intimidating force of the hindrance of death—Nichiren triumphed with composure. His statement, "I survived even the Tatsunokuchi Persecution" (*Gosho zenshu*, p. 843),[34] is his declaration of victory as an individual, an ordinary person who has won outright in the ultimate struggle with the devil king.

"Nichiren taught us that *kosen-rufu* spreads with the appearance of disciples, who, with the same spirit as their teacher, are committed to pursuing the path of Buddhahood based on the correct teaching."

Concerning this triumph, Nichiren also says, "By now, the devil king must be thoroughly discouraged" (GZ, 843). This is an important assertion. This utter demoralization of the powerful and wickedly ingenious devil king, I believe, signaled not only Nichiren's own victory but meant that he could secure and pass on to people of future generations the key to genuine wisdom for conquering fundamental darkness. This is also evident in Nichiren's statement that, although after his death the remaining forces of the devil king might raise fresh armies, the vast majority have doubtlessly already surrendered to him.[35] How indebted we are to Nichiren.

What, then, is this key Nichiren bequeathed to us so that we could generate the wisdom to subdue fundamental darkness? It is the Gohonzon, the object of devotion, which embodies the oneness of the Person and the Law.[36] The primary difference between Nichiren's pre-Sado and post-Sado teachings lies in his establishment of the Gohonzon.

SPREADING THE GREAT TEACHING FOR THE ENLIGHTENMENT OF ALL PEOPLE

Highlights

- While on Sado, Nichiren revealed both the object of devotion in terms of the Person and the object of devotion in terms of the Law.
- Nichiren Buddhism is a powerful teaching that gives people the means to break through darkness and offers hope in times when society is pervaded with negativity.
- Nichiren Buddhism upholds the teaching that life is infinitely precious and respectworthy.

The section from "Letter to Misawa" that begins "As for my teachings, regard those before my exile to the province of Sado as equivalent to the Buddha's pre-Lotus Sutra teachings" is extremely well known, as it contains Nichiren Daishonin's

"Nichiren Buddhism is a philosophy of hope that teaches that each person's life is infinitely precious and respectworthy and that all can come to shine brightly like the sun."

personal specification that a clear distinction be made between his pre-Sado and post-Sado teachings.

Here, having triumphed over the devil king and revealed his true identity as the Buddha of the Latter Day, Nichiren declares to his followers that he will devote himself even more earnestly to spreading the great teaching for the enlightenment of all people.

The great teaching of Nam-myoho-renge-kyo propagated by the Daishonin is the timeless, eternal and ultimate truth of life. It is deeply significant that while on Sado, he chose to reveal both the object of devotion in terms of the Person and the object of devotion in terms of the Law.[37]

In this section, Nichiren proclaims to the effect: "The time to spread this great teaching has arrived! Until a sage appears, I will spread it!" We can view this passage as clarifying that, for all practical purposes, Nichiren is the "lord of teaching of the Latter Day of the Law."[38] He also declares the significance of the teaching he is spreading.

Nichiren Buddhism is the Buddhism of the sun. Nichiren confidently predicts the rise of the correct teaching and the decline of the provisional teachings, explaining that when the great teaching of Nam-myoho-renge-kyo appears, all the once-influential Buddhist teachings of the Former and Middle Days of the Law will be "like stars after sunrise" (WND-1, 896). The sun impartially shines its light on all. The light of the sun has the power to vanquish darkness.

Dark times call for a teaching that can unlock the infinite potential in people's lives, for a powerful teaching that can give people the means to break through the pervasive darkness and negativity in society and vanquish the workings of the devil king, the embodiment of fundamental darkness.

Nichiren Buddhism is a philosophy of hope that teaches that each person's life is infinitely precious and respect-worthy and that all can come to shine brightly like the sun.

The world today yearns for a truly humanistic philosophy. The time has at last arrived for Nichiren Buddhism to burst forth on the brilliant stage of human history like the rising sun.

The Daishonin concludes this section by saying, "Since all of you have a bond with this teaching, you should feel reassured" (WND-1, 896). He always treasured his followers to the utmost.

The SGI is an organization directly connected to Nichiren Daishonin. Our members everywhere are courageous Bodhisattvas of the Earth, valiantly struggling against all kinds of negativity and illuminating our troubled world with the light of the Mystic Law, a teaching of hope and revitalization. May glory, happiness and victory be yours! This is my ardent prayer and heartfelt cry.

This lecture was published in the July 2008 Daibyakurenge, *the Soka Gakkai study journal.*

NOTES:

1. Devil king of the sixth heaven: Also, devil king or heavenly devil. The king of devils who dwells in the highest or the sixth heaven of the world of desire. He is also named Freely Enjoying Things Conjured by Others, the heavenly devil who, for his own pleasure, freely makes use of the fruits of others' efforts.

2. The threefold world of desire, form and formlessness: The threefold world refers to the world of unenlightened beings who transmigrate within the six paths (from hell through the realm of heavenly beings). The threefold world consists of, in ascending order, the world of desire, the world of form (or matter) and the world of formlessness (or spirit): (1) The world of desire comprises the four evil paths (the realms of hell, hungry spirits, animals and *asuras*), the four continents surrounding Mount Sumeru (that contain the realm of human beings) and the first six divisions of heaven (the lowest part of the realm of heavenly beings). The beings in this world are ruled by various cravings, such as those for food, drink and sex. (2) The world of form consists of the four meditation heavens, which are further divided into 18 heavens (16 or 17 according to other explanations). The beings here are free from desires, cravings and appetites, but still have physical form and thus are subject to certain material restrictions. (3) The world of formlessness comprises the four realms of Boundless Empty Space, Boundless Consciousness, Nothingness and Neither Thought Nor No Thought. Here, beings are free from desires and from physical form with its material restrictions.

3. This is not an actual quotation but rather the expression of Nichiren's view of what various passages in the Lotus Sutra mean.

4. A "sage" here indicates Bodhisattva Superior Practices, whom Shakyamuni Buddha entrusted with the mission of propagating the Mystic Law in the Latter Day of the Law, as stated in the "Supernatural Powers" chapter of the Lotus Sutra. In several writings, Nichiren refers to himself in humble terms as the forerunner of Bodhisattva Superior Practices.

5. Jambudvipa: According to the ancient Indian worldview, Jambudvipa indicates the entirety of the realm where people dwell and where Buddhism will spread.

6. Three obstacles and four devils: Various obstacles and hindrances to the practice of Buddhism. They are listed in the Nirvana Sutra and Nagarjuna's *The Treatise on the Great Perfection of Wisdom*. The three obstacles are (1) the obstacle of earthly desires, or obstacles arising from the three poisons of greed, anger and foolishness; (2) the obstacle of karma, obstacles due to bad karma created by committing any of the five cardinal sins or ten evil acts; and (3) the obstacle of retribution, obstacles caused by the negative karmic effects of actions in the three evil paths (the realms of hell, hungry spirits and animals). The four devils are (1) the hindrance of the five components, obstructions caused by one's physical and mental functions; (2) the hindrance of earthly desires, obstructions arising from the three poisons; (3) the hindrance of death, meaning one's own untimely death obstructing one's practice of Buddhism, or the premature death of another practitioner causing one to doubt; and (4) the hindrance of the devil king of the sixth heaven, who is said to assume various forms or take possession of others in order to cause people to discard their Buddhist practice. This hindrance is regarded as the most difficult to overcome.

7. For their refusal to compromise their religious beliefs, Tsunesaburo Makiguchi, president of the Soka Kyoiku Gakkai (forerunner of the Soka Gakkai), and his disciple, Josei Toda (later the Soka Gakkai's second president), were arrested by the Japanese militarist government during World War II on charges of violating the notorious wartime Peace Preservation Law and committing lèse-majesté—treason against the state. President Makiguchi was arrested during a propagation trip to Shimoda on July 6, 1943, while Mr. Toda was arrested on the same day at his home in Tokyo. Mr. Makiguchi died in prison on November 18, 1944, but Mr. Toda survived and was released on July 3, 1945. In an unusual coincidence, on that same date 12 years later—July 3, 1957—President Ikeda, then youth division chief of staff, was arrested on trumped-up charges by the authorities and detained in jail in Osaka. He was later exonerated of all charges.

8. For example, while en route to Minobu following his departure from Kamakura (in May 1274), Nichiren deliberately refrained from visiting lay priest Takahashi Rokuro Hyoe, a central figure among his followers in Fuji District of Suruga Province. This province was the domain of the regent Hojo Tokimune (also known as the lord of Sagami), and the Fuji area in particular was filled with relatives of the regent's mother, who felt great rancor toward Nichiren because she regarded him an enemy of the late Shigetoki and Tokiyori. Nichiren had been concerned that visiting Takahashi at his residence might result in the latter being persecuted by the government (see WND-1, 607–09).

9. Atsuhara Persecution: A series of threats and acts of violence against Nichiren's followers in Atsuhara Village, in Fuji District of Suruga Province, beginning around 1275 and continuing until around 1283. In 1279, 20 farmers were unjustly arrested and sent to Kamakura, where they were interrogated by Hei no Saemon, the deputy chief of the Office of Military and Police Affairs. He demanded they renounce their faith, but not one yielded. Eventually, three of these followers were executed—the peasant brothers Jinshiro, Yagoro and Yarokuro. They are known as the three martyrs of Atsuhara.

10. The pre-Lotus Sutra teachings and the Lotus Sutra: The pre-Lotus Sutra teachings refer to those teachings Shakyamuni Buddha expounded during the first 42 years of his preaching life, from the time following his enlightenment until he began to expound the Lotus Sutra. According to the Great Teacher T'ien-t'ai's classification of the Buddha's teachings into five periods, the teachings of the first four periods—the Flower Garland, Agama, Correct and Equal, and Wisdom periods—constitute the pre-Lotus Sutra teachings. He identified all of these as provisional teachings, or expedient means, to lead people to the Lotus Sutra, the teaching in which he directly reveals the ultimate truth to which he had become enlightened.

11. Pre-Sado and post-Sado: A reference to the teachings and writings of Nichiren before and after the Tatsunokuchi Persecution and his subsequent exile to Sado Island. The Tatsunokuchi Persecution took place on September 12, 1271, and his exile lasted two-and-a-half years, from October 1271 through March 1274. Before Tatsunokuchi, Nichiren spread the invocation, or *daimoku*, of Nam-myoho-renge-kyo, but did not mention anything about the object of devotion known as the Gohonzon or about the Three Great Secret Laws. After Tatsunokuchi, however, he revealed the object of devotion in terms of both the Person and the Law. He implicitly revealed his identity as the Buddha of the Latter Day of the Law (Person) in "The Opening of the Eyes," and the object of devotion in his teachings (the Law) in "The Object of Devotion for Observing the Mind." He completed both works during his exile. He referred to the Three Great Secret Laws as "the three important matters of the 'Life Span' chapter of the essential teaching" of the Lotus Sutra in his 1272 letter titled "Earthly Desires Are Enlightenment"—his earliest reference to the Three Great Secret Laws in his extant writings.

12. The Person and the Law: Nichiren revealed and spread the Law of Nam-myoho-renge-kyo and inscribed it in the form of a mandala known as the Gohonzon in order to enable all people in the Latter Day of the Law to reveal their inherent Buddhahood; for this reason, he is regarded as the Buddha of the Latter Day of the Law. The Gohonzon is the object of devotion in terms of the Law, or the physical embodiment of the eternal and intrinsic Law of Nam-myoho-renge-kyo that Nichiren realized and manifested within his own life. Hence, Nichiren Daishonin is the object of devotion in terms of the Person. Nichikan, the 26th high priest, established the principle of the oneness of the Person and the Law, indicating that the object of devotion in terms of the Person and the object of devotion in terms of the Law are one in essence. In other words, the Law is inseparable from the Person and vice versa.

13. Casting off the transient and revealing the true: Revealing one's true status as a Buddha, and setting aside that Buddha's provisional or transient identity. Here it refers to Nichiren, at the time of the Tatsunokuchi Persecution, discarding his "transient status" as "an ordinary person at the stage of hearing the name and words of the truth" and revealing his "true identity" as "the Buddha of limitless joy who has been enlightened from time without beginning," while remaining an ordinary person.

14. True Word school: A Buddhist school in Japan established by Kobo (774–835), also known as Kukai, that follows the esoteric doctrines and practices found in the Mahavairochana and Diamond Crown sutras.

15. The arrival of an official letter from the Mongol Empire demanding fealty in 1268 signaled the impending crisis of foreign invasion that Nichiren had predicted in his 1260 treatise "On Establishing the Correct Teaching for the Peace of the Land." The government, however, instead of heeding Nichiren's warnings and acting in accord with the correct teaching of Buddhism, had continued to rely on the True Word and other erroneous Buddhist schools, ordering them to perform extensive prayers for the defeat of the Mongols. After the Mongols actually invaded in 1274, the government, fearing a second invasion, again had the True Word and other schools perform prayers for the Mongols' defeat.

16. This refers to the holding of a formal debate in a public venue, with an officer of the government or imperial court presiding, in order to determine which was the correct and superior teaching.

17. See footnote 6 for an explanation of the specific obstacles and hindrances included in the three obstacles and four devils.

18. Translated from Japanese. Josei Toda, *Toda Josei zenshu* (Collected Writings of Josei Toda) (Tokyo: Seikyo Shimbunsha, 1987), vol. 7, p. 409.

19. The principle of prolonging one's life through faith: This is based on the passage in the "Life Span" chapter of the Lotus Sutra that reads: "We beg you to cure us and let us live out our lives!" (LSOC, 269). This is in the section that explains the parable of the outstanding physician, who gives "good medicine" to his children who have "drunk poison" (that is, succumbed to delusion), and who implore him to cure their illness. Through taking this good medicine (that is, embracing faith in the wonderful Law of the Lotus Sutra), they are cured and can enjoy many more years of life.

20. Fundamental darkness: Also, fundamental ignorance or primal ignorance—the inability to recognize the truth, particularly the true nature of one's life. Nichiren interprets fundamental darkness as ignorance of the ultimate Law, or ignorance of the fact that one's life is essentially a manifestation of the Law, which he identifies as Nam-myoho-renge-kyo.

21. Three Great Secret Laws: The core principles of Nichiren Buddhism: (1) the object of devotion, (2) the invocation, or *daimoku*, of Nam-myoho-renge-kyo and (3) the sanctuary, or the place where one chants the *daimoku* before the object of devotion. See footnote 11 for a detailed explanation.

22. Substituting faith for wisdom: The principle that faith is the true cause for gaining supreme wisdom, and faith alone leads to enlightenment. In general, Buddhism describes supreme wisdom as the cause of enlightenment. According to the Lotus Sutra, however, even Shariputra, who among the Buddha's 10 disciples was revered as foremost in wisdom, could attain enlightenment only through faith, not through wisdom.

23. See footnote 2 for an explanation of the threefold world of desire, form and formlessness.

24. These ten kinds of troops or ten armies of the devil king are described in Nagarjuna's *Treatise on the Great Perfection of Wisdom*.

25. Devadatta: Shakyamuni's cousin, who first followed Shakyamuni but later out of arrogance became his enemy and committed various actions of extreme evil, such as attempting to kill the Buddha. As a result of his offenses, he is said to have fallen into hell alive.

26. Sunakshatra: One of Shakyamuni's sons from the period before he renounced secular life. Although Sunakshatra also embarked on a religious life and became Shakyamuni's disciple, under the influence of evil teachers he became attached to mistaken views and is said to have fallen into hell alive.

27. King Ajatashatru: A king of Magadha in India in the time of Shakyamuni. Incited by Devadatta, he gained the throne by killing his father, King Bimbisara, a follower of Shakyamuni. He also made attempts on the lives of the Buddha and his disciples by releasing a drunken elephant upon them, again at Devadatta's urging.

28. Sammi-bo: One of Nichiren's earliest disciples. Although he was highly esteemed for his learning and debating skill and assisted Nikko's propagation efforts in the Fuji area, he was arrogant about his knowledge and desirous of social recognition and status. Nichiren found it necessary to admonish him about this on several occasions. During the Atsuhara Persecution, Sammi-bo renounced his belief in Nichiren's teachings and turned against him and his supporters. In several letters, Nichiren refers to Sammi-bo's untimely and tragic death, though the details are unknown.

29. Lay nun of Nagoe: Nichiren's follower who lived in Nagoe in Kamakura. She is thought to have taken faith in Nichiren's teachings relatively early on. While the details are not known, she later abandoned her faith along with Sho-bo and Noto-bo, two other disciples who eventually turned against Nichiren.

30. Nichiren writes, "With the lay nun of Nagoe, Sho-bo, Noto-bo, Sammi-bo, and the like, who are cowardly, unreasoning, greedy, and doubting, my words have no more effect than pouring water on lacquer ware or slicing through air" ("On Persecutions Befalling the Sage," WND-1, 998).

31. A passage from the "Encouraging Devotion" chapter of the Lotus Sutra reads, "Evil demons will take possession of others" (LSOC, 233). This means that devilish functions enter the lives of various people causing them to speak ill of and insult those who protect the correct teaching and to obstruct their Buddhist practice.

32. A passage from the Benevolent Kings Sutra, which reads, "It is the spirits that first show signs of rampancy" (see "On Establishing the Correct Teaching for the Peace of the Land," WND-1, 8). It means that in a country that slanders the Law, devilish functions become rampant, causing various disasters to arise.

33. Great citadel of the hell of incessant suffering: Also, hell of incessant suffering. The lowest realm of hell into which people who have committed the most serious offenses of slandering the Law or those of incorrigible disbelief are said to fall.

34. "Oko kikigaki" (The Recorded Lectures); not translated in WND, vols. 1 and 2.

35. Nichiren states: "[Despite the personal interference of the devil king of the sixth heaven,] it is because the heavenly deities came to my aid that I survived even the Tatsunokuchi Persecution and emerged safely from other great persecutions. By now, the devil king must be thoroughly discouraged. After my death, his surviving minions may arouse their armies, but they will not be able to succeed in defeating my followers. This is because the minions of the devil king of the sixth heaven have become the 4,994,828 people of Japan, who now for the most part have yielded to Nichiren" (GZ, 843).

36. See footnote 12.

37. The object of devotion in terms of the Person is revealed in "The Opening of the Eyes," composed by Nichiren on Sado in February 1272. In it, he clarifies that he is the Buddha of the Latter Day of the Law who possesses the three virtues of sovereign, teacher and parent, and who will lead the people of the Latter Day to enlightenment. The object of devotion in terms of the Law, meanwhile, is revealed in "The Object of Devotion for Observing the Mind," composed on Sado in April 1273. Nichiren clarifies that Nam-myoho-renge-kyo is the fundamental Law for attaining Buddhahood that all people of the Latter Day should revere.

38. Lord of teaching of the Latter Day of the Law: Also, teacher of the Latter Day of the Law. The person who in the time of the Latter Day of the Law—an evil age 2,000 years after Shakyamuni's passing when Shakyamuni's teaching loses its power to benefit people—instructs and guides people through propagating Nam-myoho-renge-kyo, which is the essence of the Lotus Sutra, in accord with the sutra's predictions.

(11)

"The Essentials for Attaining Buddhahood"

The Great Path of Mentor and Disciple—Working Together for Kosen-rufu To Enrich Humanity With the Wisdom of the Mystic Law

The Passage for Study in This Lecture

The Lotus Sutra states that Bodhisattva Superior Practices and the others[1] will appear in the first five hundred years of the Latter Day of the Law to propagate the five characters [of the Mystic Law, Nam-myoho-renge-kyo], the embodiment of the two elements of reality and wisdom. The sutra makes this perfectly clear. Who could possibly dispute it? I, Nichiren, am neither Bodhisattva Superior Practices nor his envoy, but I precede them, spreading the five characters to prepare the way. Bodhisattva Superior Practices received the water of the wisdom of the Mystic Law from the Thus Come One Shakyamuni and causes it to flow into the wasteland of the people's lives in the evil world of the latter age. This is the function of wisdom. Shakyamuni Buddha transferred this teaching [the five characters of the Mystic Law that are the embodiment of the two elements of reality and wisdom] to Bodhisattva Superior Practices, and now Nichiren propagates it in Japan. With regard to the transfer of teachings, it is divided into two categories: general and specific. If you confuse the general with the specific even in the slightest, you will never be able to attain Buddhahood and will wander in suffering through endless transmigrations of births and deaths. . . .

[T]o forget the original teacher

who had brought one the water of wisdom from the great ocean of the Lotus Sutra and instead follow another would surely cause one to sink into the endless sufferings of birth and death.

One should abandon even one's teacher if he or she is misguided, though there will be cases where this is not necessary. One should decide according to the principles both of the world and of Buddhism. Priests in the Latter Day of the Law are ignorant of the principles of Buddhism and are conceited, so they despise the correct teacher and fawn on patrons. True priests are those who are honest and who desire little and yet know satisfaction. Volume one of *The Words and Phrases of the Lotus Sutra* [by the Great Teacher T'ien-t'ai][2] states: "Those who have yet to attain the truth should humble themselves before the highest principle [the ultimate truth], which is comparable to heaven, and feel abashed before all the sages. Then they will be monks with a sense of shame. When they manifest insight and wisdom, then they will be true monks."

The Nirvana Sutra states: "If even a good monk sees someone destroying the teaching and disregards him, failing to reproach him, to oust him, or to punish him for his offense, then you should realize that that monk is betraying the Buddha's teaching. But if he ousts the destroyer of the Law, reproaches him, or punishes him, then he is my disciple and a true voice-hearer." You should etch deeply in your mind the two words "see" and "disregard" in the phrase "sees someone destroying the teaching and disregards him, failing to reproach him."

Both teacher and followers will surely fall into the hell of incessant suffering if they see enemies of the Lotus Sutra but disregard them and fail to reproach them. The Great Teacher Nan-yüeh[3] says that they "will fall into hell along with those evil persons."[4] To hope to attain Buddhahood without speaking out against slander is as futile as trying to find water in the midst of fire or fire in the midst of water. No matter how sincerely one believes in the Lotus Sutra, if one is guilty of failing to rebuke slander of the Law, one will surely fall into hell, just as a single crab leg will ruin a thousand pots of lacquer. This is the meaning of the passage in the sutra, "Because the poison has penetrated deeply and their minds no longer function as before" [*The Lotus Sutra and Its Opening and Closing Sutras*, p. 269].

The sutra states, "Those persons who had heard the Law dwelled here and there in various Buddha lands, constantly reborn in company with their teachers" [see LSOC, 178]. . . . Above all, be sure to follow your original teacher so that you are able to attain Buddhahood. Shakyamuni Buddha is the original teacher for all people, and moreover, he is endowed with the virtues of sovereign and parent. Because I have expounded this teaching, I have been exiled and almost killed. As the saying goes, "Good advice grates on the ear." But still I am not discouraged. The Lotus Sutra is like the seed, the Buddha like the sower, and the people like the field. If you deviate from these principles, not even I can save you in your next life. (*The Writings of Nichiren Daishonin*, vol. 1, pp. 746–48)

LECTURE

Highlights

Written: August 1276

Recipient: Believed to be addressed to the lay priest Soya, a samurai and lead disciple in Shimosa Province

- This letter highlights the indivisible bonds shared by teacher and disciple.

Key points of this letter:

- The elements of both reality and wisdom are necessary for revealing our Buddhahood.

- Buddhist practitioners need to seek the correct teacher who propagates the Law of Nam-myoho-renge-kyo, the embodiment of these two elements.

- A correct teacher demonstrates a firm commitment to rebuke slander of the Law.

- Following such a teacher is key to attaining enlightenment in this defiled age.

No matter how famous or successful one might be, a life without a teacher or mentor is sad and lonely indeed. Genuine victory as a human being will also remain elusive. To have a lifelong mentor is one of life's greatest blessings. In August 1947, I met my mentor, Josei Toda, who later became the second president of the Soka Gakkai. That summer of my 19th year, I made a conscious decision to become his disciple. I instinctively felt that I could trust Mr. Toda and that he was the person I should take as my mentor in life. Based on that firm conviction, I embarked on a journey together with him toward achieving a religious revolution and lasting world peace—a journey that I continue with unabated passion to this day.

Throughout my five-decade leadership of *kosen-rufu* following Mr. Toda's death [in April 1958], I have fought my way through all kinds of difficulties, continually carrying on an inner dialogue with my mentor. And together with all of you, my fellow members everywhere, I have established the foundations for worldwide *kosen-rufu* on an unprecedented scale. Today, I have not a single regret. I have won in every sphere. For me, there is no greater satisfaction in life than reporting my successes to my mentor.

The profoundest life is one dedicated to pursuing a shared ideal with one's mentor. The loftier the ideal, the more valuable and enduring a legacy such a life can leave behind.

To realize happiness for oneself and others—this is the eternal ideal of all humankind. It represents the ultimate wisdom waiting to be found in the depths of each person's life. It is the genuine yearning that underlies all life's workings. At the same time, no goal is more difficult to achieve. This is because the dark clouds of ignorance and greed blanket our lives and obscure the sun of wisdom and idealism.

Nichiren Buddhism provides us with the philosophy and practice for realizing genuine happiness for ourselves and others. Its driving spirit is to undertake this difficult challenge and never give up trying to achieve it. And the mentor-disciple relationship lies at the very heart of the human network and the united efforts so vital to succeeding.

To live in accord with this path of mentor and disciple is to lead an unsurpassed life, one committed to opening the way to peace and happiness for all humanity.

To bring the "nourishment of wisdom" and the "moisture of compassion" to the "parched fields" of people's lives that have been devitalized by greed, anger and ignorance and restore them to "lush green fields"—this is the vow of mentor and disciple in Buddhism. And in one respect, improving the human condition in this way could be called a fervent wish of all humankind.

In the writing we are studying this time, "The Essentials for Attaining Buddhahood," Nichiren Daishonin describes the heart of a genuine Buddhist teacher by sharing his own spirit of striving selflessly, no matter the hardship, to cause the water of the infinite wisdom of the Buddha "to flow into the wasteland of people's lives in the evil world of the latter age" (WND-1, 746–47). Written in August 1276, it seems this letter was addressed to a follower known as the lay priest Soya.[5]

In the first half of the letter, Nichiren indicates that "the way to Buddhahood lies within the two elements of reality and wisdom" (WND-1, 746), and emphasizes the importance of seeking the correct teacher in the Latter Day who propagates the Law of Nam-myoho-renge-kyo, which is the embodiment of these two elements (WND-1, 746–47). In the second half, the Daishonin asserts that the correct teacher will demonstrate, both in spirit and action, a firm commitment to rebuking slander of the

"The profoundest life is one dedicated to pursuing a shared ideal with one's mentor. The loftier the ideal, the more valuable and enduring a legacy such a life can leave behind."

Law, and he further explains that following such a teacher is key to attaining enlightenment in this defiled age. [See March–April 2006 *Living Buddhism*, pp. 80–92, for more on this topic.]

The entire letter can be viewed as highlighting the indivisible bonds shared by teacher and disciple. Let us study the great path of disciples working wholeheartedly alongside their teacher to cause the Law to flow unimpeded in people's lives, thereby paving the way for the happiness of all humanity.

THE MYSTIC LAW IS THE KEY TO AN INEXHAUSTIBLE WELLSPRING OF WISDOM

Highlights

- By awakening to the existence of the Mystic Law, which exists equally in all people, we can overcome the four sufferings and gain lasting happiness.

- The path of mentor and disciple is indispensable in transmitting and spreading this great Law.

- *Reality* means the objective reality or truth that includes all things spiritual and physical, and *wisdom* means the subjective wisdom to perceive or illuminate that truth.

- Nam-myoho-renge-kyo encompasses these two elements. When we dedicate our lives (Jpn *nam* or *namu*) to Myoho-renge-kyo, we become one with the eternal and unchanging truth and can bring forth boundless life force.

Fundamentally, the lives of all human beings are supremely noble and respect-worthy entities of the Mystic Law, and they are all endowed with immeasurable wisdom. How can we bring that wisdom to shine? How can we draw forth the infinite latent potential we each possess? Buddhism answers these questions by teaching the eternal and universal Law that pulses within life. This Law exists equally in all people. By awakening to the existence of this Law that pervades life and the universe, anyone can overcome the four sufferings—birth, aging, sickness and death—and gain lasting happiness. In Buddhism, the path of teacher and disciple is indispensable in transmitting and spreading this great Law of happiness that exists within us.

At the beginning of this letter, Nichiren Daishonin describes the Law as embodying "the two elements of reality and wisdom" (WND-1, 746). This is a crucial principle explaining the Buddha's enlightenment. *Reality* means the objective reality or truth and includes all things spiritual and physical. *Wisdom* means the subjective wisdom to perceive or illuminate that truth. The towering wisdom of the Buddha not only illuminates the true nature of all universal phenomena but also makes us aware that we ourselves are entities of the Mystic Law.

The essential point regarding these two elements—reality and wisdom—is the illumination of our true self with the light of great wisdom. This is the fusion of reality and wisdom, through which means we can attain the expansive and perfectly serene state of mind of a Buddha. Once we awaken to our

THE FUSION OF REALITY AND WISDOM

Enlightenment is defined as the state in which one fully manifests the wisdom to perceive the objective truth of the Buddha nature inherent within life.

Nichiren states: "Life at each moment encompasses the body and mind and the self and environment of all sentient beings in the Ten Worlds as well as all insentient beings in the three thousand realms, including plants, sky, earth, and even the minutest particles of dust. Life at each moment permeates the entire realm of phenomena and is revealed in all phenomena. To be awakened to this principle is itself the mutually inclusive relationship of life at each moment and all phenomena" ("On Attaining Buddhahood in This Lifetime," WND-1, 3).

Nichiren identifies the Law that underlies the fusion of reality and wisdom as Nam-myoho-renge-kyo, and asserts that he embodied his enlightenment to the fusion of reality and wisdom in the form of the Gohonzon.

Nichiren maintains that when we chant Nam-myoho-renge-kyo with deep faith in the Gohonzon, we achieve the fusion of reality and wisdom within our own lives and are thus able to manifest the Buddha nature. According to Nichiren, the Buddha nature constitutes reality, while faith in the Gohonzon—the embodiment of that nature—corresponds to wisdom.

true self—that is, our greater self—we can gain the immeasurable wisdom to break through and surmount all delusions and sufferings that arise from our attachment to our lesser self. Herein lies the path to realizing genuine happiness.

The elements of reality and wisdom constitute none other than Nam-myoho-renge-kyo, the Law propagated by Nichiren. In other words, when we "dedicate our lives" (Jpn *nam* or *namu*) to Myoho-renge-kyo, the ultimate Law of the universe, we become one with "the principle of eternal and unchanging truth," thereby manifesting the life-state of Buddhahood through which we can base all our activities on "the wisdom of the truth that functions in accordance with changing circumstances"[6] (*The Record of the Orally Transmitted Teachings*, p. 3). And the water of immeasurable wisdom that issues forth from our greater self will then flow powerfully in our lives.

The Law of Nam-myoho-renge-kyo enables us to bring forth the boundless life force or vitality of our greater self. Accordingly, Nichiren writes: "What then are these two elements of reality and wisdom? They are simply the five characters of Nam-myoho-renge-kyo"[7] (WND-1, 746).

To use a simile, our greater self is like a broad and deep spring overflowing with the water of wisdom. Nam-myoho-renge-kyo serves as the means for tapping this water and bringing it to flow richly in the fields of our lives. To live in accord with the limited wisdom of our lesser self, in contrast, is like drawing water from a vast spring with a tiny ladle. No matter how much effort we make, we can only scoop up a small amount. In this situation, there is a disconnect between reality and wisdom; they are definitely not fused.

In this letter, Nichiren refers to the fact that the sutras expounded prior to the Lotus Sutra teach various kinds of reality and wisdom as appropriate to the capacities of the people of the nine worlds (the life-states from hell through bodhisattva), but that none teach the principle of the fusion of reality and wisdom, which constitutes the Buddha's enlightenment. He states that because they separate reality and wisdom, these teachings cannot possibly convey to people the state of true happiness that is Buddhahood (see WND-1, 746).

NICHIREN DAISHONIN IS THE "ORIGINAL TEACHER" OF THE LATTER DAY OF THE LAW

Highlights

- Because he presented and propagated the two elements of reality and wisdom as Nam-myoho-renge-kyo for the enlightenment of all people, Nichiren should be considered the "original teacher" for all people in the Latter Day.

- Nichiren established the practice of chanting Nam-myoho-renge-kyo and teaching others to do the same and bequeathed to us the Gohonzon, a concrete expression of his enlightened state and a representation of the fusion of reality and wisdom.

- With the Gohonzon (reality) and faith in Nam-myoho-renge-kyo (wisdom), we can achieve the same fusion of reality and wisdom as the Buddha; we can find inexhaustible wisdom.

In the history of humankind, it was Shakyamuni who first became enlightened to the two elements—reality and wisdom—and widely taught them to others. It was Nichiren Daishonin, however, who presented and propagated these two elements as Nam-myoho-renge-kyo for the enlightenment of all people, who suffer in the evil latter age after the Buddha's passing. Consequently, in this writing, the Daishonin reveals that he should be considered the "original teacher" for all people in the Latter Day (see WND-1, 748).

He writes, "The Lotus Sutra states that Bodhisattva Superior Practices and the others will appear in the first five hundred years of the Latter Day of the Law to propagate the five characters [of the Mystic Law, Nam-myoho-renge-kyo], the embodiment of the two elements of reality and wisdom" (WND-1, 746). It should be clear to all that the Daishonin is the one who had actually embarked on propagating the Mystic Law in the Latter Day, the task that had been entrusted to Bodhisattva Superior Practices in the Lotus Sutra. Nichiren bequeathed to us the Gohonzon—a concrete expression of his enlightened state that fused reality and wisdom—and the practice of chanting Nam-myoho-renge-kyo and teaching others to do the same. His purpose was to enable the water of the wisdom of the Mystic Law to flow in the lives of people throughout the world into the eternal future of the Latter Day, and thereby allow all to realize genuine happiness.

With the Gohonzon that embodies the life of Nichiren as our *reality* and faith in Nam-myoho-renge-kyo based on the Gohonzon as our *wisdom* (in accordance with the principle of "substituting faith for wisdom"[8]), we can achieve the same fusion of reality and wisdom (or enlightenment) as the Buddha. All we require is the strong faith to withstand and repel obstacles and devilish functions that are a manifestation of darkness or ignorance. All we require is persistent faith that never wavers under any circumstances.

Mr. Toda said: "The Gohonzon (Nam-myoho-renge-kyo) is the fundamental entity of life that powers change

GENERAL AND SPECIFIC TRANSFER OF THE TEACHINGS

In one sense, *general* refers to an overall or surface view of a particular teaching or doctrine, and *specific* to a more sharply delineated and profound view.

In Nichiren Daishonin's doctrine, Shakyamuni's teachings can be categorized from the general to the specific. The entire body of teaching is the general truth, the Lotus Sutra is more specific, and the Law shown in the "Life Span" chapter is the most specific teaching.

The terms *general* and *specific* also apply to the transfer or entrustment of the teachings of the Lotus Sutra as described in the sutra. In the "Entrustment" chapter, Shakyamuni makes a general transfer of the sutra to all the bodhisattvas present, but in the "Supernatural Powers" chapter, he entrusts it specifically to the Bodhisattvas of the Earth. While he transfers the sutra to the Bodhisattvas of the Earth in general, he specifically entrusts it to Bodhisattva Superior Practices.

in the universe. By achieving the fusion of reality and wisdom in our lives (by chanting Nam-myoho-renge-kyo with faith in the Gohonzon), we can change our lives and bring forth benefit." The beneficial power of the Gohonzon is infinitely profound and immeasurable. The Buddhist Law is eternal, boundless and untrammeled. By chanting to the Gohonzon and taking action based on faith in the Mystic Law, we can bring this inexhaustible wisdom to well forth in our lives. Thus, we can never be truly deadlocked in life.

Nichiren writes, "Bodhisattva Superior Practices received the water of the wisdom of the Mystic Law from the Thus Come One Shakyamuni and causes it to flow into the wasteland of the people's lives in the evil world of the latter age" (WND-1, 746–47). As these words indicate, through the Daishonin—who fulfills the mission of Superior Practices—the "water of the wisdom of the Mystic Law" flowed into, nourished and enriched the parched lives of people of the Latter Day, who were bereft of good fortune and benefit.

Nichiren then touches on the subject of the transfer of teachings in Buddhism, clarifying that there are two kinds of transfer—general and specific—and that a clear distinction should be made between them. Why should he emphasize this point? We can surmise that it is a solemn reminder not to forget who brought "the water of wisdom from the great ocean of the Lotus Sutra" and who is therefore the original teacher of the Latter Day. This is because, as Nichiren writes, following an erroneous teacher "would surely cause one to sink into the endless sufferings of birth and death" (WND-1, 747).

If we forget the original teacher and follow a teacher who functions as a negative influence, leading people astray—what Buddhism terms an "evil friend"[9]—the water of the wisdom of the Buddha will stop flowing. This is why the path of teacher and disciple is so important in Buddhism.

A CORRECT TEACHER CONSCIENTIOUSLY UPHOLDS THE LAW

Highlights

- The Latter Day is filled with misguided teachers, corrupt priests and evil friends. Erroneous teachers are both ignorant of the principles of Buddhism and conceited; they despise the correct teacher and fawn on patrons.

- A correct teacher advances straight ahead along the path of the correct teaching, valuing the Law above all and striving actively in Buddhist practice without begrudging his or her life.

- Those who sincerely seek the Law bring forth wisdom and continue on the path of self-improvement and growth.

- As Nichiren Buddhist practitioners, we must always ask ourselves: Are we practicing in direct connection with Nichiren, grounded in his writings and centered on the Gohonzon?

In the passage beginning "One should abandon even one's teacher if he or she is misguided, though there will be cases where this is not necessary" and ending "When they manifest insight and wisdom, then they will be true monks" (WND-1, 747), Nichiren Daishonin outlines the essential requirements for a good, or correct, teacher in the Latter Day of the Law. In the preceding passage, he had discussed, from the perspective of his inner enlightenment, who the correct teacher of the Latter Day was with regard to the elements of reality and wisdom. In this passage, however, he discusses this same question from the perspective of his conduct with regard to correctly spreading the Law.

First, he writes, "One should abandon even one's teacher if he or she is misguided" (WND-1, 747). The Latter Day is an age filled with misguided teachers, corrupt priests and evil friends. It is particularly difficult to discern the true nature of corrupt priests and evil friends. Therefore, in this writing, to clearly distinguish between a correct teacher and an erroneous teacher, Nichiren sets as a standard the qualifications of a correct teacher and explains the characteristics of an erroneous teacher.

Describing erroneous teachers, he writes, "Priests in the Latter Day of the Law are ignorant of the principles of Buddhism and are conceited, so they despise the correct teacher and fawn on patrons" (WND-1, 747). In contrast, referring to the characteristics of a correct teacher, he cites such qualities as "honesty" and "desiring little yet knowing satisfaction" (see WND-1, 747). Honesty generally means being morally upright, sincere and genuine. While in Buddhism, the term *honesty* includes these meanings, it also has the meaning of advancing straight ahead on the path of the correct teaching. In the truest sense, it means earnestly seeking and correctly spreading the Law. "Desiring little yet knowing satisfaction," meanwhile, means controlling one's desires, but it can be taken further to mean having the spirit to value the Law above all and demonstrating this by striving actively in Buddhist practice and efforts to propagate the Law without begrudging your life.

Those who sincerely seek the Law can bring forth wisdom and continue on the path of self-improvement and growth by humbly comparing their present situation and state of life to those of sages in the past and applying themselves all the more diligently to their Buddhist practice.

In short, the Law is the ultimate criterion. From our standpoint, it is a question of whether we are basing ourselves on Nichiren Buddhism, whether we are practicing faith directly connected to Nichiren—grounded in his writings and centered on the Gohonzon.

In recent times, corrupt priests and a few self-serving former Soka Gakkai leaders have strayed from this path of faith and acted counter to the teachings of Nichiren Buddhism. Common to both we find an arrogance that prevents them from maintaining a correct attitude toward the Law. The arrogant and conceited invariably veer from the path of mentor and disciple. Instead of the Law, these few made their own misguided selves their foundation. Ultimately, they found it impossible to remain in the strict realm of Buddhism centered on the Law. Jealous and resentful of the harmonious community of believers who base their practice on the Law, they had no option but to depart.

"Honesty generally means being morally upright, sincere and genuine. While in Buddhism, the term *honesty* includes these meanings, it also has the meaning of advancing straight ahead on the path of the correct teaching. In the truest sense, it means earnestly seeking and correctly spreading the Law."

REBUKING SLANDER OF THE LAW IS CRUCIAL TO ATTAINING BUDDHAHOOD

Highlights

- In order to reveal our Buddhahood, we must be willing to rebuke slander of the Law, because slander can be a virulent poison in terms of faith.

- Therefore, a correct teacher in the Latter Day is one who strictly rebukes such slander.

- If we fail to fight against evil, we become accomplices to evil.

- Evil friends intensify others' ignorance and heighten the workings of the three poisons.

- Unless we take a firm stand against slander and error in terms of Buddhism, we cannot attain Buddhahood.

Nichiren Daishonin quotes the following well-known passage from the Nirvana Sutra, and then stresses the importance of taking a firm stand against erroneous priests who go against the teachings of Buddhism: "If even a good monk sees someone destroying the teaching and disregards him, failing to reproach him, to oust him, or to punish him for his offense, then you should realize that that monk is betraying the Buddha's teaching. But if he ousts the destroyer of the Law, reproaches him, or punishes him, then he is my disciple and a true voice-hearer" (WND-1, 747).

The Daishonin says that we should deeply engrave in our hearts the words *see* and *disregard* in "sees someone destroying the teaching and disregards him, failing to reproach him." And he declares that both teacher and disciple are certain to fall into the hell of incessant suffering if they encounter enemies of the Lotus Sutra but let them go unchallenged. Further, he says, it is meaningless to hope to reveal Buddhahood without making any effort to rebuke slander of the Law; indeed without such efforts, no matter how much one may believe in the Lotus Sutra, he or she will be destined to fall into a state of hell.

He then uses the metaphor of "a single crab leg ruining a thousand pots of lacquer." Japanese lacquer is made from the sap of the lacquer tree. The sap is bled by making cuts in the tree's trunk, a very time-consuming process. It seems a substance in shellfish had such an adverse effect on the properties of lacquer that even an amount as small as a crab leg would be enough to ruin a thousand pots. Similarly, even one drop of poison added to a vessel of pure water will render that water unfit for drinking. Slander of the Law can be a virulent poison in terms of faith; it can instantly change the water of wisdom of the Mystic Law in a person's life into poison.

Therefore, a correct teacher in the Latter Day is one who strictly rebukes such slander. The evil age, as I mentioned earlier, is a time filled with evil friends or negative influences who lead others astray, specifically causing them to turn against the correct teaching. Moreover, it is a time when Buddhist priests who wield religious authority especially become such negative influences. Therefore, a correct teacher is one who courageously speaks out against slander and error, unafraid of those who hold power and authority, in order to cause the water of wisdom of the Mystic Law to flow correctly in people's lives.

Fighting against evil in Buddhism is an important part of our Buddhist practice because if we fail to do so, we become accomplices to that evil. Regarding this frightening reality, Nichiren cites the Great Teacher Nanyüeh, who says that those who turn a blind eye to evil will fall into hell along with those who actually commit that evil (see WND-1, 747). "Failing to do good is the same as doing evil"—this is the undying credo of Tsunesaburo Makiguchi, the founding president of the Soka Gakkai.

Evil friends serve to intensify others' ignorance or darkness by heightening the workings of the three poisons—greed, anger and foolishness[10]—in their lives. That is the fearful nature of such negative influences. Allowing evil to go unchallenged, therefore, ultimately spells suffering and pain for many people. As long as Buddhism is a philosophy that teaches the inherent dignity of human life, it is crucial that its practitioners fight resolutely against those tendencies that promote disrespect for human life, discrimination and the destruction of life.

Unless we put a stop to evil, we cannot achieve genuine, lasting good.

Likewise, unless we take a firm stand against slander and error in terms of Buddhism, we cannot reveal our Buddhahood. Our efforts in this sphere must not be halfhearted. Mr. Toda also urged us to thoroughly defeat evil.

Next, Nichiren cites the Lotus Sutra, "Because the poison has penetrated deeply and their minds no longer function as before" (LSOC, 269). It is vital that we fight against the poison of erroneous teachings or ways of thinking that cause people to lose sight of their Buddha nature and that destroy their humanity. Then, as the Nirvana Sutra teaches, we will be practicing as true disciples of the Buddha and upholding a truly humanistic teaching.

THE GREAT VOW WELLS FORTH FROM A SPIRIT OF COMPASSION

Highlights

- Teacher and disciple have striven together from the distant past with the same great bodhisattva vow.
- Those who follow the path of mentor and disciple come to enjoy an indestructible state of life pervaded by the four virtues in rhythm with the eternal Mystic Law.

In the last section of the selected passage, Nichiren Daishonin clarifies that the correct teacher who spreads the Law for people's happiness in the Latter Day is also the original teacher with whom all people have a profound karmic connection, in that they have followed that teacher in past lifetimes.

First, he cites the passage from the "Parable of the Phantom City" chapter of the Lotus Sutra, "Those persons who had heard the Law dwelled here and there in various Buddha lands, constantly reborn in company with their teachers" (see LSOC, 178). It is one of four passages that he cites here from the sutra and its commentaries—all four of which indicate that people can attain Buddhahood only through the instruction of a teacher with whom they have formed profound karmic bonds in their past lives.[11]

The passage "Those persons who had heard the Law dwelled here and there in various Buddha lands, constantly reborn in company with their teachers" isn't simply emphasizing the long duration of these bonds of teacher and disciple, but it is also explaining that teacher and disciple have striven together from the distant past with the same great bodhisattva vow to realize happiness for self and others. This bodhisattva spirit is the summation of Mahayana Buddhism. Also, viewed from the essential teaching (latter half) of the Lotus Sutra, this spirit is embodied in the vow made by the Bodhisattvas of the Earth as well as in the great vow that wells forth from the compassion that is the very essence of the life of the eternal Buddha revealed in the "Life Span" chapter [see "The Heritage of the Ultimate Law of Life" (11) and (12) in the March–April 2008 *Living Buddhism*, pp. 46–79].

COMPASSION AND REFUTATION

From SGI President Ikeda's lecture series on "The Opening of the Eyes"

Hypocrisy is the exact opposite of compassion—especially, the hypocrisy of knowing when wrong is being committed in the realm of Buddhism but doing nothing to address it. If such hypocrisy prevails, lies and pretense will become the norm and no one will speak the truth. This will ultimately lead to the spiritual and moral decay of society. Without a sound spiritual underpinning like that provided by a humanistic religion, the fabric of society will crumble. If erroneous teachings spread to where they enslave and exploit people, they will exert a harmful and poisonous effect on people's hearts and minds. That is why Nichiren Daishonin stresses the importance of steadfastly and resolutely battling the "enemies of the Lotus Sutra." He writes: "Even those with profound faith do not reproach the enemies of the Lotus Sutra. However great the good causes one may make, or even if one reads and copies the entirety of the Lotus Sutra a thousand or ten thousand times, or attains the way of perceiving three thousand realms in a single moment of life, if one fails to denounce the enemies of the Lotus Sutra, it will be impossible to attain the way" ("Encouragement to a Sick Person," WND-1, 78).

(March–April 2006 Living Buddhism, p. 80)

On the second anniversary of Mr. Makiguchi's death (commemorated in November 1946), Mr. Toda addressed his late mentor, saying: "In your vast and boundless compassion, you let me accompany you even to prison. As a result, I could read with my entire being the passage from the Lotus Sutra: 'Those persons who had heard the Law dwelled here and there in various Buddha lands, constantly reborn in company with their teachers' (see LSOC, 178). The benefit of this was coming to know my former existence as a Bodhisattva of the Earth and to absorb with my very life even a small degree of the sutra's meaning. Could there be any greater happiness than this?"[12]

These solemn words of Mr. Toda have stayed with me ever since I first learned of them in my youth. Now, I share the same spirit of gratitude toward my own mentor, Mr. Toda.

What a truly sublime life it is to serve and support one's mentor and strive to actualize that mentor's great aspiration. Those who follow the path of mentor and disciple come to enjoy an indestructible state of life pervaded by the noble virtues of eternity, happiness, true self and purity in rhythm with the eternal Mystic Law. It is a path filled with boundless joy that comes from striving to fulfill the noblest mission in life. And I wish to convey this joy to the youth. The heart of the Lotus Sutra and Buddhism is remaining true to the vow to lead others to enlightenment by striving together unceasingly on the path of mentor and disciple throughout the three existences of past, present and future.

"STILL I AM NOT DISCOURAGED"— THE ETERNAL SOKA GAKKAI SPIRIT

Highlights

- Even with the population of Japan almost entirely turned against him, Nichiren resolutely put forth his fearless lion's roar, "But still I am not discouraged."
- The ability to awaken the Buddha nature in each person is possible because the Daishonin is the original teacher with whom people share profound karmic ties from past lifetimes.
- The first three presidents of the Soka Gakkai—united by the bonds of mentor and disciple—have worked for *kosen-rufu* with the same spirit and intent as Nichiren, directly carrying on his legacy.
- The path of mentor and disciple found in the Soka Gakkai originates from our mission to uphold faith in the Gohonzon and work for the realization of *kosen-rufu*.

The immense compassion of Nichiren Daishonin as the original teacher for people in the Latter Day of the Law is encapsulated in the words, "Still I am not discouraged" (WND-1, 748).

Having lost sight of Shakyamuni Buddha, the Lotus Sutra and the fundamental spirit of Buddhism, people of the Daishonin's day had largely placed their faith in Amida Buddha of the Pure Land (Nembutsu) school; Mahavairochana Buddha, who was revered by the True Word (Shingon) school; and various other Buddhas who appear in the provisional, pre-Lotus Sutra teachings. Nichiren dared to speak out about the error and confusion existing in the realm of Buddhism at that time. But as goes the proverb "Good advice grates on the ear," he incurred the wrath of the secular and religious authorities of the day. As a result, he was exiled twice and nearly executed at Tatsunokuchi. Yet, with the entire population of Japan virtually turned against him, the Daishonin resolutely declared, "But still I am not discouraged." This fearless lion's roar was an irrepressible cry issuing forth from the boundless compassion of the Buddha of the Latter Day.

Fighting against error and slander of the Law, without begrudging one's life, in order to protect the correct teaching of Buddhism and safeguard the people's welfare is the compassion of the original teacher of the Latter Day. This struggle is vital if the water of wisdom of the

Mystic Law is to flow unhindered into people's lives.

In the final part of this letter, Nichiren likens efforts toward this end to planting the seeds of the Mystic Law in the fields of people's hearts. He writes, "The Lotus Sutra is like the seed, the Buddha like the sower, and the people like the field" (WND-1, 748). To plant the seeds of the Lotus Sutra in the fields of people's hearts simply means activating people's Buddha nature. This effort to touch and awaken the Buddha nature in each person is possible because the Daishonin is the original teacher with whom people share profound karmic ties from past lifetimes.

And it is the first three presidents of the Soka Gakkai—united by the bonds of mentor and disciple—who have worked for *kosen-rufu* with the same spirit and intent as Nichiren, directly carrying on his legacy. Together with them, the noble members of the Soka Gakkai—not least, our pioneering members in the Many Treasures Group [the Golden Stage Group in the SGI-USA]—have proclaimed the correct teaching of Nichiren

"Those who follow the path of mentor and disciple come to enjoy an indestructible state of life pervaded by the noble virtues of eternity, happiness, true self and purity in rhythm with the eternal Mystic Law."

Buddhism far and wide. Fervently seeking to break through the thick walls of fundamental darkness that prevent the Buddha nature from shining forth, they have devoted themselves to planting the seeds of the Mystic Law in people's lives. None are stronger than those who have fought with this invincible spirit. They have developed into people of towering character who enjoy unshakable trust and are admired and respected inside and outside the organization. The mentors and disciples of Soka have won!

I have heard our pioneering members say: "The Daishonin's declaration 'Still I am not discouraged' is itself the Soka Gakkai spirit"; and "I have walked the great path of mentor and disciple with the determination, 'No matter what happens, I will dedicate my life to *kosen-rufu.*'" In these words, we can find the very heart of the Soka Gakkai. The selfless effort to cause the water of wisdom of the Mystic Law to flow in people's lives in this evil latter age—an endeavor first begun by just one person, Nichiren Daishonin—is being carried on and amplified by countless heroic ordinary people. It was the correct teachers of the Soka Gakkai, our mentors Mr. Makiguchi and Mr. Toda, who taught us how to live our lives in this way as noble champions of humanity.

Nichijun, the 65th high priest, wrote about the path of mentor and disciple that exists in the Soka Gakkai:

The Daishonin writes, "Nichiren's teaching represents the third doctrine"[13] (WND-1, 855). President Toda truly embraced this teaching

with his life. I believe that the path of mentor and disciple originates from the great object of devotion, from which the water of the Law flows forth and is now beginning to spread across the Soka Gakkai. Because of this, the Soka Gakkai enjoys a great variety of benefits and blessings.[14]

He is clearly stating that the path of mentor and disciple found in the Soka Gakkai originates from our mission to uphold faith in the Gohonzon and work for the realization of *kosen-rufu.*

Buddhist practice should always accord with the time (see "The Opening of the Eyes," WND-1, 287). Mr. Makiguchi laid down his life to protect the integrity of Nichiren Buddhism, Mr. Toda actualized an unprecedented membership of 750,000 households, and we of the SGI today have spread the Mystic Law to 192 countries and territories around the globe. There could be no more eloquent proof than this that we, the mentors and disciples of Soka, are the ones who are directly connected to Nichiren Daishonin, the Buddha of the Latter Day, and who are actively working to realize his decree of worldwide *kosen-rufu.*

As long as each member maintains the Soka spirit of mentor and disciple and remains dedicated to fulfilling the vow to lead others to enlightenment, the SGI movement will continue to grow and flourish into the eternal future.

This lecture was published in the August 2008 Daibyakurenge, the Soka Gakkai study journal.

NOTES:

1 This refers to the Bodhisattvas of the Earth, who are led by Bodhisattva Superior Practices. All are disciples of Shakyamuni from the remote past. Shakyamuni entrusts these bodhisattvas with the sutra's propagation after his passing. See also following footnote.

2. *The Words and Phrases of the Lotus Sutra:* One of three major works of the Great Teacher T'ien-t'ai (538–97; also known as Chih-i). A 10-volume commentary on the Lotus Sutra.

3. Nan-yüeh (515–77): Also known as Hui-ssu. T'ien-t'ai's teacher and the third patriarch of the T'ien-t'ai school in China, in the tradition that counts Nagarjuna as the school's founder.

4. This phrase is found in a passage from Nan-yüeh's *On the Peaceful Practices of the Lotus Sutra,* which reads: "If there should be a bodhisattva who protects evil persons and fails to chastise them . . . then, when his life comes to an end, he will fall into hell along with those evil persons."

5. Lay priest Soya (1224–91): Also known as Soya Kyoshin. His full name and title were Soya Jiro Hyoe-no-jo Kyoshin. A samurai who lived in Soya of Katsushika District in Shimosa Province (part of present-day Chiba Prefecture), Japan. Having converted to Nichiren's teachings around 1260, he was a leading believer in the area along with Toki Jonin and Ota Jomyo. In 1271, he became a lay priest, and the Daishonin gave him the Buddhist name Horen Nichirai.

6. According to Nichiren's *Record of the Orally Transmitted Teachings,* the act of devotion (Jpn *nam* or *namu*) has two aspects: One is to devote ourselves to, or fuse our lives with, the eternal and unchanging truth; the other is that, through this fusion of our lives with the ultimate truth, we simultaneously draw forth inexhaustible wisdom that functions in accordance with changing circumstances.

7. Nichiren often regards Myoho-renge-kyo as the equivalent of Nam-myoho-renge-kyo. While Myoho-renge-kyo consists of five Chinese characters, Nam-myoho-renge-kyo consists of seven. In his writing "The Daimoku of the Lotus Sutra," for instance, the Daishonin mentions "the five or seven characters of Nam-myoho-renge-kyo" (WND-1, 141).

8. Substituting faith for wisdom: The principle that faith is the true cause for gaining supreme wisdom, and faith alone leads to enlightenment. In general, Buddhism describes supreme wisdom as the cause of enlightenment. According to the Lotus Sutra, however, even Shariputra, who among the Buddha's ten major disciples was revered as foremost in wisdom, could attain enlightenment only through faith, not through wisdom.

9. Evil friend: Also, evil companion or evil teacher. One who causes others to fall into the evil paths by misleading them in terms of Buddhism. An evil friend deludes others with false teachings in order to obstruct their correct Buddhist practice.

10. Three poisons—greed, anger and foolishness. The fundamental evils inherent in life that give rise to human suffering. In *The Treatise on the Great Perfection of Wisdom* [by Nagarjuna], the three poisons are regarded as the source of all illusions and earthly desires. The three poisons are so called because they pollute people's lives and obstruct them from turning their hearts and minds to goodness.

11. The other three passages are: (1) "If one stays close to the teachers of the Law, one will speedily gain the bodhisattva way. By following and learning from these teachers one will see Buddhas as numerous as Ganges sands" (LS, 169). (2) "Originally one followed this Buddha and for the first time conceived the desire to seek the way. And by following this Buddha again, one will reach the stage where there is no retrogression" (T'ien-t'ai's *Profound Meaning of the Lotus Sutra*). (3) "In the beginning one followed this Buddha or bodhisattva and formed a bond with him, and so it will be through this Buddha or bodhisattva that one will attain one's goal" (Miao-lo's *Annotations on "The Words and Phrases of the Lotus Sutra"*).

12. Translated from Japanese. Josei Toda, *Toda Josei zenshu* (Collected Writings of Josei Toda) (Tokyo: Seikyo Shimbunsha, 1983), vol. 3, p. 386.

13. Third doctrine: A categorization of Nichiren's teachings according to the three standards of comparison outlined in the Great Teacher T'ien-t'ai's *Profound Meaning of the Lotus Sutra.* The three standards comprise: (1) whether people of all capacities can attain Buddhahood through a particular sutra; (2) whether the process of teaching, i.e., the process of planting the seed of Buddhahood in people's lives and finally harvesting its fruit by leading them to Buddhahood, is revealed in full; and (3) whether the original relationship between teacher and disciple is revealed. Whereas the first two standards show the superiority of the Lotus Sutra over the other sutras, the third standard demonstrates the superiority of the essential teaching of the Lotus Sutra over the theoretical teaching.

In the writing titled "The Third Doctrine," the Daishonin states, "Nichiren's teaching represents the third doctrine" (WND-1, 855), indicating that his teaching is the doctrine transferred to the Buddha's eternal disciples; that is to say, it is the essential Law transferred to the Bodhisattvas of the Earth.

In terms of the threefold secret teaching—the threefold comparison of true Mahayana versus provisional Mahayana, the essential teaching of the Lotus Sutra versus the theoretical teaching of the Lotus Sutra, and the Buddhism of sowing versus the Buddhism of the harvest—the 26th high priest Nichikan Shonin concludes from the third part of the threefold secret teaching that the Daishonin's teaching is the Buddhism of sowing hidden in the depths of the sutra. In other words, Nam-myoho-renge-kyo, the teaching implicit in the depths of the "Life Span" chapter, is the third teaching, or third doctrine.

14. From the original speech text that Nichijun prepared for the 19th Soka Gakkai General Meeting in November 1958.

(1 2)

"Many in Body, One in Mind"

The Spirit of "Many in Body, One in Mind"
Is the Path to Victory

The Passage for Study in This Lecture

Hoki-bo and Sado-bo, and the believers in Atsuhara, have proved the strength of their resolve.

If the spirit of many in body but one in mind prevails among the people, they will achieve all their goals, whereas if one in body but different in mind, they can achieve nothing remarkable. The more than three thousand volumes of Confucian and Taoist literature are filled with examples. King Chou of Yin led seven hundred thousand soldiers into battle against King Wu of Chou and his eight hundred men.[1] Yet King Chou's army lost because of disunity while King Wu's men defeated him because of perfect unity. Even an individual at cross purposes with himself is certain to end in failure. Yet a hundred or even a thousand people can definitely attain their goal, if they are of one mind. Though numerous, the Japanese will find it difficult to accomplish anything, because they are divided in spirit. In contrast, although Nichiren and his followers are few, because they are different in body but united in mind, they will definitely accomplish their great mission of widely propagating the Lotus Sutra. Though evils may be numerous, they cannot prevail over a single great truth, just as many raging fires are quenched by a single shower of rain. This principle also holds true with Nichiren and his followers. (*The Writings of Nichiren Daishonin*, vol. 1, p. 618)

LECTURE

Songs can unite; they can bring people together. Soka Gakkai songs—songs for *kosen-rufu*—unite our members in the cause of widely spreading the ideals and principles of Nichiren Buddhism. Throughout Japan and countries around the globe, SGI members are singing songs energetically as they forge ahead valiantly to create a new era.

Songs provide the rhythm for victory. Songs express the solidarity of mentor and disciple.

My mentor, second Soka Gakkai president Josei Toda, would frequently ask youth to get up and sing; he had us lead songs and dance to the music. At times, he would even stand up himself and lead a song by performing a solemn Japanese dance in rhythm with the melody.

Often, when visiting our members in areas near and far, I would also sing along with everyone, lead them in songs or perform a dance to encourage them. Firmly united with the members, I aligned my life with that of Mr. Toda, our mentor in the struggle for *kosen-rufu*, and set into motion a powerful impetus for peace, culture and harmony.

TWO WHEELS OF A CART

Highlights

- Aligning our hearts with our mentor while uniting in our efforts for *kosen-rufu* is the key to victory for our movement.

- It is vital that we take a firm stand against any person or negative influence that seeks to destroy the oneness of mentor and disciple and the unity of many in body, one in mind.

The Soka Gakkai has emphasized the importance of songs and their ability to unite people's hearts because the heart-to-heart bonds shared between mentor and disciple and among fellow members together make up the unchanging formula for absolute victory—victory toward *kosen-rufu* and in our lives as practitioners of Nichiren Buddhism. These two kinds of unity—known respectively as the "oneness of mentor and disciple" and the "unity of many in body, one in mind"—are essential to the deepening of each individual's faith and to the progress of *kosen-rufu*. Indeed, it is not too much to say that the ongoing development of the Soka Gakkai will depend on whether these vital elements are preserved and passed on to future generations.

In every major campaign I waged for *kosen-rufu*—be it in Ota and Bunkyo wards in Tokyo, in Japan's northern island of Hokkaido, in Osaka or in Yamaguchi Prefecture—I did all I could to share Mr. Toda's guidance and vision with the members and urged them to join me in achieving victory as his disciples. I realized that the future of our movement hinged on us uniting solidly for the sake of *kosen-rufu* and living as our mentor taught us. That was why I built a rhythm of victory through the unity of many in body, one in mind, centering on the oneness of mentor and disciple.

Suppose there is a 10-million-horsepower motor. By engaging the gears of a machine with the engine, that 10-million horsepower will be transmitted to the entire machine. In much the same way, aligning our hearts with our mentor while uniting in our efforts for *kosen-rufu* is the key to victory for our movement.

In that respect, it is vital that we take a firm stand against any person or negative influence that seeks to destroy the oneness of mentor and disciple or the unity of many in body, one in mind. Mr. Toda often said that the Soka Gakkai was more precious to him than his own life, and he sternly exhorted us to show the door to anyone who dared disrupt the pure organization of the Soka Gakkai.

The oneness of mentor and disciple and the spirit of many in body, one in mind are essentially inseparable

SGI PRESIDENT IKEDA ON UNITY

[Nichiren] Daishonin states, "Both oneself and others together will take joy in their possession of wisdom and compassion" (*The Record of the Orally Transmitted Teachings*, p. 146). To possess both wisdom and compassion is the heart of our human revolution. If you have wisdom alone and lack compassion, it will be a cold, perverse wisdom. If you have compassion alone and lack wisdom, you cannot achieve your own happiness or give happiness to others. You are even likely to lead them in the wrong direction.

As we advance together in the pursuit of our human revolution—on the paths of unsurpassed joy and self-improvement—we deepen both our wisdom and compassion with the passing of time. This is our way of life in the SGI. (*My Dear Friends in America*, second edition, pp. 253–54)

principles; they are like the two wheels of a cart. If we do not share our mentor's heart or spirit to realize *kosen-rufu*, there will be no genuine unity of purpose among our diverse membership. Nor can we be called disciples who truly embody our mentor's spirit if we fail to cherish our harmonious community of practitioners and to make continuous efforts to forge and maintain unity.

Nichiren teaches his followers that if they persevere in faith with the same spirit as his and unite in heart and mind, the goal of *kosen-rufu* will definitely be realized.

The key to victory in all spheres of our movement lies in building and maintaining an organization whose members are united in spirit. To reaffirm this important point, I will discuss here the Daishonin's writing "Many in Body, One in Mind." Together, let us study these principles for successful leadership in Buddhism, using them as a guide in fulfilling our own unique missions and scaling new summits of victory.

UNITY IS THE KEY TO OVERCOMING GREAT OBSTACLES

Highlights

Written: Most likely between the late Bun'ei era (1264–75) and the Kenji era (1275–78).

Recipient: Unknown

- For disciples to take on challenges and strive to win with the same spirit as their teacher is the essence of the spirit of many in body, one in mind.

- *Many in body* refers to people's diverse personalities and characteristics, and the roles they fulfill.

- *One in mind* means sharing the same purpose or values and cherishing a shared wish or aspiration to realize a lofty goal or ideal.

- Only when we rise above our attachment to self and reveal our highest potential and individuality can we achieve harmonious unity.

It is not known precisely when this letter was written or to whom it was addressed. Nichiko Hori—the 59th high priest, who compiled and edited the text of the collected writings of Nichiren Daishonin—speculated that it was actually composed of two separate letters that may have been mistakenly combined when they were transcribed in later centuries. He reached this conclusion because of the lack of substantial connection between the first half of the letter (concerning the importance of unity) and the second half (concerning the likelihood of a Mongol invasion).

In this lecture, let's examine the first half of the writing, focusing mainly on Nichiren's teaching about unity of purpose.

The Daishonin mentions "Hoki-bo"—a reference to his disciple Nikko Shonin, who was actively leading propagation efforts in Suruga Province (present-day central Shizuoka Prefecture)—and "the believers in Atsuhara." From this, it is believed that the letter may have been sent to one of the Daishonin's key followers in the province, such as the lay priest Takahashi Rokuro Hyoe, and been composed sometime between the late Bun'ei era (1264–75)—when trouble first began in Atsuhara—and the Kenji era (1275–78).[2]

In light of this view, the government harassment of Nichiren's followers that would later escalate into the Atsuhara Persecution[3] was already under way.

SGI President Ikeda warmly greets University College South of Denmark Rector Søren Vang Rasmussen, who bestowed an honorary doctorate upon President Ikeda, Soka University Auditorium, Tokyo, March 21, 2009.

Accordingly, we can conclude that this letter was written to confirm that unity, or the spirit of many in body, one in mind, was the key to overcoming this great difficulty. In other words, because of the major persecution about to descend upon his followers in Suruga at any moment, Nichiren succinctly explains that unity based upon faith is the only way for them to prevail over such devilish functions. Indeed, it is the only "weapon" for thwarting the schemes of the devil king of the sixth heaven,[4] the most malevolent of devilish functions.

To quickly reconfirm the meaning of the concept of "many in body, one in mind," *many in body*—which can also be expressed as "different in body"— refers to people's diverse personalities and characteristics, and the roles they have to fulfill. *One in mind*—which can also be expressed as "same in heart or spirit"—generally means sharing the same purpose or values. It also means cherishing a shared wish or aspiration to realize a lofty goal or ideal.

In terms of Buddhism, the core of "being one in mind" is faith based on the oneness of mentor and disciple— that is, each person taking *kosen-rufu*, the Buddha's will and intent, as a personal mission and actively working for its realization. For disciples to take on challenges and strive to win with the same spirit as their teacher is the essence of the spirit of many in body, one in mind.

The explicit acknowledgment here that though we unite in spirit, we are many or different in body is very important. I find it profoundly significant that Nichiren doesn't use the term *one in body, one in mind*—which is commonly used in Japanese to signify unity in conformity—rather he uses *many in body, one in mind*, signaling unity in diversity. In other words, though we may share the same purpose or aspiration, we do not suppress or deny our own individuality. When we each fully express our unique potential through the power of the Mystic Law, we can manifest the invincible strength of the unity of many in body, one in mind.

The Buddha became enlightened to the fundamental power that connects all phenomena in the universe—namely, the Mystic Law. He also awakened to the fact that all people have the potential to manifest the power of this Law in their own lives. Buddhism calls this potential the Buddha nature (or Dharma nature). Only when we each bring forth the wisdom of our enlightened Buddha nature can we truly actualize the unity of many in body, one in mind as taught in Nichiren Buddhism. Because we rise above our attachment to self and reveal our highest potential and individuality, the path of many in body, one in mind becomes a path for absolute victory.

Here, we should also remember that, through manifesting the wisdom of our Buddha nature, we can break free from the fundamental darkness or ignorance that would keep us trapped in the paths of evil and suffering. The spirit of many in body, one in mind is not a unity achieved through external constraints or demands for conformity. Rather, it is an expression of the wisdom of our Buddha nature arising from a fundamental liberation occurring in the depths of each person's life. It is a unity based on aligning our own hearts with the heart of the Buddha.

"Many in body" or "different in body" are expressions supported by the

In terms of Buddhism,
the core of "being one in mind"
is faith based on the oneness of mentor
and disciple—that is, each person taking
kosen-rufu, the Buddha's will and intent,
as a personal mission and actively
working for its realization.

guiding principle of Buddhism that all people have boundless potential and can lead the most wonderful lives.

Emphasizing that the spirit of many in body, one in mind is the key to victory, Nichiren says, "The more than three thousand volumes of Confucian and Taoist literature are filled with examples [of this]" (WND-1, 618). He asserts that in China, a land with a rich cultural and philosophical heritage, it was a well-established principle that the unity of many in body, one in mind is crucial to any great achievement. As a classic example of this, he cites a famous battle in Chinese history.

BECOME UNIFYING LEADERS

Highlights

- The king of Yin was defeated because his despotic rule had fueled resentment and turned the hearts of his soldiers against him.

- In contrast, the forces of King Wu of Chou were firmly united in their righteous cause of toppling a tyrannical ruler.

- Unity begins with leaders rising into action with a stand-alone spirit to empower the people. If leaders are earnest and dedicated, they will find resonance with many others, and this will enable many diverse individuals to unite with a common sense of purpose.

This battle is known as the Yin-Chou War and is documented in *Records of the Historian* by Sima Qian and other writings. We can surmise that Nichiren Daishonin chose this example because it offers an eloquent and thought-provoking illustration of the importance of the principle of many in body, one in mind.

The battle took place more than three millennia ago, in the 11th century BCE. King Chou, the last ruler of the Yin dynasty [also known as the Shang dynasty], possessed a great army of 700,000 men. Rising up against the misruling of the Yin dynasty's king, King Wu of Chou—a vassal state of Yin—had a force consisting of only 800 feudal lords and their respective warriors. Though it is not possible today to know the exact figures, one source puts the size of this force at around 45,000 men.

One might conclude that the forces of Yin, given their sheer superiority in numbers, held an overwhelming advantage. But the Yin soldiers had no will to fight. They are said to have turned their weapons upside down and parted their ranks to let the Chou forces make their way through. The King of Yin was defeated because his despotic rule had fueled resentment and turned the hearts of his soldiers against him. Thus, as the Daishonin writes: "King Chou of Yin led seven hundred thousand soldiers into battle . . . [yet his army] lost because of disunity" (WND-1, 618). In contrast, the forces of King

Wu of Chou were firmly united in their righteous cause of toppling a tyrannical ruler. They demonstrated the spirit of many in body, one in mind.

Though by all outward appearances, the Yin forces were there to defend King Chou, they shared neither his heart nor spirit; they were at cross purposes—in other words, "one in body but different in mind."

From an organizational perspective, vital to maintaining the condition of many in body, one in mind is the attitude of leaders. This may seem somewhat contradictory, but unity begins with a central figure taking a solitary stand. If leaders are earnest and dedicated, they will find resonance with others, and this will enable many diverse individuals to unite with a common sense of purpose. On the other hand, if leaders are cowardly or authoritarian, they cannot foster authentic unity. A clear example of this is seen in the difference between King Chou of Yin and King Wu of Chou, as I have just outlined.

In *Records of the Historian,* King Chou is described as being "skilled in oratory," "shrewd and quick-witted" and "having prodigious strength."[5] And precisely because he possessed such exceptional abilities, he was always "justifying his abuses" and in the habit of "denigrating his ministers as useless and boasting of his own prowess."[6] History teaches us that there is no true or lasting unity under arrogant leaders.

Among the rulers of states who paid fealty to King Chou of Yin, three were particularly capable and influential. The king, however, had two of them executed and the third placed under house arrest and then banished. This last ruler was the Earl of the West, later known as King Wen, the father of King

Everything begins with
leaders rising into action with a
stand-alone spirit to empower the people.
Sharing that ideal, our members join together
for its realization, and with unshakable unity
of purpose, they rise up to confront
and defeat evil.

Wu. King Chou ruthlessly purged any ministers or retainers who dared speak out against his oppressive rule. As a result, only sycophants skilled in the arts of flattery and subterfuge remained around him.

In the meantime, the state of Chou—a dominion of Yin—was administered fairly under the central leadership of the Earl of the West [who had eventually been pardoned from banishment]. Whenever there was some quarrel or dispute among the rulers of neighboring states, they would ask him to mediate. Once, an intractable dispute broke out between two particular states, so the rulers of both kingdoms traveled all the way to Chou to seek the earl's mediation. The episode is related in *Records of the Historian* as follows: "Setting foot inside the state of Chou, they saw that farmers lived so peaceably as to concede the boundaries of paddy fields in favor of their neighbors. Not only that, but everyone overflowed with the spirit of freely and voluntarily deferring to the elderly. Seeing this, the two rulers felt utterly ashamed. 'Our conflict would only be a source of merriment in this kingdom. We'd just end up embarrassing ourselves to mention it,' they thought. The two immediately turned back. Making mutual concessions, they each returned to their own lands fully reconciled."[7]

In another writing, Nichiren observes, "The Chou dynasty lasted for seven hundred years because of the propriety and filial devotion of its

SECOND SOKA GAKKAI PRESIDENT JOSEI TODA ON CREATING UNITY

"No matter how much you may drum on the need for unity, it's quite hard to make people unite since each has a different mind. Suppose here is a bottle of sake . . . ," Toda said, pantomiming the act of setting a large bottle full of wine in the center of his desk and smiling mischievously. "When it comes to the matter of drinking this sake, you will instantly agree with each other and join in beautiful unity. That's unity centered on a bottle of liquor. Again, suppose there is a large, delicious-looking cake. You'll immediately and joyfully become unified in one mind: to eat it. But the sake or the cake will be quickly gone and with it your unity. You'll return once again to your individual frames of mind. It's easy to form unity centered on something like liquor or a cake. The unity we need to fight the forthcoming campaign cannot be achieved with such ease, however. Not only are there so many members with so many different ideas about how to wage this campaign, but they differ widely in their understanding of its significance. How can you unite them in one mind?"

"Just think about it. What kind of unity has enabled the Soka Gakkai to become what it is today? It is the unity of faith and nothing else."

(*The Human Revolution*, p. 1335)

founder, King Wen" ("On Repaying Debts of Gratitude," WND-1, 736). The fundamental merit that led to the long prosperity of the state of Chou resided in the well-known respect and veneration the king always accorded to his outstanding teacher and general, T'ai-kung Wang,[8] as well as other esteemed elders.

After King Wen's death, his son took over as King Wu, ruler of the state of Chou. King Wu appointed T'ai-kung Wang as his military strategist and appointed his own younger brother, Tan, the Duke of Chou, as his second in command.

Mr. Toda often spoke about T'ai-kung Wang and how the Chinese general led King Wu's forces, toppling King Chou.

In other writings, Nichiren notes how King Wu went into battle with a carriage bearing a wooden image of his deceased father, King Wen.[9] He describes King Wu as a person of great filial devotion and a ruler who governed the people wisely and benevolently with the support and assistance of such able ministers as T'ai-kung Wang.

In terms of our efforts, everything begins with leaders rising into action with a stand-alone spirit to empower the people. Sharing that ideal, our members join together for its realization, and with unshakable unity of purpose, they rise up to confront and defeat evil. This could be called the formula for the victory of the people in the realm of *kosen-rufu*.

THE IMPORTANCE OF BUILDING A UNITED ORGANIZATION

Highlights

There are several vital requirements for genuine leaders striving to create a united organization:

- listening to the sincere opinions of many others;

- freely discussing things with other core leaders in order to expand and strengthen solidarity;

- giving thought to what needs to be done and what needs to be discussed so that everyone is satisfied and inspired to continue striving for *kosen-rufu* with joy and conviction; and

- accurately transmitting information to central figures.

A leader taking action based on a stand-alone spirit is fundamentally different from a leader behaving as a dictator. At times, based on their towering sense of responsibility, courageous leaders may need to take a stand in making bold decisions for their organization. Unlike dictators, however, genuine leaders will listen to the sincere opinions of many others. It is especially important in this day and age for key leaders at all levels of the organization to freely discuss things with other core leaders. When our leaders engage in frank and open dialogue with other leaders who share the same sense of responsibility, and when they work to expand and strengthen solidarity through the power of dialogue, the Soka Gakkai will achieve even greater growth.

Accordingly, leaders should constantly give thought to what they need to do and what they need to discuss so that everyone is satisfied and inspired to stand up with joy and conviction and can continue making wonderful strides toward *kosen-rufu*. This is the responsibility of leaders of a united organization—an organization where the spirit of many in body but one in mind prevails.

Another vital requirement for maintaining a united organization is the accurate transmission of information to the central figures. Mr. Toda often declared that those who fail to report on matters of crucial importance to the organization are like enemies. Those who lack unity of purpose and refuse to support the central figures are, bluntly speaking, people who "destroy their own castle from within" (see "The Heritage of the Ultimate Law of Life," WND-1, 217) in that through their actions they end up aiding and abetting the real enemies.

Let us forever engrave in our lives the motto: Win through perfect unity (see WND-1, 618). With this resolve, let's continue to build a united organization through our faith and our concerted efforts, and create a rhythm of unceasing victory.

TRUE UNITY BEGINS WITH A FUNDAMENTAL CHANGE IN ONE'S OWN RESOLVE

Highlights

- A person conflicted about which course to pursue can accomplish nothing meaningful.
- Everything begins with changing our own mind-set.
- A mind prone to making distinctions of self and other leads one to isolation, to self-attachment and to regarding the self as faultless, giving rise to evil and misery.
- Those who transcend attachment to the self and bring forth the power of the Mystic Law free themselves from this negative tendency that confines people to evil and suffering.
- As we strive to accomplish human revolution while working to forge the unity of many in body, one in mind, we can conquer our attachment to self and establish faith based on the Mystic Law.

Nichiren Daishonin emphasizes the importance of being "of one mind"—that is, sharing the same purpose or spirit.

First, he notes, "Even an individual at cross purposes with himself is certain to end in failure" (WND-1, 618). Certainly, nothing meaningful can be accomplished by a person conflicted, or of two minds, about which course to

ALWAYS BEGIN WITH FRESH RESOLVE

On May 3, 1951, when Josei Toda was inaugurated second Soka Gakkai president, he made a dramatic declaration to achieve 750,000 member-households in his lifetime.

The flame of fighting spirit burned brightly in the hearts of mentor and disciple. A tremendous struggle thus began, to which both [Josei Toda and Daisaku Ikeda] devoted their entire beings day after day. Their passionate determination eventually spread to the hearts of all members, inspiring people across the entire Japanese archipelago.

Finally, almost seven years later, in December 1957, this unprecedented goal had been reached—750,000 households, comprising some two million members, united under the banner of Soka. It was truly a splendid achievement. In his New Year's poem, President Toda highlighted the key to their success—that is, to start each year with fresh resolve. The pioneer members never complacently assumed that they always had the following year or the year after that to achieve their goals. They took action with the strong determination that this year was decisive, that this year was all they had. Each day was an earnest struggle in which they fought with all their might. That was how the solid foundation of *kosen-rufu* was built. (*The New Human Revolution*, vol. 17, pp. 2–3)

pursue. That only stands to reason. If we cannot make up our minds, we cannot have firm resolve. We will be swayed by our environment and lose our direction. Such is the folly of human beings.

Especially, if we suffer such confusion in relation to the all-important question of attaining Buddhahood, we will not only fail to gain the Buddha way but travel a path leading to unhappiness and suffering.

The heart is what matters most. Having a firm and concrete resolve is what secures the path to victory.

Everything begins with changing our own attitude, or mind-set. This applies equally to creating the unity of many in body, one in mind. If members of an organization are constantly at loggerheads, always blaming and criticizing one another, then they will always remain disunited, in the condition of many in body, different in mind. Since organizations are made up of people, we are bound to encounter all kinds of people. At times, our personalities may not mesh with those of other individuals. That is why unless we each ground ourselves within our own human revolution, we cannot create genuine unity. In "The Heritage of the Ultimate Law of Life," the Daishonin urges his followers to unite "in the spirit of many in body but one in mind, transcending all differences among themselves[10] to become as inseparable as fish and the water in which they swim" (WND-1, 217).

It is only natural that people have different personalities and temperaments. But we must never use someone's being different as an excuse to discriminate against, exclude or reject such a person. The important thing is that we accept one another's diverse qualities with the spirit of "transcending all differences" among ourselves.

A mind prone to making distinctions of self and other leads one to self-isolation, to self-attachment and to regarding the self as faultless, which gives rise to evil and misery. Depending on the person and the situation, such negative traits as contempt, hatred, jealousy, resentment, indignation, arrogance, malice, sullenness, gloom, stubbornness, impatience, disloyalty and ingratitude may arise. People who transcend attachment to the self and bring forth the power of the Mystic Law free themselves from a negative life tendency that confines one to evil and suffering.

The Daishonin also urges us "to become as inseparable as fish and the water in which they swim" ("The Heritage of the Ultimate Law of Life," WND-1, 217). This means developing a sense of affinity or fellowship with everyone who joins us in studying and practicing Nichiren Buddhism and working for *kosen-rufu*, and indeed with all people with whom we have a connection.

Those who have conquered the tendency to focus on differences come to manifest in their lives the workings of the Mystic Law, which connects and harmonizes all things. At times, they will play a leading role and freely take initiative for *kosen-rufu*, while at other times, they will work behind the scenes to support other central figures. Moreover, whatever capacity they fulfill, their lives will pulse vibrantly due to the Mystic Law, the fundamental power of the universe.

As we strive to accomplish human revolution while working to forge the unity of many in body, one in mind, we can conquer our attachment to self and establish faith based on the selfless spirit of "valuing the Law more highly than

> The heart is what matters most. Having a firm and concrete resolve is what secures the path to victory. Everything begins with changing our own attitude, or mind-set. This applies equally to creating the unity of many in body, one in mind.

our own lives."[11] Making the Law the basis of our practice is the true essence of the spirit of many in body, one in mind.

Nichiren further says, "Yet a hundred or even a thousand people can definitely attain their goal, if they are of one mind" (WND-1, 618). Being "of one mind" is the same as being "inseparable as fish and the water in which they swim" ("The Heritage of the Ultimate Law of Life," WND-1, 217). To achieve victory ourselves and for others, while advancing harmoniously together, united in faith—this is the essence of the Soka Gakkai spirit.

Mr. Toda often remarked: "If we ask what kind of unity has enabled the Soka Gakkai to realize the development it has today, the answer is the unity of faith and nothing else. It is the unity of many diverse individuals who share the same purpose or commitment. The human heart is very fickle, easily swayed by changing circumstances. It is an extraordinary thing for people's hearts to be united in a shared goal. It's not something that can simply be achieved by ordering people to unite."

Without the spirit of many in body but one in mind, we cannot accomplish *kosen-rufu*. Those who turn their backs on this spirit are turning their backs on the teachings of Nichiren Daishonin.

Let's engrave in our hearts Nichiren's teaching about being "of one mind." We mustn't forget that realizing any victory depends on tenacious united efforts.

THE CONDITION OF MANY IN BODY, ONE IN MIND IS PROOF OF THE VICTORY OF KOSEN-RUFU

Highlights

- The success or failure of *kosen-rufu* is not dependent on the number of people involved in that undertaking but whether those who strive to accomplish it are united in spirit.

- Those who attacked Nichiren and his followers were "one in body" in terms of being against the Lotus Sutra; but they were "different in mind" holding varying agendas and not earnestly aspiring for any particular ideal. Thus they could not achieve anything worthwhile.

- The Atsuhara followers had resolute faith that no authority could restrain. Centuries later, they remain a lasting reference point for Nichiren Buddhists and continue to inspire us in our efforts for worldwide *kosen-rufu*.

With regard to the circumstances facing him and his followers, Nichiren Daishonin clearly states that the spirit of many in body, one in mind is crucial if good is to triumph.

At the time, people throughout Japan viewed Nichiren and his followers with animosity and abused and harassed them. But, here, he emphasizes that what determines the success or failure of *kosen-rufu* is not the number of people involved in that undertaking. He assures his followers that even if their ranks are small, as long as they are united in spirit, they can definitely achieve *kosen-rufu*.

The Daishonin observes, "Though numerous, the Japanese will find it difficult to accomplish anything, because they are divided in spirit" (WND-1, 618). "The Japanese" here means the people of Japan during the Daishonin's time who were hostile to the efforts he and his followers were making to propagate the Lotus Sutra. These propagation efforts were directed toward actualizing the ideals of the Lotus Sutra—namely, happiness for oneself and others (the universal attainment of enlightenment) and establishing the correct teaching for the peace of the land (establishing a nation or society in which the humane ideals of Buddhism predominate and peace prevails). The people of the day, however, failed to appreciate these ideals. As a result, they vehemently opposed them and attacked Nichiren and his followers. Yet they had no ideals of their own that were capable of changing the reality of the times and improving the world.

The religions to which many Japanese of the time subscribed were such established Buddhist schools as the Pure Land (Nembutsu) school, which taught that one should despise and reject the real world as impure; the

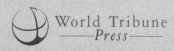

Zen school, which emphasized pursuing enlightenment through austere practices as a monk; and the True Word (Shingon) and Tendai schools, which were devoted almost exclusively to conducting prayer rituals for the defeat of the enemies of the rulers. Ultimately, all these schools merely exacerbated the existing conflicts of the age, which could be described as the karma created by the warrior government.

Having no sound religion or philosophy as their foundation, the leaders of society had little hope of realizing a happy and prosperous society. As Nichiren states, "Though numerous, the Japanese will find it difficult to accomplish anything, because they are divided in spirit" (WND-1, 618).

The people of Japan who attacked the Daishonin and his followers could perhaps be described as "one in body" in terms of being against the Lotus Sutra; but because they held varying goals and agendas and aspired toward no particular ideals, they could also be described as being "different in mind." As a result, they could achieve nothing worthwhile. In contrast, the Daishonin writes, "Although Nichiren and his followers are few, because they are different in body but united in mind, they will definitely accomplish their great mission of widely propagating the Lotus Sutra" (WND-1, 618). It is a declaration that he and his followers, though few in number, could definitely prevail and realize *kosen-rufu* because they were united in spirit.

The followers in Atsuhara steadfastly embraced this teaching of Nichiren. Showing actual proof of faith, they courageously refused to give in to

A Buddha is one whose life is dedicated to value creation. In a world wracked by schism and human misery, a Buddha makes every effort to bring people together and actualize the ideal of a peaceful society, while aiming for the overarching goal of peace for all humankind.

authoritarian persecution and achieved a monumental spiritual victory. Their strong spirit, which no authority could restrain, has become a lasting reference point for Nichiren Buddhism of the people and continues to inspire us in our efforts for worldwide *kosen-rufu* today.

In "The True Aspect of All Phenomena," Nichiren writes: "At first only Nichiren chanted Nam-myoho-renge-kyo, but then two, three, and a hundred followed, chanting and teaching others. Propagation will unfold this way in the future as well. Does this not signify '[bodhisattvas] emerging from the earth'? At the time when the Law has spread far and wide, the entire Japanese nation will chant Nam-myoho-renge-kyo, as surely as an arrow aimed at the earth cannot miss the target" (WND-1, 385).

He declares that the goal of *kosen-rufu* is certain to be achieved if a steady stream of Bodhisattvas of the Earth continues to emerge to follow Nichiren—the teacher who first chanted Nam-myoho-renge-kyo—and, with the spirit of oneness with their mentor and the solidarity of many in body but one in mind, to chant and teach others as well.

The many examples of powerful unity evident in our Soka Gakkai activities give eloquent testimony to the success of our *kosen-rufu* movement and are the essence of its growth and development. In other words, unity of purpose in the realm of faith is not only the key to victory but also the proof of that victory.

Furthermore, those who are dynamically striving together in such unity have already freed themselves from the mind-set that discriminates between self and other, which would have kept them encumbered by suffering and evil. There is no greater victory than this.

All those who vibrantly unite in the spirit of many in body, one in mind based on the Mystic Law blossom as victorious "human flowers" (see *The Lotus Sutra and Its Opening and Closing Sutras*, p. 142). Victory in the realm of Buddhism equals victory in all areas of life.

THE SINGLE GREAT TRUTH OF THE MYSTIC LAW

Highlights

- In a world wracked by schism and human misery, a Buddha makes every effort to bring people together and actualize the ideal of a peaceful society, while aiming for the overarching goal of peace for all humankind.

- When the influence of ultimate good increases, the darkness of evil, no matter how deep, will instantly vanish.

- Humanity as a whole is searching for the unity of spirit exemplified by that of many in body, one in mind.

In this writing, Nichiren Daishonin and his followers—who manifest the power of the Mystic Law, battle slander and persecution, and advance the cause of *kosen-rufu*—are described as representing "a single great truth [or good]" (WND-1, 618). This is because the Mystic Law represents a single truth, or ultimate good, that links all life and phenomena and can vanquish evil. That is to say, division is evil; unity is good.

The state of Buddhahood allows us to live amid the reality of society with the enlightened wisdom to perceive the true nature of the universe in which all phenomena are interconnected. A Buddha is one whose life is dedicated to value creation. In a world wracked by schism and human misery, a Buddha makes every effort to bring people together and actualize the ideal of a peaceful society, while aiming for the overarching goal of peace for all humankind.

Therefore, Nichiren says, "Though evils may be numerous, they cannot prevail over a single great truth [good]" (WND-1, 618). When the sun of ultimate good rises, the darkness of evil, no matter how deep, will instantly vanish. Nichiren and his followers embody this single great truth, or good. This is demonstrated by their resolve and efforts to propagate the Mystic Law, the most fundamental good, unafraid of confronting devilish functions or obstacles.

As modern-day practitioners of the Daishonin's philosophy, we also dedicate our lives to *kosen-rufu*, the realization of the ideals envisaged in the Lotus Sutra. No one has worked harder or devoted themselves more selflessly than the members of the Soka Gakkai—through sheer effort and perseverance amid abuse and criticism—in the cause of unleashing the power of the people and building an age of the people. That is why our movement is applauded throughout the world.

We are now at a stage where people around the globe are taking positive note of our philosophy and practice as a result of the unparalleled unity we have forged.

Today, intercultural and interfaith dialogue are becoming increasingly indispensable for the future development of humankind. It could be said that humanity as a whole is searching for the kind of unity of spirit exemplified by that of many in body, one in mind. Many leaders today recognize the growing importance of dialogue in transcending cultural differences and nurturing people's essential goodness. I feel that we are at the forefront of this endeavor.

The world is counting on our united efforts to forge an alliance of people dedicated to good. Let us advance with pride and confidence, and write a history of truly brilliant achievement.

This lecture was published in the September 2008 Daibyakurenge, *the Soka Gakkai monthy study journal.*

NOTES:

1. Nichiren uses the expression "eight hundred men," but to be precise it was actually "a force led by eight hundred feudal lords," which includes their respective warriors.

2. Eras in Japanese history correspond to the beginning and ending of each emperor's rule.

3. A series of threats and acts of violence against followers of Nichiren in Atsuhara Village, in Fuji District of Suruga Province, beginning around 1275 and continuing until around 1283. In 1279, 20 farmers were unjustly arrested and sent to Kamakura, where they were interrogated by Hei no Saemon, the deputy chief of the Office of Military and Police Affairs. He demanded that they renounce their faith; not one of them yielded, however. Eventually, three of these followers were executed—the brothers Jinshiro, Yagoro and Yarokuro. They are known as the three martyrs of Atsuhara.

4. Devil king of the sixth heaven: Also, devil king or heavenly devil. The king of devils who dwells in the highest or the sixth heaven of the world of desire. He is also named Freely Enjoying Things Conjured by Others because he makes free use of the fruits of others' efforts for his own pleasure.

5. Translated from Japanese. *Shiki* (Records of the Historian), translated by Hiroshi Ichikawa and Tatsuo Sugimoto (Tokyo: Tokuma Shoten, 1972), p. 34.

6. *Shiki*, p. 34.

7. *Shiki*, p. 42.

8. T'ai-kung Wang is the title of a general who served under King Wen and King Wu of the state of Chou dynasty. Also known as Chiang Tzu-ya (Jiang Ziya), he was King Wen's teacher and advisor. His strategies are said to have enabled King Wen's son, King Wu, to overthrow the state of Yin.

9. Nichiren writes: "We have the example of King Wu of the ancient land of Chou, who carved a wooden image of his deceased father and placed it in a carriage, designating it as the general who would lead his troops into battle. Heaven, moved by such conduct, lent him protection, and thus he succeeded in overthrowing his enemy, Chou, the king of Yin" ("The Tripitaka Master Shan-wu-wei," WND-1, 170–71). He also writes: "King Wu of the Chou dynasty made a wooden image of his father, the Earl of the West. . . . [He and others like him were all] models of filial piety" ("The Opening of the Eyes," WND-1, 220).

10. "Transcending all differences among themselves" could also be rendered literally as "without any thought of self or other, this or that." This is not a denial of individuality but rather urges the bridging of divisions among people that arise from self-centeredness.

11. A rewording of a passage from Chang-an's *Annotations on the Nirvana Sutra:* "One's body is insignificant while the Law is supreme" ("Letter to Akimoto," WND-1, 1021).

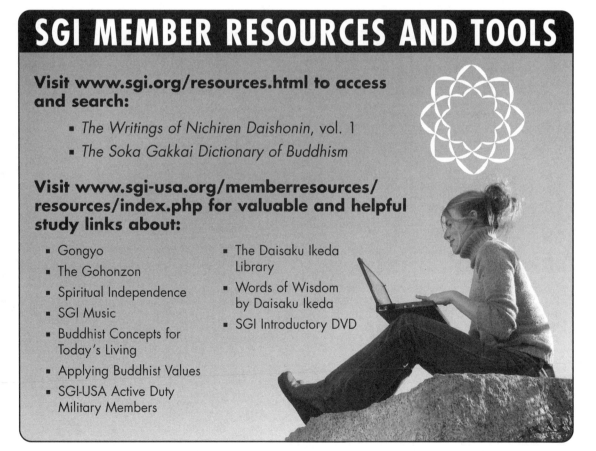

SGI MEMBER RESOURCES AND TOOLS

Visit www.sgi.org/resources.html to access and search:

- *The Writings of Nichiren Daishonin*, vol. 1
- *The Soka Gakkai Dictionary of Buddhism*

Visit www.sgi-usa.org/memberresources/ resources/index.php for valuable and helpful study links about:

- Gongyo
- The Gohonzon
- Spiritual Independence
- SGI Music
- Buddhist Concepts for Today's Living
- Applying Buddhist Values
- SGI-USA Active Duty Military Members
- The Daisaku Ikeda Library
- Words of Wisdom by Daisaku Ikeda
- SGI Introductory DVD

(13)

"On Repaying Debts of Gratitude"

Kosen-rufu: A Great River Enriching Humanity Eternally—Our Victory as Disciples Is the Greatest Way To Repay Our Gratitude to Our Mentor

The Passage for Study in This Lecture

In Japan, China, India, and all the other countries of Jambudvipa, every person, regardless of whether wise or ignorant, will set aside other practices and join in the chanting of Nam-myoho-renge-kyo. This teaching has never been taught before. Here in the entire land of Jambudvipa, in all the 2,225 years since the passing of the Buddha, not a single person chanted it. Nichiren alone, without sparing his voice, now chants Nam-myoho-renge-kyo, Nam-myoho-renge-kyo.

The size of the waves depends upon the wind that raises them, the height of the flames depends upon how much firewood is piled on, the size of the lotuses depends upon the pond in which they grow, and the volume of rain depends upon the dragons that make it fall. The deeper the roots, the more prolific the branches. The farther the source, the longer the stream.

The Chou dynasty lasted for seven hundred years because of the propriety and filial devotion of its founder, King Wen. The Ch'in dynasty (211–206 B.C.E.), on the other hand, lasted hardly any time at all, because of the perverse ways of its founder, the First Emperor of the Ch'in. If Nichiren's compassion is truly great and encompassing, Nam-myoho-renge-kyo will spread for ten thousand years and more, for all eternity, for it has the beneficial power to open the blind eyes of every living being in the country of Japan, and it blocks off the road that leads to the hell of incessant suffering. Its benefit surpasses that of Dengyo[1] and T'ien-t'ai,[2] and is superior to that of Nagarjuna[3] and Mahakashyapa.[4]

A hundred years of practice in the Land of Perfect Bliss[5] cannot compare to the benefit gained from one day's practice in the impure world. Two thousand years of propagating Buddhism during the Former and Middle Days of the Law are inferior to an hour of propagation in the Latter Day of the Law. This is in no way because of Nichiren's wisdom, but simply because the time makes it so. In spring the blossoms open, in autumn the fruit appears. Summer is hot, winter is cold. The season makes it so, does it not? (*The Writings of Nichiren Daishonin*, vol. 1, p. 736)

LECTURE

To repay one's debts of gratitude is the highest virtue. Neglecting gratitude is a reflection of a life controlled by innate negativity.

As we each deepen our faith in the Mystic Law, break through our fundamental darkness[6] and live true to our greater self, we will come to feel boundless appreciation for all those around us and for all who have nurtured and helped us become who we are. And we will confidently make our way along the invigorating path of recognizing and repaying our debts of gratitude.

In contrast, those who fail to refresh their faith, who give in to negativity and are shackled by attachments to the lesser self invariably become ruled by arrogance, cowardice or anger. As they descend, their ability to appreciate the goodness of others wanes until, eventually, they neither recognize nor repay the kindnesses others have done for them.

It all comes down to either living based on the greater self or remaining attached to the lesser self. Ultimately, this difference in the fundamental orientation of our attitude determines whether we will lead lives of gratitude or ingratitude.

THE LIVES OF GENUINE BUDDHIST PRACTITIONERS SHINE WITH APPRECIATION AND GRATITUDE

Highlights

Written: on July 21, 1276, in honor of Nichiren's late teacher, Dozen-bo

- Nichiren vowed to "become the wisest person in Japan," with the firm belief that through thoroughly studying the teachings of Buddhism and identifying the key to solving the sufferings of birth and death, he could enable his parents to realize true happiness.

- To repay his debt of gratitude to all living beings, he established the teaching of Nam-myoho-renge-kyo, taking on the arduous battle of refuting the erroneous and revealing the true in the realm of Buddhism.

- In addition, he recognized and made efforts to repay his gratitude to his country, the three treasures and his former teacher Dozen-bo.

Recognizing debts of gratitude expresses the Buddhist spirit of cultivating the richest possible humanity, while *repaying* that gratitude is the hallmark of a life of wisdom that comes from conquering fundamental ignorance. Hence, the lives of genuine Buddhist practitioners always shine with the inner light of appreciation and gratitude.

Throughout his life, Nichiren Daishonin demonstrated an extraordinary commitment to repaying his gratitude as a human being and as a Buddhist. He writes, "Ever since I began to study the Law handed down from Shakyamuni Buddha and undertook the practice of the Buddhist teachings, I have believed it is most important to understand one's obligations to others, and made it my first duty to repay such debts of kindness" ("Conversation between a Sage and an Unenlightened Man," WND-1, 122).

Nichiren vowed to "become the wisest person in all Japan" ("The Tripitaka Master Shan-wu-wei," WND-1, 175) and, upon entering Seicho-ji[7] at a young age, diligently applied himself to his studies in order to repay his debt of gratitude to his mother and father. With firm conviction, Nichiren thoroughly studied the teachings of Buddhism and identified the key to solving the sufferings of birth and death, and he sought to help his parents realize true happiness.

Moreover, it was to repay his gratitude to all living beings that, after two decades of intensive Buddhist study, he established the teaching of Nam-myoho-renge-kyo and, understanding the scope of his perilous battle, he "refuted the erroneous and revealed the true" (see sidebar, p. 229) in the realm of Buddhism. Discovering in the depths of the Lotus Sutra the universal Law of life for the enlightenment of all people and of all living beings, Nichiren lived as the sutra taught, embodying it in his own life.

GRATITUDE LEADS TO HAPPINESS

SGI President Ikeda: People who can express their gratitude are truly happy. A life that is always filled with appreciation is a bright and cheerful one—be it when you are meeting with people, when someone gives you a lift in his or her car, or when you are at home with your family. Sincerely offering thanks is a sign of living truly happy lives. Where people embody such a sense of appreciation, they send out waves of happiness that envelop both themselves and others.

To voice your appreciation, it is important to say "thank you" to your fellow members and to your friends. Leaders who take the members' sincere efforts for granted and assume a highhanded attitude toward them inevitably come to a deadlock because of their own arrogance. They bring bleakness and unhappiness to both themselves and others.

The expression *thank you* contains the essence of happiness. Those who appreciate the heart of these two words and use them generously are surely more eloquent than the most skilled of speakers. (*My Dear Friends in America*, second edition, pp. 291–92)

Furthermore, because he recognized his debt of gratitude to his country, he strictly admonished various schools of Buddhism that slandered the Law and went against the Buddha's original intent. And he remonstrated with the rulers of Japan, who stood idly by while the people suffered and the country fell into confusion and disorder.

Repaying one's debt of gratitude to one's country does not mean slavish submission to the ruler or the state. In modern terms, we can consider *country* as referring to society. Nichiren's effort to "establish the correct teaching for the peace of the land"—bringing about the fundamental reformation needed for creating a better society—can be considered a means of repaying the debt of gratitude to the country.

After surmounting life-threatening persecutions and casting off his transient status as an ordinary person to reveal his true identity as the Buddha of the Latter Day of the Law,[8] Nichiren revealed the Gohonzon as the object of devotion and manifestation of his enlightened state of life. He also revealed and established the Three Great Secret Laws (see sidebar, p. 232) as the framework for spreading the teachings of the Lotus Sutra throughout the Latter Day. Determinedly carrying out the struggle to reveal the correct Law hidden in the depths of the Lotus Sutra that would lead all people to enlightenment, he took on the momentous battle of repaying his gratitude to the three treasures (see sidebar, p. 226).

In addition, the revelation of the Three Great Secret Laws is said to signify Nichiren fully repaying his debts of gratitude to his parents, to all living beings and to the nation, as well as marking a fresh undertaking in his life toward the realization of worldwide *kosen-rufu*—the means for repaying gratitude owed to humankind and the world.

We can view Nichiren's entire life, then, as a grand endeavor to repay debts of gratitude. In this treatise, "On Repaying Debts of Gratitude," he discusses this in detail in order to express his appreciation to his former teacher Dozen-bo.[9]

A TREATISE CONTAINING "MATTERS OF THE UTMOST IMPORTANCE"

Highlights

- Nichiren describes his ardent pursuit of Buddhism in his youth and gives a comprehensive account of his subsequent efforts to spread the Mystic Law.

- He explains Nam-myoho-renge-kyo of the Three Great Secret Laws, which are: the object of devotion of the essential teaching, the *daimoku* of the essential teaching and the sanctuary of the essential teaching.

In June 1276, Nichiren Daishonin received news of the death of Dozen-bo, under whom he had first studied Buddhism at Seicho-ji. He immediately set about composing this treatise in honor and appreciation of his late teacher. In late July, he sent the completed work to the priests Joken-bo and Gijo-bo[10]—who, during his early years of study under Dozen-bo, had been Nichiren's seniors and who later became his followers. Nichiren attached a message instructing that they should have the text read aloud before Dozen-bo's grave.

In the cover letter to "On Repaying Debts of Gratitude," the Daishonin writes, "In the enclosed treatise, I have written matters of the utmost importance" (WND-1, 737). This writing contains a detailed description of his ardent pursuit of Buddhism in his youth, along with a comprehensive account of his subsequent efforts to spread the Mystic Law. He also clarifies the immeasurable benefits of Nam-myoho-renge-kyo of the Three Great

As we each deepen our faith in the Mystic Law, break through our fundamental darkness and live true to our greater self, we will come to feel boundless appreciation for all those around us and for all who have nurtured and helped us become who we are.

Secret Laws, which constitutes the great Law that will lead all people to enlightenment and that is to be propagated throughout the eternal future of the Latter Day. And he pays tribute to his first teacher by stating that this benefit in its entirety will return to Dozen-bo.

This treatise can be viewed as a record of Nichiren's lifetime struggles to refute the erroneous and reveal the true. It closes with the triumphant proclamation that the path to enlightenment in the Latter Day is open to all through the Buddhism of the Three Great Secret Laws.

THE THREE TREASURES

The three treasures in Nichiren Buddhism are the three things that all Buddhists should revere and serve. They are the Buddha, the Law (the Buddhist teachings) and the Buddhist Order (community of believers). In Sanskrit, they are known as the Buddha, Dharma and *Sangha*.

The Buddha is one who is awakened to the truth of life and the universe. The Dharma, or Law, means the teachings that the Buddha expounds in order to lead all people to enlightenment. The *Sangha*, or Buddhist Order, is the group of believers that practices the Buddha's teachings, preserves the Law, spreads it and transmits it to future generations.

The three treasures are endowed with the power to free people from all sufferings and lead them to enlightenment. Traditionally, upon becoming Buddhists, people vowed to believe in and devote themselves to the three treasures.

The culmination of the Daishonin's struggle to propagate the Law is the revelation of the foundation of *kosen-rufu*, which is Nam-myoho-renge-kyo of the Three Great Secret Laws.

The first of the Three Great Secret Laws is the object of devotion of the essential teaching. In the Gohonzon, Nichiren embodied the supremely noble life-state of his own enlightenment. He did so in order to enable each person to become aware of this state of life that inherently and equally exists in all human beings.

The second of the Three Great Secret Laws is the *daimoku* of the essential teaching. This consists of our chanting Nam-myoho-renge-kyo and teaching others to do the same—Nam-myoho-renge-kyo being the name of this noble state of life, or Buddha nature.[11]

The sanctuary of the essential teaching, the third of the Three Great Secret Laws, serves as the foundation for constructing a harmonious community of believers (Skt *sangha*) in which members encourage one another to maintain firm faith in Nam-myoho-renge-kyo, vow to propagate the Law and actualize the principle of establishing the correct teaching for the peace of the land.

Based on these three elements, practitioners of Nichiren Buddhism strive to realize *kosen-rufu* by bringing the brilliance of the infinitely precious Mystic Law to shine in people's lives and in the land where they reside.

In the short passage we are studying, Nichiren first explains that Nam-myoho-renge-kyo of the Three Great

Secret Laws is the great teaching that will spread throughout the diverse countries of the world. He also states that this universal teaching transcends distinctions and can be practiced by anyone, irrespective of their understanding of Buddhism.

CHANTING AND SPREADING THE MYSTIC LAW "WITHOUT SPARING ONE'S VOICE"

Highlights

- To cause the teachings of the Lotus Sutra to spread widely in the defiled age of the Latter Day, we must defeat the fundamental darkness in our own lives and teach others to do likewise.

- After declaring the establishment of his teaching, Nichiren, while encountering many severe persecutions, continued to chant and teach others to do the same.

- The power of Nam-myoho-renge-kyo will endure for eternity because the Law itself is infinitely profound and because of the selfless struggles Nichiren underwent to establish and propagate it.

Nichiren Daishonin observes: "Here in the entire land of Jambudvipa, in all the 2,225 years since the passing of the Buddha, not a single person chanted it. Nichiren alone, without sparing his voice, now chants Nam-myoho-renge-kyo, Nam-myoho-renge-kyo" (WND-1,

736). A universal teaching will only spread when the time is right and when a person willing to give his or her life to propagating it appears.

Nichiren worked tirelessly "without sparing his voice" to teach people about the path he had pioneered. As a result, he established the Three Great Secret Laws, the core principles of the supreme teaching to be propagated in the Latter Day. We must never forget that Nichiren's people-centered Buddhism has flourished solely because of unceasing efforts to spread the Law.

Merely chanting Nam-myoho-renge-kyo by oneself without encouraging others to do the same will not cause the Law to spread widely among the people in the evil age of the Latter Day. Unless we can defeat our own fundamental darkness and teach others to do likewise, there will be no concrete transformation in people's lives. Therefore, after declaring the establishment of his teaching, Nichiren continued to chant and teach others to do the same—"without sparing his voice." Consequently, he encountered tremendous persecution. Undeterred, he advanced fearlessly along the path of his mission to propagate the Mystic Law in the Latter Day. His unrelenting efforts to speak out and spread the correct teaching epitomize the spirit of not begrudging one's life.

He then uses an example of natural phenomena—such as how the strength of the wind determines the size of the waves—words by the Great Teacher T'ien-t'ai and events from Chinese history to substantiate his prediction that Nam-myoho-renge-kyo will spread far into the future as a result of his selfless efforts to spread the Law.

Among these examples, let's look at the following metaphors: "The deeper the roots, the more prolific the branches. The farther the source, the longer the stream." Originally found in T'ien-t'ai's *Words and Phrases of the Lotus Sutra,* these aphorisms illustrate that the wisdom of the Buddhas is infinitely profound and immeasurable. The "roots" and the "source" symbolize this wisdom, while the prolific "branches" and the length of the "stream" represent its broad and far-reaching workings. In *The Record of the Orally Transmitted Teachings,* Nichiren states that Nam-myoho-renge-kyo is the essence of this wisdom of the Buddhas (see OTT, 26).

T'ien-t'ai uses this metaphor of "roots" and "branches" to teach the principle that the more profound a teaching, the more people it will have the power to lead to enlightenment over a long period of time.

The Chinese history cited by Nichiren offers a similar point. He explains that the Chou dynasty flourished for 700 years because its founder, King Wen, was a person of propriety and filial devotion. By contrast, the Ch'in dynasty, which was the first to unify China, fell after a mere 15 years. Nichiren declares that this was because of the tyrannical rule of its founder, the First Emperor of the Ch'in.

In other words, success hinges on whether the founder cherishes above all the welfare of the people and establishes

Nichiren worked tirelessly "without sparing his voice" to teach people about the path he had pioneered. . . . We must never forget that Nichiren's people-centered Buddhism has flourished solely because of unceasing efforts to spread the Law.

this compassion as a lasting tradition. Enduring prosperity depends on the depth of the country's guiding ideals and principles and the earnestness of those who inherit them.

Since the earliest times, religious teachings have been expounded with the aim of relieving human suffering. There is a significant difference, however, between a teaching that clarifies the fundamental cause of suffering and one that fails to do so. Teachings that offer only a shallow understanding of life's truths will have a limited scope and be short-lived. In contrast, the teaching of Nam-myoho-renge-kyo is the fundamental Law of life. Therefore, at present and for eternity, it will lead people to enlightenment. The power of Nam-myoho-renge-kyo will endure for eternity because the Law itself is infinitely profound and because of the selfless struggles Nichiren underwent to establish and propagate it. Because there is depth in the teaching accompanied by a profound struggle, *kosen-rufu* will advance and be achieved.

Our *kosen-rufu* movement today reaches 192 countries and territories. This was realized because the SGI members around the world have striven tirelessly in the same spirit as the first three Soka Gakkai presidents, who inherited their unyielding commitment in faith directly from Nichiren Daishonin. Such strong faith is the wellspring of *kosen-rufu* and happiness for oneself and others.

How is it that millions of SGI

REFUTING THE ERRONEOUS, REVEALING THE TRUE

To "refute the erroneous and reveal the true" means to challenge and prove false erroneous Buddhist teachings and viewpoints and bring to light the correct teachings.

Nichiren Daishonin writes, "If one fails to denounce the enemies of the Lotus Sutra, it will be impossible to attain the way" ("Encouragement to a Sick Person," *The Writings of Nichiren Daishonin*, vol. 1, p. 78). He teaches that the way to attain Buddhahood in this lifetime and achieve the widespread propagation of the Law is found in the struggle to denounce falsehood and proclaim truth.

Expanding on how this applies to our daily lives, SGI President Ikeda states: "We must raise our voices loudly in protest against any scheme or design that tramples on human dignity, insults decent ordinary people and undermines humanity's concerted efforts for peace. We must courageously fight back, through dialogue and the written and spoken word, making ourselves heard like fearless lions" (February 2, 2001, *World Tribune*, p. 10). Such actions not only lead us to eliminating negativity within, they help us eradicate negative karma.

As Nichiren stated, those who fail to stand up against slander of the Law when necessary become slanderers of the Law themselves. Such people cannot attain Buddhahood. Only by battling supreme evil can we draw forth the brilliant life-state of Buddhahood.

members around the globe now strive for the lofty cause of *kosen-rufu*? It is because Tsunesaburo Makiguchi and Josei Toda, our first and second presidents, dedicated themselves to propagating the Law in exact accord with Nichiren's spirit and taught us to do the same.

For us, "the deeper the roots" and "the farther the source" mean having faith that is deep and firm. With the power of faith, we can definitely triumph over any of the three obstacles and four devils[12] that may assail us in the course of our life struggles and in our work for *kosen-rufu*. If we maintain a strong sense of purpose and determination to fight for *kosen-rufu*, we will see negativity or devilish functions for what they are and prevail over them. Belief is the sharp sword that cuts through any and all obstacles.

In addition, "the more prolific the branches" and "the longer the stream" indicate that if we have courageous faith to remain undefeated by obstacles, we will enjoy not only success and prosperity in our own lives, but our victory in turn will form the foundation for the success and prosperity of our descendants for generations to come.

Accordingly, striving for *kosen-rufu*, here and now, becomes the cause for happiness and prosperity in the present and the future. All our hard work and effort to share Nichiren Buddhism is transformed into good fortune for our families and loved ones throughout eternity. This is the law of causality based on the Mystic Law.

The power of Nam-myoho-renge-kyo will endure for eternity because the Law itself is infinitely profound and because of the selfless struggles Nichiren underwent to establish and propagate it.

THE THREE VIRTUES OF NICHIREN DAISHONIN FUNCTION TO ACTUALIZE KOSEN-RUFU

Highlights

- Widespread propagation of the correct teaching is the fundamental wish of Shakyamuni, Many Treasures and all Buddhas throughout time and space.

- Nichiren declares that he has actualized this wish and explains that to propagate the Law, he has manifested the three virtues—those of parent (nurturing and caring for people), teacher (guiding people) and sovereign (protecting people).

Based on the principle "the farther the source, the longer the stream," Nichiren Daishonin declares that, driven by his profound compassion for his fellow human beings, he has secured the foundation for the enlightenment of all people into the eternal future through his own unflagging efforts. He proclaims in the following well-known passage: "If Nichiren's compassion is truly great and encompassing, Nam-myoho-renge-kyo will spread for ten thousand years and more, for all eternity, for it has the beneficial power to open the blind eyes of every living being in the country of Japan, and it blocks off the road that leads to the hell of incessant suffering" (WND-1, 736).

His immensely compassionate struggle to identify and spread the correct teaching led to his revelation of Nam-myoho-renge-kyo. In this, we can see his towering conviction that, because of his deep resolve, Nam-myoho-renge-kyo will eternally spread and lead people throughout the world to enlightenment in the Latter Day.

The Buddha vows to save all people. And widespread propagation of the correct teaching that continues after the Buddha's passing is the fundamental wish of Shakyamuni, Many Treasures and all Buddhas throughout time and space. This passage is Nichiren's declaration that he has actualized this vow. It also points to the Daishonin's three virtues—those of parent, teacher and sovereign. "If Nichiren's compassion is truly great and encompassing" indicates the virtue of the parent; "it has the beneficial power to open the blind eyes of every living being" indicates the virtue of the teacher; and "it blocks off the road that leads to the hell of incessant suffering" indicates the virtue of the sovereign.

The virtue of parent represents the function of nurturing and caring for people. Nichiren succeeded in establishing the supreme Law for the enlightenment of all people into the eternal future of the Latter Day precisely because he himself repeatedly overcame daunting opposition and persecution. The great and encompassing compassion of which he speaks in this passage did not arise out of his living in a peaceful, tranquil society. It was

THE THREE GREAT SECRET LAWS

The Three Great Secret laws, the core principles of Nichiren Daishonin's teaching, are:

the object of devotion of the essential teaching;

the *daimoku* [invocation of Nam-myoho-renge-kyo] of the essential teaching; and

the sanctuary of the essential teaching.

Here, "essential teaching" refers to the teaching of Nam-myoho-renge-kyo. Nichiren established these three principles to enable all people in the Latter Day of the Law to attain Buddhahood.

They are called secret because they are implicit in the text of the "Life Span" chapter of the Lotus Sutra and remained hidden or unknown until Nichiren revealed them. Nichiren regarded them as the vital or essential teaching that Shakyamuni Buddha transferred to Bodhisattva Superior Practices in the "Supernatural Powers" chapter of the sutra.

The Three Great Secret Laws are related to three types of learning set forth in Buddhism—precepts, meditation and wisdom. The object of devotion corresponds to meditation, the sanctuary to precepts and the *daimoku* to wisdom.

Because embracing the object of devotion—the Gohonzon—is the only precept in Nichiren's teaching, the place where it is enshrined corresponds to the place where one vows to observe the Buddhist precepts.

The *daimoku* of the essential teaching indicates the chanting of Nam-myoho-renge-kyo with faith in the object of devotion; it includes chanting Nam-myoho-renge-kyo for oneself and teaching it to others. Thus, both the sanctuary and the *daimoku* are contained in the object of devotion.

during an evil age steeped in the three poisons—greed, anger and foolishness[13]—and while battling the three powerful enemies[14] of Buddhism that he initiated the flow of *kosen-rufu* for the sake of future generations. The depth and breadth of his compassion are without comparison.

The virtue of the teacher represents the function of correctly guiding people. The Daishonin speaks of "the blind eyes of every living being in the country of Japan." Naturally, by "blind eyes," he is not referring to physical disability but rather to being oblivious to the Dharma nature inherent in life due to ignorance, the fundamental cause of delusion. He wanted to break through this ignorance, or fundamental darkness, in people's lives. Through exemplifying, as the votary of the Lotus Sutra, how to battle the three obstacles and four devils, he sought to "upset people's attachment and arouse doubts"[15]—in other words, to cause people to question their assumptions and doubt their misguided beliefs—so they could awaken to and embrace the correct teaching.

The virtue of the sovereign represents the function of protecting others. Nichiren speaks of "blocking off the road that leads to the hell of incessant suffering." This is a manifestation of his profound and irrepressible wish to not let even one person fall into the hell of incessant suffering. It is impossible to secure the welfare of all people without an unwavering commitment to eradicating suffering and misery from the face of the earth.

We must never forget that Nichiren demonstrated a living example of the virtues of parent, teacher and sovereign through his fierce and selfless struggle to propagate the correct teaching in the evil age of the Latter Day.

Buddhism always comes down to action. People who flaunt their authority and claim to possess the "same inner enlightenment as the Buddha" without taking action that

lends credence to this are certainly spiritual descendants of the six non-Buddhist teachers[16] in Shakyamuni's time.

Inheriting Nichiren's selfless spirit, our first two presidents, Mr. Makiguchi and Mr. Toda, stood up to actualize *kosen-rufu* in society. Thanks to the appearance of the Soka Gakkai, an organization dedicated to carrying out the Buddha's decree, the "great river of *kosen-rufu*" with Nichiren's teachings as its source now flows powerfully throughout the world in the 21st century. This is indisputable. The establishment of the foundation of worldwide *kosen-rufu* is complete. The time has at last arrived to extend this great river into an ocean of *kosen-rufu* encompassing the globe.

The most trying times represent the most wonderful opportunities for challenging ourselves in our Buddhist practice and for deepening our faith. All of our arduous efforts during those times will turn into incalculable benefit.

A TEACHING OF TRANSFORMATION: "THE BENEFIT GAINED FROM ONE DAY'S PRACTICE IN THE IMPURE WORLD"

Highlights

- Striving to free people from suffering at the most fundamental level in this defiled Latter Day of the Law brings immeasurable benefit.

- The most trying times are the most wonderful opportunities for challenging ourselves in our Buddhist practice and deepening our faith.

- Chanting Nam-myoho-renge-kyo enables us to bring forth within our lives the state of supreme enlightenment of the Buddha.

- A daily practice in which we challenge our obstacles head-on by chanting and taking action over time produces the great benefit of attaining Buddhahood in this lifetime.

Nichiren Daishonin further explains that the benefit received from widely propagating Nam-myoho-renge-kyo during the Latter Day of the Law surpasses that of Dengyo, T'ien-t'ai, Nagarjuna and Mahakashyapa.

Striving to free people from suffering at the most fundamental level in this defiled latter age is an action that brings immeasurable benefit. Hence,

Nichiren says, "A hundred years of practice in the Land of Perfect Bliss cannot compare to the benefit gained from one day's practice in the impure world."

The most trying times represent the most wonderful opportunities for challenging ourselves in our Buddhist practice and for deepening our faith. All of our arduous efforts during those times will turn into incalculable benefit. Quite simply, "a hundred years of practice in the Land of Perfect Bliss" signifies Buddhist practice in a comfortable environment free of hardships. Such circumstances would make it difficult for us to accomplish our human revolution. And without polishing and forging our lives, the goal of attaining the Buddha way would remain out of reach even if we practiced for a hundred years.

Nichiren intended this statement as a sharp refutation of the teaching of the Pure Land (Nembutsu) school of Buddhism of his day, which emphasized carrying out Buddhist practice *after* gaining rebirth in the Pure Land. While many religious traditions encourage aspiring for some otherworldly paradise, the Daishonin teaches that this world, the here and now, is the true place for carrying out Buddhist practice. He explains that opening the way to victory amid severe trials and tribulations is itself genuine Buddhist practice for polishing and forging our lives.

"One day's practice in the impure world" may also be interpreted as meaning a teaching of transformation that truly leads those living in a defiled age to happiness. Nam-myoho-renge-kyo is the great Law that enables us to instantly bring forth within our lives the state of supreme enlightenment of the Buddha. By transforming our minds or attitude, we can immediately transform our state of life.

Because this is an evil age, various problems and difficulties arise in the course of daily life. It stands to reason, then, that we who dedicate our lives to a grand mission will face even more daunting obstacles. The key, however, is to use these obstacles as a powerful impetus to chant Nam-myoho-renge-kyo and actively challenge ourselves to overcome the problems we face. Each day we spend engaged in this manner is one of life-changing practice, and the continuation of such practice over time produces the great benefit of attaining Buddhahood in this lifetime.

Only a Buddhist teaching of fundamental transformation—one that teaches the importance of taking action amid the turmoil of society—can offer the means for genuinely changing this strife-filled *saha* world into a Buddha land and for actualizing the principle of establishing the correct teaching for the peace of the land.

In addition, Nichiren says that 2,000 years of propagating Buddhism during the Former and Middle Days of the Law[17] are inferior to even a brief time spent doing so during the Latter Day of the Law. Buddhism during the Former and Middle Days was basically a teaching for people of superior capacity,[18] and benefit could be gained through even the partial or implicit teachings.

The Latter Day, however, is an age of quarrels and disputes,[19] when the proponents of various partial and

Striving to free people from suffering at the most fundamental level in this defiled latter age is an action that brings immeasurable benefit.

implicit teachings will all proclaim their particular school of Buddhism to be perfect and absolute. These teachings will function as negative influences that obstruct the spread of the correct teaching. In such a confused and disordered age, only the teaching of Nam-myoho-renge-kyo of the Buddhism of sowing—which directly activates the Buddha nature—will lead people to enlightenment. That is why propagating the correct teaching of Nam-myoho-renge-kyo for even a brief time in the Latter Day is superior to spreading partial or implicit teachings for a long period during the Former and Middle Days of the Law.

THE TIME TO OPEN THE WAY FOR KOSEN-RUFU IS THE LATTER DAY

Highlights

- Buddhism attaches special importance to the time, or era. It teaches that when the people of a land require spiritual change, a sage will appear who can propel that change.

- Nichiren appeared at a time of transition moving from an age of aristocracy toward an age of the people.

- The Soka Gakkai was founded against the backdrop of unprecedented developments in history, when humankind was in need of fresh wisdom.

Nichiren Daishonin explains that he could establish the Law to be widely propagated in the Latter Day not because he possessed unsurpassed wisdom, but simply because the time had come to do so. In writing that this achievement is not attributable to his wisdom, Nichiren is, of course, merely being modest. But his comment that his establishment of the Law had accorded with the time expresses a profound truth. Generally speaking, too, there is a sense that truly great individuals in every sphere appear in the right place at the right time or are summoned forth by the times.

Buddhism attaches special importance to the time, or era. It teaches that when the people of a land require spiritual change, a sage will appear who can propel that change. In other words, a defiled age requires the appearance of a genuine Buddha who can expound a great teaching capable of freeing the people of suffering and positively transforming the times. Nichiren emphasizes the importance of the time because he is absolutely confident that Nam-myoho-renge-kyo is the teaching that accords with the age of the Latter Day.

If we overlay the history of Buddhism and the history of humankind, we could say that the time of the Latter Day when Nichiren Daishonin appeared marked a crossroads—a transition from an age of aristocracy toward an age of the people. It also preceded an age of great exchange between peoples of different nations traveling across vast continents and oceans, which gave rise to a more global view and brought about dynamic changes. In the vanguard of this era, he revealed and spread the Law of Nam-myoho-renge-kyo. This teaching constitutes the heart of his Buddhism of the people and a universal religion.

Turning to modern times, the Soka Gakkai appeared in the first half of the 20th century. That this organization that has spearheaded the worldwide propagation of Nichiren Buddhism should have appeared at this juncture is not unrelated to the 20th century being a major turning point in human history. Witnessing two world wars and the birth of nuclear weapons that continue to threaten our very survival, the 20th century signaled the start of an entirely new epoch. Humankind embarked on economic and other activities on a global scale and even took flight into outer space. Further, the recognition that the earth is finite—as seen, for example, in growing awareness of environmental destruction—is another unmistakable development of the 20th century. That century also saw a burgeoning awareness of human rights, as is evident in the dismantling of slavery and colonial rule and in the creation of the United Nations and other world agencies dedicated to peace.

The Soka Gakkai was founded against the backdrop of such unprecedented developments in history—at a time when humankind was in need of fresh wisdom. Holding high the banner of a humanistic religion, we have shared

NICHIREN DAISHONIN ON COMPASSION

The great mercy refers to the sowing of the seeds of Buddhahood through Nam-myoho-renge-kyo. Because of this mercy of sowing the seeds, all other kinds of mercy follow just as shadows follow a form. And now Nichiren too dispenses this kind of mercy. (*The Record of the Orally Transmitted Teachings*, p. 61)

At what time, what moment, should we ever allow ourselves to forget the compassionate vow of the Buddha, who declared, "At all times I think to myself: [How can I cause living beings to gain entry into the unsurpassed way and quickly acquire the body of a Buddha]?" ("Questions and Answers about Embracing the Lotus Sutra," WND-1, 62)

I, Nichiren, have done nothing else, but have labored solely to put the five or seven characters of Myoho-renge-kyo into the mouths of all the living beings of the country of Japan. In doing so, I have shown the kind of compassion that a mother does when she labors to put milk into the mouth of her infant child. ("On Reprimanding Hachiman," WND-2, 931)

with people around the globe the wisdom of Nichiren Buddhism—a wisdom that can block off the path to misery and open the way to realizing true happiness.

Mr. Makiguchi espoused a philosophy of value creation and formulated a system of value-creating education as a basic foundation for building character. His disciple, Mr. Toda, meanwhile, through advocating the ideal of global citizenship, the abolition of nuclear weapons and human revolution—or inner transformation— offered profound wisdom to combat the fundamental darkness of humankind that characterized the 20th century. And as Mr. Toda's dedicated disciple, I have been striving through humanistic dialogue to bridge gaps between civilizations and between different faiths, to expand our network of good and to make the 21st century a century of humanity, a century of life and a century of peace.

I believe that the age of Soka has truly arrived "because the time makes it so."

"I PRAY TO THE BUDDHA FOR FINAL VICTORY"

Highlights

- Nichiren concludes this treatise expressing his conviction that the Buddha's ardent wish is the widespread propagation of Nam-myoho-renge-kyo and that he has accomplished this wish.

- The benefits of opening the path for *kosen-rufu* will all return to his late teacher, Dozen-bo.

- The best way to repay our mentor is through our own victories.

Nichiren says that the disciple is
like the plant, and the teacher, the earth.
The flower of victory that the disciple causes
to blossom will unfailingly return to the earth
as the good fortune of the mentor.

At the end of this treatise, Nichiren Daishonin expresses confidence that the Buddha's ardent wish is the widespread propagation of Nam-myoho-renge-kyo in the evil age after the Buddha's passing, and that he has accomplished that wish. And he states that his benefit in establishing the great Law for the enlightenment of all people and opening the path for *kosen-rufu* into the eternal future of the Latter Day will all return to his former teacher, Dozen-bo.[20]

In another writing, he says that the disciple is like the plant, and the teacher, the earth.[21] The flower of victory that the disciple causes to blossom will unfailingly return to the earth as the good fortune of the mentor. And without doubt a new flower of victory will fragrantly bloom from this earth of mentor and disciple. I have served Mr. Toda with that conviction for the past 61 years. Even now, every day I am devoting myself to *kosen-rufu* with a fresh determination to reply to his expectations. That's why I'm not afraid of anything.

Mr. Toda used to always say, "To have an honorable disciple is a mentor's greatest happiness." I am confident that Mr. Toda would be pleased by my efforts.

In December 1957, just after he had fulfilled his vow of realizing a membership of 750,000 households, Mr. Toda presented me with this poem. It was the last one I received from him.

> *Winning and losing*
> *are both*
> *part of life,*
> *but I pray to the Buddha*
> *with determination for*
> *final victory.*

Win without fail! Triumph in the end even over the harshest reality through prayer based on a vow! Break through all hardships to ring the bell of victory!

I always recall the compassionate visage of Mr. Toda, who believed in the triumph of his disciples.

The best way to repay our mentor is through our own victories. Let's set our sights on November 18, the Soka Gakkai's 78th anniversary. The time has arrived to create a fresh record of victories of mentor and disciple. I believe in the absolute victory of my beloved disciples. And I am especially looking forward to the victory of the youth who will carry on as my genuine disciples.

This lecture was published in the October 2008 Daibyakurenge, the Soka Gakkai study journal.

NOTES:

1. Dengyo (767–822): Also known as Saicho. The founder of the Tendai (T'ien-t'ai) school in Japan. He refuted the errors of the six schools of Nara—the established Buddhist schools of the day—elevated the Lotus Sutra and dedicated himself to the establishment of a Mahayana ordination center on Mount Hiei.

2. T'ien-t'ai (538–97): Also known as Chih-i, commonly referred to as the Great Teacher T'ien-t'ai, a name taken from Mount T'ien-t'ai where he lived. He founded the T'ien-t'ai school of Buddhism in China. He criticized the scriptural classifications formulated by the 10 major Buddhist schools of his time, which either regarded the Flower Garland Sutra or the Nirvana Sutra as the highest Buddhist teachings. Based on his studies, he classified all of Shakyamuni's sutras into "five periods and eight teachings," and through this demonstrated the superiority of the Lotus Sutra. He also established the practice of threefold contemplation in a single mind and the principle of the "three thousand realms in a single moment of life."

3. Nagarjuna: A Mahayana scholar of southern India, thought to have lived between the years 150 and 250. Nagarjuna wrote many important treatises, including *The Treatise on the Middle Way*, and had a major impact on the development of Buddhist thought in China and Japan. Nichiren identifies Nagarjuna as a successor who correctly understood Shakyamuni's true intent.

4. Mahakashyapa: One of Shakyamuni's ten major disciples, known as the foremost in ascetic practices. After Shakyamuni's death, he served as head of the Buddhist Order, and is said to have been the first of the Buddha's successors.

5. Land of Perfect Bliss: The name of the land of Amida Buddha, said to be located in a western region of the universe. It is also called the Pure Land, the Pure Land of Perfect Bliss and the Western Paradise.

6. Fundamental darkness: Also fundamental ignorance or primal ignorance. The most deeply rooted illusion inherent in life, said to give rise to all other illusions. *Darkness* in this sense refers to the inability to see or recognize truth, particularly, the true nature of one's life. The term *fundamental darkness* is contrasted with the fundamental nature of enlightenment, which is the Buddha nature inherent in life. According to the

Shrimala Sutra, fundamental darkness is the most difficult illusion to surmount and can only be eradicated by the wisdom of the Buddha. Nichiren interprets fundamental darkness as ignorance of the ultimate Law, or ignorance of the fact that one's life is essentially a manifestation of that Law, which he identifies as Nam-myoho-renge-kyo.

7. Seicho-ji: The temple in Awa Province (present-day southern Chiba Prefecture), where Nichiren was ordained at the age of 12 and where he later proclaimed his teaching.

8. At the time of the Tatsunokuchi Persecution (on September 12, 1271), Nichiren discarded his transient status as "an ordinary person at the stage of hearing the name and words of the truth" and revealed his true identity as "the Buddha of limitless joy who has been enlightened from time without beginning," while remaining an ordinary person.

9. Dozen-bo (d. 1276): A priest of Seicho-ji, a temple in Awa Province (present-day southern Chiba Prefecture), under whom Nichiren studied from age 12. When Nichiren first declared his teaching at Seicho-ji (in 1253), his refutation of the Nembutsu teaching of the Pure Land school enraged Tojo Kagenobu, the steward of the area and an ardent Pure Land believer, who ordered his arrest. Dozen-bo helped Nichiren escape at that time, but he was nevertheless afraid to oppose Kagenobu. After the Komatsubara Persecution (in 1264), Dozen-bo sent a message to the Daishonin asking whether it was possible for him to attain Buddhahood. In response, the Daishonin issued a refutation of the Nembutsu teaching and encouraged Dozen-bo to devote himself to the correct teaching. It seems that Dozen-bo did arouse a measure of faith in Nichiren's teaching from that time; however, he died without formally converting.

10. Joken-bo and Gijo-bo: Priests at Seicho-ji who, as disciples of Dozen-bo, had supported the Daishonin during his early studies. When the Daishonin declared the establishment of his teaching at Seicho-ji in 1253, they helped him escape when his life was threatened by the local steward, Tojo Kagenobu, who was enraged by his denunciation of the Pure Land teachings. Later, they became Nichiren's followers and received several of his writings.

11. Nichiren writes: "Myoho-renge-kyo is the Buddha nature of all living beings. The Buddha nature is the Dharma nature, and the Dharma nature is enlightenment. . . . The Buddha nature that all these beings possess is called by the name Myoho-renge-kyo. Therefore, if you recite these words of the daimoku once, then the Buddha nature of all living beings will be summoned and gather around you. At that time the three bodies of the Dharma nature within you—the Dharma body, the reward body, and the manifested body—will be drawn forth and become manifest. This is called attaining Buddhahood" ("Conversation between a Sage and an Unenlightened Man," WND-1, 131).

12. Three obstacles and four devils: Various obstacles and hindrances to the practice of Buddhism. The three obstacles are (1) the obstacle of earthly desires, (2) the obstacle of karma and (3) the obstacle of retribution. The four devils are (1) the hindrance of earthly desires, (2) the hindrance of the five components, (3) the hindrance of death and (4) the hindrance of the devil king.

13. Three poisons—greed, anger and foolishness: The fundamental evils inherent in life that give rise to human suffering. The three poisons are so called because they pollute people's lives and work to prevent them from turning their hearts and minds to goodness.

14. Three powerful enemies: Three types of arrogant people who persecute those who propagate the Lotus Sutra in the evil age after Shakyamuni Buddha's death, described in the "Encouraging Devotion" chapter of the Lotus Sutra. The Great Teacher Miao-lo summarizes them as arrogant lay people, arrogant priests and arrogant false sages.

15. "Upsetting attachments and arousing doubts": a way of teaching employed by the Buddha to lead people toward the correct teaching. It means "to disturb the mind that is attached to inferior teachings, thereby arousing doubt in those attachments and causing the person to aspire for a deeper understanding of the correct teaching."

16. Six non-Buddhist teachers: Influential thinkers in India during Shakyamuni's lifetime who openly broke with the old Vedic tradition and challenged Brahman authority in the Indian social order. Their teachings ran counter to those of Shakyamuni Buddha.

17. Former and Middle Days of the Law: According to various sutras, during the Former Day Shakyamuni's teaching and its practice are maintained, during the Middle Day the Buddha's teaching becomes rigid and formalized, and during the Latter Day Shakyamuni's teaching loses its efficacy. While there are various explanations as to the duration of each of these periods, in Nichiren's time it was commonly held that the Former and Middle Days each consisted of 1,000 years.

18. Shakyamuni Buddha's disciples are divided into three groups according to their capacity to understand his teaching: superior, intermediate and inferior. This traditional division of capacity was employed by T'ien-t'ai (see note # 2) and others in interpreting the Lotus Sutra.

19. Age of quarrels and disputes: Also, age of conflict. The last of the five 500-year periods following Shakyamuni's death, which are described in the Great Collection Sutra. It corresponds to the beginning of the Latter Day of the Law. In the Great Collection Sutra, Shakyamuni speaks to Bodhisattva Moon Storehouse about the first four of the five 500-year periods following his death, and then says that, in the next 500 years, quarrels and disputes will arise among the followers of his teachings, and that the pure Law will be obscured and lost.

20. "Since the [Lotus Sutra's] prediction was not made in vain, then it is certain that all the people of Japan will chant Nam-myoho-renge-kyo! Thus the flower will return to the root, and the essence of the plant will remain in the earth. The benefit [of propagating the Mystic Law in the Latter Day] will surely accumulate in the life of the late Dozen-bo" ("On Repaying Debts of Gratitude," WND-1, 736–37).

21. "If a tree is deeply rooted, its branches and leaves will never wither. If the spring is inexhaustible, the stream will never run dry. Without wood, a fire will burn out. Without earth, plants will not grow. I, Nichiren, am indebted solely to my late teacher, Dozen-bo, for my having become the votary of the Lotus Sutra and my being widely talked about now, in both a good and bad sense. Nichiren is like the plant, and my teacher, the earth" ("Flowering and Bearing Grain," WND-1, 909).

(14)

"Letter to Jakunichi-bo"

The Shared Struggle of Mentor and Disciple—Leading
a Profound and Hope-filled Life of Mission, Illuminating
the Darkness With the Great Light of Buddhism

The Passage for Study in This Lecture

deeply appreciate your sending a letter to this distant place [of Mount Minobu[1]]. It is extremely rare to be born as a human being. Not only are you endowed with human form, but you have had the rare fortune to encounter Buddhism. Moreover, out of the Buddha's many teachings you have encountered the daimoku,[2] or the title, of the Lotus Sutra and become its votary. Truly you are a person who has offered alms to a hundred thousand million Buddhas in his past existences!

Nichiren is the supreme votary of the Lotus Sutra in Japan. In this land only he has lived the twenty-line verse[3] of the "Encouraging Devotion" chapter. The eight hundred thousand million nayutas of bodhisattvas[4] pledged with this verse to propagate the Lotus Sutra, but not one of them fulfilled the pledge. ...

My giving myself the name Nichiren (Sun Lotus) derives from my own enlightenment regarding the Buddha vehicle. This may sound as though I think I am wise, but there are specific reasons for what I say. The sutra reads, "As the light of the sun and moon can banish all obscurity and gloom, so this person as he advances through the world can wipe out the darkness of living beings." Consider carefully what this passage signifies. "This person as he advances through the world" means that the first five hundred years of the Latter Day of the Law will witness the advent of Bodhisattva Superior Practices,[5] who will illuminate the darkness of ignorance and earthly desires with the light of the five characters of Nam-myoho-renge-kyo. In accordance with this passage, Nichiren, as this bodhisattva's envoy, has urged the people of Japan to accept and uphold the Lotus Sutra. His unremitting efforts never slacken, even here on this mountain [of Minobu].

The sutra then goes on to say, "After I [Shakyamuni] have passed into extinction, [one] should accept and uphold this sutra. Such a person assuredly and without doubt will attain the Buddha way." Therefore, those who become Nichiren's disciples and lay believers should realize the profound karmic relationship they share with him and spread the Lotus Sutra as he does. ...

Believe in [this] Gohonzon with all your heart, for it is the robe to protect you in the world after death. No wife would ever leave her husband unclothed, nor could any parents fail to feel pity for their child shivering in the cold. Shakyamuni Buddha and the Lotus Sutra are like one's wife and parents. You have helped me and thereby saved me from disgrace in this life; in return, I will protect you from disgrace in the next. What one has done for another yesterday will be done for oneself today. Blossoms turn into fruit, and brides become mothers-in-law. Chant Nam-myoho-renge-kyo, and be always diligent in your faith.

I cannot thank you enough for your frequent letters. Jakunichi-bo, please convey all these teachings in detail to that believer. (*The Writings of Nichiren Daishonin*, vol. 1, pp. 993–94)

LECTURE

What is the purpose of life? It is to become happy. What, then, is genuine happiness? It is to establish within our lives an indestructible state of supreme dignity through upholding faith in the Mystic Law—a state of life pervaded by the Buddha's four noble virtues of eternity, happiness, true self and purity[6] that will endure eternally throughout the cycle of birth and death. The essential aim of Nichiren Buddhism is to polish and forge our lives through faith. This is the path pursued by the Bodhisattvas of the Earth,[7] the true protagonists of *kosen-rufu*—the widespread propagation of the Law. While challenging their own spiritual development, they endeavor to lead all people to the sure path for genuine happiness. Bodhisattvas of the Earth follow a path of practice aspiring for the happiness of themselves and others, a path of mission dedicated to advancing *kosen-rufu.*

In "Letter to Jakunichi-bo," Nichiren Daishonin indicates that he is fulfilling the function of Bodhisattva Superior Practices, the leader of the Bodhisattvas of the Earth, and he teaches us how noble it is to devote one's life to propagating the Mystic Law in the same spirit as one's teacher.

Dated September 16, 1279, it is believed that this letter was sent to a lay follower through Jakunichi-bo, one of Nichiren's priest disciples.[8] The letter's content and language strongly suggest that the recipient was a woman who had some close connection to the Daishonin's parents, and that this recipient was most likely from his birthplace of Awa Province.[9]

At the end of this writing, the Daishonin explains that the benefit of embracing the Gohonzon will adorn one's life in both present and future existences, writing, "[This] Gohonzon ... is the robe to protect you in the world after death" (WND-1, 994). These words can also be read as an indication that the letter probably accompanied the Daishonin's conferral of a Gohonzon upon the recipient.

He urges his disciple to spread the Lotus Sutra just as he does and to live out her life as a votary of the Lotus Sutra. We can infer that his bestowal of the object of devotion prompts him to explain to her what it truly means to persevere in faith as a Bodhisattva of the Earth.

SGI President Ikeda delivers his acceptance speech for the Honorary Doctorate of Laws from Queen's University of Belfast at the Soka University Central Tower in Hachioji, Tokyo, Japan, May 18, 2009.

PRACTITIONERS OF THE LAW POSSESS "IMMEASURABLE BLESSINGS"

Highlights

Written: September 16, 1279

Recipient: This letter was most likely sent through Jakunichi-bo to a woman living in Awa Province, the area in which Nichiren was born.

- Those who chant Nam-myoho-renge-kyo and teach others to do the same—votaries of the Lotus Sutra who desire to lead those who are suffering to enlightenment—truly possess "immeasurable blessings."

Nichiren Daishonin begins this letter by pointing out the rarity of our lives. In effect, he is saying: "You've had the rare fortune to be born a human being. And you've had the still rarer fortune of encountering Buddhism. Furthermore, out of all the Buddha's teachings, you've become a votary of the *daimoku*[10] of the Lotus Sutra. This is no doubt the reward of your having made offerings to countless millions of Buddhas in past existences."

The "Teacher of the Law" chapter of the Lotus Sutra states that those who have gained immeasurable blessings from making offerings to untold Buddhas in past lifetimes voluntarily choose to be born in the human world as "teachers of the Law" out of a desire to lead those who are suffering to enlightenment. These teachers of the Law practice the Lotus Sutra themselves and also share it with others. The Daishonin, therefore, says that the votaries of the *daimoku*, those who chant Nammyoho-renge-kyo and teach others to do the same, are people who truly possess "immeasurable blessings."

A LIFE-STATE PERVADED BY ETERNITY, HAPPINESS, TRUE SELF AND PURITY

Highlights

- Chanting Nam-myoho-renge-kyo is the practice for transforming the four sufferings of birth, aging, sickness and death into the four virtues of eternity, happiness, true self and purity.

- *Nam* equates to the "paramita of happiness"; *myoho* equates to the "paramita of true self"; *renge* equates to the "paramita of purity"; *kyo* equates to the "paramita of eternity."

- Votaries of the Mystic Law can bring forth these four virtues through their nobility of character and humanity, and make their lives shine to the fullest.

Through the practice of chanting and spreading Nam-myoho-renge-kyo for the happiness of oneself and others, votaries of the *daimoku* forge within themselves the supremely noble life-state

of Buddhahood imbued with the four virtues of eternity, happiness, true self and purity.

In *The Record of the Orally Transmitted Teachings,* Nichiren Daishonin says: "When, while in these four states of birth, aging, sickness, and death, we chant Nam-myoho-renge-kyo, we cause them to waft forth the fragrance of the four virtues.[11] *Nam* stands for the paramita of happiness, *myoho* for the paramita of true self, *renge* for the paramita of purity, and *kyo* for the paramita of eternity" (p. 90).

Chanting Nam-myoho-renge-kyo is the practice for transforming lives steeped in the four universal sufferings of birth, aging, sickness and death into lives of supreme inner dignity and worth exuding the fragrance of the four virtues of eternity, happiness, true self and purity.

The "paramita of happiness" means attaining true inner peace and happiness. *Nam* [meaning "to devote one's life"] corresponds to this paramita, because through the power of faith based on dedicating our lives to the Mystic Law, we can break through the ignorance or darkness[12] that is the source of all suffering and delusion. The Daishonin writes, "There is no true happiness for human beings other than chanting Nam-myoho-renge-kyo" ("Happiness in This World," WND-1, 681).

The "paramita of true self" means gaining true autonomy or self-identity. Our Buddhist practice of chanting enables us to overcome our shallow, limited ego and our attachment to our lesser self, and reveal our greater or higher self that is one with the Mystic Law. Therefore, *myoho*, or Mystic Law, corresponds to the "paramita of true self."

The "paramita of purity" means establishing a life-state of genuine purity and integrity embodying the principle of "earthly desires are enlightenment."[13] *Renge* means lotus flower and is characterized by the image of pristine lotus blossoms rising unsullied from the muddy water in which they grow.[14] It is a symbol or metaphor for the Mystic Law, which has the power to bring forth pure and unsurpassed wisdom from the swamp of earthly desires or deluded impulses.

Lastly, the "paramita of eternity" means securing a state of true eternity in the depths of our lives by internalizing the principle of "the sufferings of birth and death are nirvana."[15] Through chanting Nam-myoho-renge-kyo, we can manifest a state of life in which, by embodying the principle of the eternal and unchanging truth, we can live from moment to moment with the wisdom derived from this truth that functions in accordance with changing circumstances.[16] *Kyo*, which is written with the Chinese character that can mean the vertical thread in a loom or fabric as well as the passage of time, represents eternity encompassing the three existences of past, present and future. It thus corresponds to the "paramita of eternity."

Though human life is transient and beset by the sufferings of birth, aging, sickness and death, the votaries of the Mystic Law can bring forth the lofty fragrance of these four virtues through their nobility of character and humanity. And to establish an inner state pervaded by the four virtues is what it means to make our precious lives as human beings shine to the fullest. It is

> The essential aim of Nichiren Buddhism is to polish and forge our lives through faith. This is the path pursued by the Bodhisattvas of the Earth, the true protagonists of *kosen-rufu*.

simply another way of expressing the concept of achieving self-perfection or attaining Buddhahood in this lifetime.

In this writing, Nichiren stresses the importance of votaries following his teachings and striving for *kosen-rufu* in the same spirit as he does—for he is not only the votary of the Lotus Sutra but, more specifically, the embodiment of Bodhisattva Superior Practices, whose advent the sutra prophecies. It may well have been that the Daishonin bestowed the Gohonzon on the letter's recipient, an evidently sincere believer, out of his wish that she deepen her faith and practice as a disciple who truly shares his commitment to *kosen-rufu*.

The Daishonin depicted in the Gohonzon his own supremely noble state of life imbued with the four virtues of eternity, happiness, true self and purity. To practice in the same spirit as the Daishonin means to base our lives on the Gohonzon and regard his triumphant life as our model and touchstone.

He concludes this writing—in which he focuses on the way to perfect our precious lives as human beings—by explaining that the benefit of embracing the Gohonzon continues on "in the world after death" (WND-1, 994), that is, throughout future existences. Thus, in its entirety, "Letter to Jakunichi-bo" elucidates the everlasting benefit derived from the Mystic Law, which embodies the principle of the oneness of life and death.

FROM THE "ENCOURAGING DEVOTION" CHAPTER OF THE LOTUS SUTRA

The following is the concluding verse section of the "Encouraging Devotion" chapter of the Lotus Sutra, which is called the 20-line verse section because it is 20 lines in the Chinese translation.

We beg you not to worry.
After the Buddha has passed into
    extinction,
in an age of fear and evil
we will preach far and wide.
There will be many ignorant people
who will curse and speak ill of us
and will attack us with swords and
    staves,
but we will endure all these things.
In that evil age there will be monks
with perverse wisdom and hearts
    that are fawning and crooked
who will suppose they have attained
    what they have not attained,
being proud and boastful in heart.
Or there will be forest-dwelling
    monks
wearing clothing of patched rags
    and living in retirement,
who will claim they are practicing
    the true way,
despising and looking down on all
    humankind.
Greedy for profit and support,
they will preach the Law to white-
    robed laymen
and will be respected and revered by
    the world
as though they were arhats who
    possess the six transcendental
    powers.
These men with evil in their hearts,
constantly thinking of worldly affairs,

(Continued on page 59)

THE "EXTRAORDINARY PERSON, NICHIREN"— TRIUMPHING OVER EVEN THE MOST FORMIDABLE OBSTACLES

Highlights

- Selflessly devoted to spreading and upholding the Lotus Sutra, and enduring the harshest persecutions, Nichiren demonstrates that he is the "supreme votary of the Lotus Sutra in Japan."

- The Lotus Sutra warns of the three powerful enemies who attack and harass those who propagate the Lotus Sutra in the evil latter age.

- Only practitioners with concrete faith in the Lotus Sutra who do not hesitate to act for the sake of the Law can defeat the formidable devil king—the essence of the three powerful enemies.

- Through waging an active struggle to vanquish the negative workings inherent in life, Nichiren brought forth the Buddha wisdom and revealed his Buddhahood.

In teaching the importance of striving in faith with the same resolve as he does, Nichiren Daishonin states first of all, "Nichiren is the supreme votary of the Lotus Sutra in Japan" (WND-1, 993). He then goes on to assert the correctness of his own practice. His intention here is to clarify that an authentic Buddhist teacher first and foremost puts the teachings and principles of Buddhism into practice.

As evidence that he is the "supreme votary of the Lotus Sutra in Japan," the Daishonin cites the fact that he alone in all the land has lived the 20-line verse section of the "Encouraging Devotion" chapter of the Lotus Sutra.

The 20-line verse section contains the pledge of the eight hundred thousand million *nayutas* of bodhisattvas, who were gathered at the assembly where the Lotus Sutra was preached. They vow to spread the sutra after the Buddha's passing, ready to endure and withstand even the most harrowing persecution from society as a whole, devoting themselves with the selfless spirit expressed in the line "we care nothing for our bodies or lives" (*The Lotus Sutra and Its Opening and Closing Sutras*, p. 233). This section also contains a description of the three powerful enemies—arrogant lay people, arrogant priests and arrogant false sages—who will attack and harass those who seek to propagate the Lotus Sutra in the evil latter age.

What is the essence of these three powerful enemies? It is the ignorance or darkness that resides in the lives of those who attack and persecute the practitioners of the correct teaching. As indicated by the sutra's assertion that "evil demons will take possession of others,"[17] this ignorance manifests as a function of what is called "the devil king of the sixth heaven"[18]—the ultimate "evil demon" or negative function in life. Only the strong faith of practitioners of the Lotus Sutra who practice with the spirit of fearless dedication can defeat this formidable devil king. For no matter how daunting this devilish function is, its true nature is none other than fundamental darkness, in other words, ignorance of the Mystic Law. Therefore, by exerting ourselves in our Buddhist practice with the invincible spirit of fearless dedication, we can bring forth within us the wisdom of the Mystic Law with which to defeat the workings of the devil king. This accords with the Buddhist teaching that unsurpassed wisdom derives from faith in the supreme Law.

While living as an ordinary person in the Latter Day, the Daishonin triumphed in the struggle against endless devilish functions by manifesting the wisdom of the Mystic Law. In other words, he prevailed in the ultimate struggle to reveal his Buddhahood. This may be one reason why he refers to himself in this writing as "this extraordinary person, Nichiren" (WND-1, 993).

He also notes, "The eight hundred thousand million nayutas of bodhisattvas pledged with this [20-line] verse to propagate the Lotus Sutra, but not one of them fulfilled the pledge" (WND-1, 993). He is implying that resolutions alone won't do, that concrete efforts to defeat devilish functions are necessary. A crucial requirement for a

will borrow the name of forest-
dwelling monks
and take delight in proclaiming our
faults,
saying things like this:
"These monks are greedy
for profit and support
and therefore they preach non-
Buddhist doctrines
and fabricate their own scriptures
to delude the people of the world.
Because they hope to gain fame and
renown thereby
they make distinctions when
preaching this sutra."
Because in the midst of the great
assemblies
they constantly try to defame us,
they will address the rulers, high
ministers,
Brahmans, and householders,
as well as the other monks,
slandering and speaking evil of us,
saying, "These are men of perverted
views
who preach non-Buddhist doctrines!"
But because we revere the Buddha
we will bear all these evils.
Though they treat us with contempt,
saying,
"You are all no doubt buddhas!"
all such words of arrogance and
contempt
we will endure and accept.
In a muddied kalpa, in an evil age
there will be many things to fear.
Evil demons will take possession of
others
and through them curse, revile, and
heap shame on us.
But we, reverently trusting in the
Buddha,
will put on the armor of perseverance.

(Continued on page 61)

genuine Buddhist teacher in the Latter Day is the ability to wage an active struggle to vanquish the negative workings inherent in life and bring forth the Buddha wisdom.

"SUN LOTUS"—A NAME REVEALING THE INNATE QUALITIES OF BODHISATTVA SUPERIOR PRACTICES

Highlights

- Nichiren, whose name consists of the two Chinese characters for "sun" and "lotus," compares his mission to that of Bodhisattva Superior Practices.

- Just as the sun—symbolized by *nichi* of Nichiren—illuminates the darkness, Superior Practices spreads the wisdom of the Mystic Law in an evil age to illuminate the darkness of ignorance of all people.

- The lotus—represented by the Chinese character *ren* in Nichiren—can be viewed as a symbol of Superior Practices, whose task is to bring the pure flowers of Buddhahood to bloom in the polluted swamp of earthly desires.

- The lotus is also a metaphor for the simultaneity of cause and effect, the essence of Nam-myoho-renge-kyo.

Nichiren Daishonin clarifies the significance of his appearance in the world in terms of Buddhism, by explaining that he is the envoy of Bodhisattva Superior Practices. Yet his explanation would seem to indicate that, rather than merely being an envoy, he is actually the one who has initiated propagation of the Lotus Sutra in the Latter Day and as such is the embodiment of Bodhisattva Superior Practices himself, predicted in the sutra as the main protagonist in spreading the Law after the Buddha's passing.

In this connection, he quotes two passages from the "Supernatural Powers" chapter of the Lotus Sutra to show that he matches the description of this great leader of the Bodhisattvas of the Earth.

First, he explains that his adoption of the name Nichiren, which is represented by the characters for "sun" and "lotus," derives from his own enlightenment regarding the Buddha vehicle—the teaching that leads all people to Buddhahood. He cites the sutra passage, "As the light of the sun and moon / can banish all obscurity and gloom, / so this person as he advances through the world / can wipe out the darkness of living beings" (LSOC, 318). This passage summarizes the activities undertaken by Bodhisattva Superior Practices in the Latter Day of the Law and their significance. What is Bodhisattva Superior Practices' mission? The Daishonin says that it is to dispel the "darkness of all living beings," just as the brightness of the sun and moon illuminates the dark.

The "darkness of all living beings" refers to the darkness or unenlightened state represented by ignorance and earthly desires. Fundamental ignorance of the Mystic Law and of the true nature of life itself, and the earthly desires that arise as a result of that ignorance, are the source of all delusion and misery. This fundamental darkness is inherent in the lives of all people. Without breaking through it, true happiness is unattainable. Thus, only by illuminating the darkness of ignorance and earthly desires that shroud people's lives in the Latter Day of the Law is it possible to lead them to enlightenment.

The light that can illuminate this darkness is the Buddha wisdom, the source of which, Nichiren says, is Nam-myoho-renge-kyo. In this writing, he refers to it as "the light of the five characters of Nam-myoho-renge-kyo"[19] (WND-1, 993).

Nam-myoho-renge-kyo is the key to the enlightenment of all Buddhas—past, present and future; it is the Law of universal enlightenment. As such, it is the great light that illuminates the darkness of ignorance of all human beings. Its function is analogous to that of the light of the sun or the moon that shines down on all things and eliminates all darkness from the world. This sutra passage about the sun and the moon, as I mentioned earlier, expresses the function of Bodhisattva Superior Practices' efforts to spread the Law in the evil age

In order to preach this sutra
we will bear these difficult things.
We care nothing for our bodies or lives
but are anxious only for the
    unsurpassed way.
In ages to come we will protect and
    uphold
what the Buddha has entrusted to us.
This the World-Honored One must
    know.
The evil monks of that muddied age,
failing to understand the Buddha's
    expedient means,
how he preaches the Law in accordance with what is appropriate,
will confront us with foul language
    and angry frowns;
again and again we will be banished
to a place far removed from towers
    and temples.
All these various evils,
because we keep in mind the
    Buddha's orders,
we will endure.
If in the settlements and towns
there are those who seek the Law,
we will go to wherever they are
and preach the Law entrusted to us
    by the Buddha.
We will be envoys of the world-
    honored one,
facing the assemblies without fear.
We will preach the Law with skill,
for we desire the Buddha to rest in
    tranquillity.
In the presence of the world-honored
    one
and of the buddhas who have
    gathered from the ten directions
we proclaim this vow.
The Buddha must know what is in
    our hearts.

(*The Lotus Sutra and Its Opening and Closing Sutras*, pp. 232–34)

SGI PRESIDENT IKEDA ON THE MISSION OF BODHISATTVAS OF THE EARTH

Today's world is sorely lacking in hope, a positive vision for the future and a solid philosophy. There is no bright light illuminating the horizon. That is precisely why we, the Bodhisattvas of the Earth, have appeared. That is why Nichiren Daishonin's Buddhism of the sun is so essential. We have stood up, holding high the torch of courage in one hand and the philosophy of truth and justice in the other. We have begun to take action to boldly break through the darkness of the four sufferings of birth, old age, sickness and death as well as the darkness in society and the world. (*Faith into Action*, p. 94)

Those who, in this evil age of the Latter Day of the Law, continue chanting Nam-myoho-renge-kyo for the happiness of themselves and others, no matter what hardships they encounter, are Bodhisattvas of the Earth who have been entrusted with propagation. (October 2002 *Living Buddhism*, p. 22)

No matter what karma others may be struggling with, one can only really lead them to enlightenment by awakening them to the fact that the power to break through that karma already exists within their lives. Only Bodhisattvas of the Earth possessing the essential or original Law are able to bring about this awakening. (*The Heritage of the Ultimate Law of Life*, p. 106)

after the Buddha's passing. It seems likely then that one of the reasons that he chose the Chinese character *nichi* (meaning "sun") for his name is because of the symbolism it has with the innate illuminating quality of Superior Practices.

The second half of this same sutra passage contains the phrase, "This person as he advances through the world" (LSOC, 318). Because the task of Bodhisattva Superior Practices is to bring the pure flowers of Buddhahood to bloom in the human world—which is likened to a polluted swamp of earthly desires—his practice is the very image of the lotus flower growing unsoiled by the muddy water, as described in the "Emerging from the Earth" chapter of the Lotus Sutra (see LSOC, 263). In that sense, the lotus—represented by the Chinese character *ren* in the name Nichiren—can be viewed as a symbol of Superior Practices.

Further, the Law that Bodhisattva Superior Practices will teach people in this defiled age after the Buddha's passing is the Law for attaining Buddhahood that simultaneously possesses both cause and effect—namely, the Mystic Law or the Law of Nam-myoho-renge-kyo. The lotus is used as a metaphor for the simultaneity of cause and effect,[20] because its flowers (cause) and fruit (effect) appear at the same time. Therefore, the lotus can also be seen as symbolic of the efforts of Superior Practices to share the essence of the Lotus Sutra—Nam-myoho-renge-kyo, the causal law for the universal attainment of Buddhahood—with people living in the swamp-like reality of the human world.

A BUDDHA IS ALWAYS TAKING ON CHALLENGES

Highlights

- The altruistic actions of Bodhisattva Superior Practices are driven by his deep determination and vow to help all those living in the evil latter age become Buddhas.

- Nichiren Daishonin ceaselessly carried out the practice of Superior Practices, never faltering in his struggle to propagate Nam-myoho-renge-kyo, the essence of the Lotus Sutra.

- Buddha is another name for one who never ceases taking up challenges.

Nichiren Daishonin cites another passage from the "Supernatural Powers" chapter to show that he fulfills the function of Bodhisattva Superior Practices: "After I [Shakyamuni] have passed into extinction / [one] should accept and uphold this sutra. / Such a person assuredly and without doubt / will attain the buddha way" (LSOC, 318). This is a declaration by the Buddha that all people in the Latter Day who embrace and practice the Lotus Sutra propagated by Superior Practices are certain to gain enlightenment.

From the standpoint of the Buddha, this passage indicates that his vow to enable all people to attain Buddhahood will be actualized by Bodhisattva Superior Practices. From the standpoint of Superior Practices, meanwhile, this passage is the basis for his personal resolve and sense of duty to lead all people in the Latter Day to enlightenment in accord with the Buddha's prophecy.

Buddha is another name for one who never ceases taking up challenges. Shakyamuni continued his journey to propagate his teaching to the very end. Nichiren Daishonin also continued to lead propagation efforts from Minobu, persevering in his great and selfless struggle until his death at Ikegami.

The altruistic actions of Bodhisattva Superior Practices are driven by his deep determination and vow to help all those living in the evil latter age become Buddhas.

Nichiren Daishonin then says that he himself has ceaselessly carried out the practice of Bodhisattva Superior Practices. He never faltered even once in his

KOSEN-RUFU OF SUBSTANTIATION

In his interpretation of a passage from "The Object of Devotion for Observing the Mind," (see WND-1, 375) Nichiren Buddhist scholar and reformer Nichikan viewed the spread of Nichiren Daishonin's teachings in two categories: *shakubuku* in terms of the entity of the Law and *shakubuku* in terms of substantiation. *Shakubuku* refers to propagating Buddhism through correcting delusions and subduing attachment to error.

The first, propagation in terms of the entity of the Law, refers to Nichiren's refutation of errors in other forms of Buddhism and establishment of the practice of chanting Nammyoho-renge-kyo to the Gohonzon.

The second category is propagation in terms of substantiation. This refers to far-reaching propagation efforts by lay believers to spread the teachings, or, in other words, efforts to make Nichiren Buddhism a world religion. The SGI's ongoing movement for peace, culture and education accords exactly with this concept.

struggle from the day he first initiated the propagation of Nam-myoho-renge-kyo, the essence of the Lotus Sutra, with the declaration of the establishment of his teaching on April 28, 1253. For 27 years, even after leaving Kamakura and moving to Mount Minobu, he waged a tireless struggle against interminable onslaughts of devilish functions seeking to obstruct his path.

He writes, "[Nichiren's] unremitting efforts never slacken, even here on this mountain" (WND-1, 993). Most people at that time probably viewed the Daishonin's move to Minobu as signifying his retirement from the world. However, he continued vigorously to hold aloft the banner of *kosen-rufu* and never wavered in the slightest in his commitment or his efforts to enable all people to attain Buddhahood. His statement above conveys his unswerving spirit to continue his all-out struggle for *kosen-rufu*, even at Minobu.

Buddha is another name for one who never ceases taking up challenges. Shakyamuni continued his journey to propagate his teaching to the very end. The Daishonin also continued to lead propagation efforts from Minobu, persevering in his great and selfless struggle until his death at Ikegami.

Similarly, in modern times, first Soka Gakkai president Tsunesaburo Makiguchi continued struggling against government persecution without retreating a single step, even in prison. When being interrogated by his jailors, he confidently affirmed the correctness of the Daishonin's teaching. A record of one of his interrogations shows that, when asked about the connection between the Lotus Sutra and Nichiren, Mr. Makiguchi cited the sutra passage I have just discussed, which begins "As the light of the sun and moon ..." He declared to the effect: "Nichiren Daishonin was born in order to lead the people of the defiled and evil age of the Latter Day of the Law to enlightenment. *Kosen-rufu* means purifying, with the truth of Nam-myoho-renge-kyo, the fallacious thinking and ideas that prevail in such an age—that is to say, a defiled and evil age like that of the present."[21] In this way, Mr. Makiguchi continued to speak out powerfully for his beliefs and nobly died for them in prison.

His successor and second Soka Gakkai president Josei Toda also continued to lead our movement up until his last breath. He died in the midst of his struggle for *kosen-rufu*, in which his greatest pleasure was looking forward to the development and growth of the young people who would carry on his work in the future. Through his example, he taught us that only in unceasing struggle for the sake of *kosen-rufu* could one genuinely experience the "boundless joy of the Law."[22]

The struggles of Bodhisattvas of the Earth who cherish the great desire to lead all people to enlightenment are without end. This sublime spirit of the Daishonin is communicated in each line of this writing.

THE KARMIC TIES LINKING TEACHERS AND DISCIPLES IN BUDDHISM TRANSCEND THE THREE EXISTENCES

Highlights

- In the first half of "Letter to Jakunichi-bo," Nichiren describes his efforts as a votary of the Lotus Sutra and as the one fulfilling the mission of Bodhisattva Superior Practices.

- In the last half of the letter, based on his wish to enable his followers, who share deep karmic ties with him, to lead lives of absolute victory, he encourages them to emulate his spirit and to "spread the Lotus Sutra as [Nichiren] does."

- To awaken to the depth of the karmic ties we share with our teacher in Buddhism means courageously standing up, here and now, and practicing with the same spirit as our teacher.

- To do so is the profound and inevitable mission of the Bodhisattvas of the Earth who pledged to propagate the Law together with Superior Practices.

In the first half of "Letter to Jakunichi-bo," Nichiren Daishonin briefly touches on how he has led efforts to propagate the Law and forged ahead to triumph over all obstacles—both as the votary of the Lotus Sutra and in fulfilling the function of Bodhisattva Superior Practices. Here, as the true teacher of Buddhism in the Latter Day, he is clarifying his identity and position. Based on this, in the final half of the letter, Nichiren encourages his followers to emulate his spirit. This is an expression of his wish to enable them, as people who share deep karmic ties with him, to lead lives of absolute victory, free of any regret.

He writes, "Those who become Nichiren's disciples and lay believers should realize the profound karmic relationship they share with him and spread the Lotus Sutra as he does" (WND-1, 994). He urges his followers to awaken to the karmic bond they share with him, the votary who has prevailed over all manner of obstacles and devilish functions. This is in effect a call to them to stand up as genuinely committed practitioners of the Lotus Sutra,

to strive to accomplish the Buddha's decree of *kosen-rufu* without begrudging their lives, and to remember their mission as fellow Bodhisattvas of the Earth, who in the sutra vowed to propagate the Mystic Law in the Latter Day together with Bodhisattva Superior Practices.

The letter's recipient must have been both greatly surprised and immensely honored by the Daishonin's words to her that stated to the effect, "You should realize the karmic relationship we share and stand up as a practitioner of the Lotus Sutra and fulfill your mission as a Bodhisattva of the Earth." I can well imagine her being deeply moved by this encouragement.

Most important is Nichiren's exhortation to "spread the Lotus Sutra as [Nichiren] does" (WND-1, 994). To awaken to the depth of the karmic ties we share with our teacher or mentor in

What matters is the present. The actions we carry out now are what count. It all comes down to whether we are earnestly practicing in a way that accords with the times and in the same spirit as our teacher or mentor.

Buddhism does not mean we should lose ourselves in idle reflections on the significance of our past existences; rather, it means we should courageously stand up, here and now, and practice with the same spirit as our teacher. What matters is the present. The actions we carry out now are what count. It all comes down to whether we are earnestly practicing in a way that accords with the times and in the same spirit as our teacher or mentor.

Therefore, hoping to inspire the letter's recipient to stand up bravely for *kosen-rufu*, the Daishonin calmly states, "Being known as a votary of the Lotus Sutra is a bitter, yet unavoidable, destiny" (WND-1, 994). "Bitter" here means unfortunate. Viewed in terms of prevailing secular values, to embark on the path of a practitioner of the Lotus Sutra might be regarded as signing up for an unending succession of hardships. But when viewed from the perspective of Buddhism, in terms of the profound karmic ties we share with the Daishonin, there is no higher honor than struggling alongside him as fellow Bodhisattvas of the Earth. This, he says, is the "unavoidable destiny" of votaries or practitioners of the Lotus Sutra, and we should clearly recognize this and accept it. "Unavoidable destiny" could also be expressed as "profound, inevitable mission."

Mr. Toda often would tell members, "To meet and encounter an auspicious time, to be in rhythm with that time, makes having been born worthwhile."

And at a gathering of Kansai members, he once declared: "What a terrible fate we have to be born in this age coinciding with Japan's crushing defeat [in World War II]. On the other hand, nothing could be a source of greater pride and joy for us than having the fortune to be alive at this time of *kosen-rufu*, which has been designated by the Buddha's decree. You mustn't be late in joining our magnificent movement for *kosen-rufu*."

Mr. Toda's inauguration as second Soka Gakkai president on May 3, 1951, took place just two years before the 700th anniversary of the establishment of Nichiren Daishonin's teaching. With this, after seven centuries, the substantive realization of *kosen-rufu* (see sidebar, p. 256) was finally under way in earnest. All of this could only be due to the wondrous decree of the Buddha.

Speaking of his good fortune to be alive at such a time, Mr. Toda said: "It gives me immense joy that I could be born in the age of the Latter Day of the Law, right at the time of the 700th anniversary of Nichiren Daishonin's establishment of his teaching, and to receive the Buddha's decree to accomplish *kosen-rufu*."

Now, 750 years have passed since the Daishonin first publicly declared his teaching of Nam-myoho-renge-kyo, and we have entered a time when a mighty, ever-growing river of *kosen-rufu* flows throughout the world. Votaries of the Lotus Sutra, noble, committed Bodhisattvas of the Earth are appearing all around the globe. In light of the passages from the "Supernatural Powers" chapter of the Lotus Sutra and in light of "Letter to Jakunichi-bo," there is absolutely no doubt that we each have our own profound and unfathomable karmic relationships and missions that accord with the Buddha's towering decree.

I can just picture Mr. Toda smiling broadly in delight to see so many wonderful, youthful Bodhisattvas of the Earth joyously emerging around the world.

We now have a vast network of Bodhisattvas of the Earth, joined together by deep karmic bonds, in 192 countries and territories. Each of us deliberately chose to be born in this tumultuous age in order to fulfill our mission from time without beginning, our "unavoidable destiny." There is no greater happiness than this. The real challenge lies yet ahead. Let's advance on the great path of our mission with even more energy and exuberance.

THOSE WHO EXERT THEM-SELVES FOR KOSEN-RUFU ARE WORTHY BEYOND MEASURE

Highlights

- The Gohonzon is a manifestation of the supreme life-state of eternity, happiness, true self and purity attained by the Daishonin.

- Those who establish a sublime inner state through faith in the Gohonzon during this lifetime will be able to keep inactive and dormant the lower life-states steeped in earthly desires, negative karma and suffering.

- Those who wholeheartedly dedicate themselves to the Law, uphold Buddhism and practice it just as the Buddha instructs are truly admirable.

- Those who continue to take action for *kosen-rufu* in the same spirit as the Daishonin can manifest the same lofty life-state he attained.

Now, 750 years have passed since Nichiren Daishonin first publicly declared his teaching of Nam-myoho-renge-kyo, and we have entered a time when a mighty, ever-growing river of *kosen-rufu* flows throughout the world.

Lastly, Nichiren Daishonin stresses to the letter's recipient the beneficial power of the Gohonzon to affect both the present and the future. He also says that her life will be adorned with dignity and nobility as a result of her sincere efforts to support and assist him.

He writes that one of the benefits of faith in the Gohonzon is being "protected from disgrace in the next life" (see WND-1, 994). "Disgrace" in this context means a life-state steeped in earthly desires, negative karma and suffering. In other words, he is referring to a future existence in the three evil paths or the four evil paths[23]—the three or four lower states of the Ten Worlds. The benefit of faith in the Gohonzon protects us from this "disgrace."

The Gohonzon is a manifestation of the supreme life-state of eternity, happiness, true self and purity attained by the Daishonin. Those who establish this sublime inner state through faith in the Gohonzon during this lifetime will be able to keep the "disgrace" of the lower states of life inactive and dormant.

Those who exert themselves for *kosen-rufu* are worthy beyond measure. The Gohonzon, Shakyamuni Buddha and the Lotus Sutra cannot fail to protect them. Truly admirable are those who wholeheartedly dedicate themselves to the Law, who uphold the supreme teaching of Buddhism and practice it just as the Buddha instructs. In another writing, the Daishonin declares, "If the Law that one embraces is supreme, then the person who embraces it must accordingly be foremost among all others" ("Questions and Answers about Embracing the Lotus Sutra," WND-1, 61). Thus, when we uphold the unsurpassed teaching of Nichiren Buddhism, we can lead unsurpassed lives. This is because the benefit of forming even a slight connection to Buddhism is everlasting. The important thing, therefore, is to unite in spirit with the teacher of Buddhism who correctly upholds and propagates the Law.

Throughout his many writings, the Daishonin repeatedly urges us to follow his example. For instance, in this letter, he says, "[You] should ... spread the Lotus Sutra as [Nichiren] does" (WND-1, 994), and elsewhere he writes, "[You] should all practice as I do" ("On Establishing the Four Bodhisattvas as the Object of Devotion," WND-1, 978).

Followers prove themselves to be true votaries of the Lotus Sutra by continuing to take action for *kosen-rufu* in the same spirit as the Daishonin. When they do so, the same lofty life-state he attained will manifest in their own lives.

When viewed from our perspective as Soka Gakkai members, these words can also be taken to mean that when we share the same purpose, mission and struggle that are the hallmarks of our Buddhist mentors—people of unwavering conviction—our lives are infused with supreme dignity and splendor. I clearly recall how my mentor, Mr. Toda, used to say: "We should be confident that we, the members of the Soka Gakkai, are noble emissaries who have been sent by the Buddha. We mustn't look down on ourselves. We are the emanations of the Daishonin. ...

"As Soka Gakkai members, all of us have been born with a great mission. We mustn't be lazy or cowardly. After all, we're Bodhisattvas of the Earth who champion the cause of *kosen-rufu*. ...

"The most important thing is *kosen-rufu*, the Daishonin's mandate; it mustn't be delayed for even a day. The Soka Gakkai is the sole body that can achieve this mission."

This lecture was published in the November 2008 Daibyakurenge, *the Soka Gakkai monthly study journal.*

NOTES:

1. Mount Minobu: Also, Minobu. Located in present-day Yamanashi Prefecture in Japan. Nichiren Daishonin lived there during the later years of his life from May 1274 through September 1282, just prior to his death. At Minobu, he devoted himself to educating his disciples, directing propagation efforts and writing doctrinal treatises.

2. *Daimoku*: The title of a sutra, in particular the title of the Lotus Sutra of the Wonderful Law (Jpn *Myoho-renge-kyo*). The title of a sutra represents the essence of the sutra. In his *Annotations on "The Words and Phrases of the Lotus Sutra,"* the Great Teacher Miao-lo of China says, "When for the sake of brevity one mentions only the title, the entire sutra is by implication included therein." In Nichiren's teaching, the *daimoku* means the invocation of Nam-myoho-renge-kyo; more precisely, it indicates the practice of chanting Nam-myoho-renge-kyo with faith in the Gohonzon, the object of devotion.

3. The 20-line verse section: The concluding verse section of the "Encouraging Devotion" chapter of the Lotus Sutra, in which countless multitudes—or, more specifically, "eight hundred thousand million nayutas"—of bodhisattvas vow to Shakyamuni to propagate the sutra in the evil age after his passing. This section is called the 20-line verse section because the Chinese translation consists of 20 lines. It describes the persecutions that will occur in the evil age designated in the sutra. Based on this section, Miao-lo classified those who persecute practitioners of the Lotus Sutra into three types of enemies—arrogant lay people, arrogant priests and arrogant false sages.

4. Eight hundred thousand million *nayutas* of bodhisattvas: The bodhisattvas gathered to hear Shakyamuni Buddha preach the Lotus Sutra at the assembly on Eagle Peak. A *nayuta* is an ancient Indian numerical unit; explanations of its magnitude differ. One well-known source defines it as 100 billion, while another defines it as 10 million. See also footnote 3.

5. Bodhisattva Superior Practices: The leader of the Bodhisattvas of the Earth. Shakyamuni entrusts Superior Practices with propagating the Lotus Sutra during the evil age of the Latter Day of the Law. In his writings, Nichiren Daishonin associates himself with Superior Practices, saying that he is fulfilling the mission entrusted to the bodhisattva by Shakyamuni, and he refers to his propagation efforts as the work of Superior Practices. Nichikan Shonin, the 26th chief priest, regarded the Daishonin as the reincarnation of Superior Practices in terms of his outward behavior, and as the Buddha of the Latter Day of the Law, in terms of his inner enlightenment.

6. Four virtues: Four noble qualities of the Buddha's life, also known as the four paramitas or four virtue paramitas—eternity, happiness, true self and purity. The word *paramita* means "perfection." "Eternity" means unchanging and eternal. "Happiness" means tranquillity that transcends all suffering. "True self" means true and intrinsic nature. And "purity" means free of illusion or mistaken conduct.

7. Bodhisattvas of the Earth: Countless bodhisattvas whom Shakyamuni calls forth in the "Emerging from the Earth" chapter of the Lotus Sutra. In the "Supernatural Powers" chapter, Shakyamuni entrusts these his true disciples, with the essential teaching that they are to spread in the evil age after his passing.

8. Jakunichi-bo (n.d.): Also known as Jakunichi-bo Nikke, a priest disciple of Nichiren Daishonin. Son of the lord of Okitsu in Isumi District in Kazusa Province (present-day Chiba Prefecture). He is said to have converted to the Daishonin's teaching along with his entire family, but details are not known.

9. Editors' Note: It was previously thought this letter was addressed to Jakunichi-bo, but recent scholarship has revealed that it was most likely sent through him to a woman living in Awa Province, the area for which Jakunichi-bo was responsible.

10. See footnote 2.

11. See footnote 6.

12. Ignorance: Also, illusion or darkness. In Buddhism, this points to ignorance about the true nature of existence. Ignorance is the first of the twelve-linked chain of causation, the sequence of causal relationships connecting ignorance with suffering. In the concept of the twelve-linked chain of causation, ignorance is the fundamental cause of delusion, suffering and transmigration in the realm of delusion and suffering.

13. "Earthly desires are enlightenment": This means that the wisdom for awakening to the ultimate truth for attaining Buddhahood (enlightenment) manifests in the lives of ordinary people who are ruled by earthly desires.

14. The Lotus Sutra states: "These sons of the Buddha are immeasurable in number! Already for a long time they have practiced the buddha way, dwelling in transcendental powers and the power of wisdom, skillfully learning the bodhisattva way, unsoiled by worldly things like the lotus flower in the water" (LSOC, 262–63).

15. "The sufferings of birth and death are nirvana": This means that the Buddha's enlightened life-state of true peace and tranquillity (nirvana) manifests in the lives of ordinary people who undergo the sufferings of birth and death.

16. *The Record of the Orally Transmitted Teachings* states: "*Namu* or *nam* [of Nam-myoho-renge-kyo] is a Sanskrit word. Here it means to dedicate one's life. … 'Dedication' means dedication to the principle of eternal and unchanging truth. … and

'life' means that one's life dedicated to that principle bases itself on the wisdom of the truth of the essential teaching that functions in accordance with changing circumstances. In essence, one dedicates one's life to Nam-myoho-renge-kyo" (p. 3). As this indicates, the act of dedicating oneself to the Mystic Law through chanting Nam-myoho-renge-kyo has two aspects: One is to devote oneself to, or to fuse one's life with, the eternal and unchanging truth; the other is that, through this fusion of one's life with the ultimate truth, one simultaneously draws forth inexhaustible wisdom that functions in accordance with changing circumstances.

17. "Evil demons will take possession of others": A line from the "Encouraging Devotion" chapter of the Lotus Sutra (LSOC, 233). This means that evil demons, or negative functions, enter the lives of various living beings, causing them to speak ill of those who protect the correct teaching and to obstruct their Buddhist practice.

18. Devil king of the sixth heaven: Also, devil king or heavenly devil. The king of devils, who dwells in the highest, or the sixth heaven, of the world of desire. He is also named Freely Enjoying Things Conjured by Others, the devil king who makes free use of the fruits of others' efforts for his own pleasure. Served by innumerable minions, he obstructs Buddhist practice and delights in sapping the life force of other beings. The devil king is a personification of the negative tendency to force others to one's will at any cost.

19. Five or seven characters: Myoho-renge-kyo is written with five Chinese characters, while Nam-myoho-renge-kyo is written with seven (*nam*, or *namu*, is composed of two characters). The Daishonin, however, often uses Myoho-renge-kyo synonymously with Nam-myoho-renge-kyo in his writings.

20. Simultaneity of cause and effect: The principle that both cause and effect exist together simultaneously in a single moment of life.

21. Translated from Japanese. Tsunesaburo Makiguchi, *Makiguchi Tsunesaburo zenshu* (Collected Writings of Tsunesaburo Makiguchi) (Tokyo: Daisanbunmei-sha, 1987), vol. 10, pp. 195, 199–200.

22. "Boundless joy of the Law": The supreme and ultimate happiness of the Buddha, the benefit of the Mystic Law.

23. The three evils paths are the worlds of hell, hunger and animality, the lowest of the 10 states of life known as the Ten Worlds. The term "four evil paths" refers to the three evil paths plus the world of anger.

(15)

"A Warning against Begrudging One's Fief"

Dauntless Confidence and Conviction: The Invincible Path of Mentor and Disciple

The Passage for Study in This Lecture

The Buddha wondered whether even bodhisattvas like Universal Worthy and Manjushri[1] could undertake the propagation of the Lotus Sutra in the latter age, and he therefore entrusted the five characters[2] of Myoho-renge-kyo to Superior Practices and the other three leaders of bodhisattvas[3] who had sprung up from the earth as numerous as the dust particles of a thousand worlds. Now, pondering the meaning of this matter [your pledge to carry through with your faith in the Lotus Sutra in spite of your lord's threats], I wonder if Bodhisattva Superior Practices has taken possession of your body in order to assist me along the way. Or could it be the design of Shakyamuni Buddha, the lord of teachings?

The fact that those retainers [of Lord Ema] who resent you are growing more presumptuous is definitely the result of the scheming of the priests Ryokan[4] and Ryuzo.[5] Should you write an oath discarding your faith, they would only become more arrogant, and they would mention it to everyone they meet. Then my disciples in Kamakura would be hounded until not a single one remained.

It is the nature of ordinary people not to know what awaits them in the future. Those who have a full understanding of this are called worthies or sages. ...

265

This life is like a dream. One cannot be sure that one will live until tomorrow. However wretched a beggar you might become, never disgrace the Lotus Sutra. Since it will be the same in any event, do not betray grief. Just as you have written in your letter, you must act and speak without the least servility. If you try to curry favor, the situation will only worsen. Even if your fiefs should be confiscated or you yourself driven out, you must think that it is due to the workings of the ten demon daughters [see sidebar, p. 83], and wholeheartedly entrust yourself to them.

Had I not been exiled, but remained in Kamakura, I would certainly have been killed in the battle. In like manner, since remaining in your lord's service will likely be to your detriment, this may well be the design of Shakyamuni Buddha. ...

I explained the teachings of the Lotus Sutra to you before. Matters of minor importance arise from [minor] good, but when it comes to a matter of great importance, great disaster without fail changes into great fortune. When people read this petition, their errors will surely come to light. You have only to speak briefly. Say rebukingly, "I will neither leave my lord's clan nor return my fief of my own accord. If my lord should confiscate it, I will regard it as an offering to the Lotus Sutra and a blessing."

You must in no way behave in a servile fashion toward the magistrate. Tell him, "These fiefs were not bestowed upon me by my lord. They were awarded to me because I saved his life with the medicine of the Lotus Sutra when he was seriously ill. If he takes them from me, his illness will surely return. At that time, even if he should apologize to me, I will not accept it." Having said so, take your leave in an abrupt manner.

Avoid all gatherings. Maintain a strict guard at night. Be on good terms with the night watchmen and make use of them. You should always be in company with them. If you are not ousted this time, the chances are nine to one that your fellow samurai will make an attempt on your life. No matter what, be sure not to die a shameful death. (*The Writings of Nichiren Daishonin*, vol. 1, pp. 823–25)

LECTURE

What defines a truly great person? Josei Toda, the second Soka Gakkai president, once remarked: "Truly great are those who live with a youthful vitality throughout their lives. Surely there are none more admirable as human beings than those who can maintain their original youthful spirit and hopes throughout their entire lives." I engraved these words in my life. I think it is just as he says.

Embodying Mr. Toda's words, countless Soka Gakkai members—noble champions of the people, especially our pioneer members—have won in life through maintaining unwavering faith. I praise and applaud them with all my heart.

It is only by maintaining our convictions throughout our lives, by not abandoning our beliefs, that we can prove them to be genuine; indeed, herein lies the essence of faith. Those who continue to uphold their beliefs through adversity are truly admirable; they are people of the highest caliber. They are honorable people of faith who would surely be praised by Nichiren Daishonin, the Buddha of the Latter Day of the Law.

WHOLEHEARTED ENCOURAGEMENT TO FACE THE GREATEST ADVERSITY

Highlights

Written: Seventh month of 1277

Recipient: Shijo Kingo

- After hearing a false allegation that Kingo had led an armed group that disrupted a debate between Nichiren's disciple Sammi-bo and Ryokan's protégé Ryuzo-bo, Kingo's lord Ema ordered him to renounce his faith in the Lotus Sutra.

- Ema threatened Kingo that if he did not discard the Lotus Sutra, he would confiscate his lands and expel him from the clan. However, Kingo refused to abandon his faith.

- In this letter, reflecting the shared commitment of mentor and disciple, Nichiren praises Kingo for resolutely pledging never to discard the Lotus Sutra.

Shijo Kingo[6] was also a person of conviction and integrity who maintained his faith at a critical crossroads in life. His greatest adversity came in June 1277, when his lord Ema ordered him to write an oath renouncing his faith in the Lotus Sutra.

This demand stemmed from a religious debate at Kuwagayatsu in Kamakura earlier that same month on June 9. On that occasion, one of Nichiren Daishonin's disciples, the priest Sammi-bo,[7] thoroughly defeated an influential priest known as Ryuzo-bo, whose fallacious teachings were misleading people. It was a debate to refute the erroneous and reveal the true in the realm of Buddhism. Kingo was present on that occasion, but simply as a silent observer. However, the false allegation that a group armed with swords led by Kingo had burst in and disrupted the proceedings later reached Lord Ema. Hearing this, Ema issued an order threatening Kingo with the confiscation of his lands and expulsion from the clan if he did not submit a written oath discarding his faith in the Lotus Sutra. Having one's lands confiscated was not only a disgrace for a member of the samurai class, but also meant the loss of one's very livelihood.

Nevertheless, Kingo unhesitatingly chose to stay true to his faith. He immediately reported these developments to Nichiren, who, with keen insight into the true nature of the situation, immediately composed a lengthy explanation in his follower's name that could be submitted to Ema. Its aim was to dispel the lord's suspicions, saying of the accusations, "What you heard must have been the fabrication of those who harbor jealousy against me" ("The Letter of Petition from Yorimoto," WND-1, 807). This "Letter of Petition from Yorimoto" (see WND-1, 803–13) also sets forth the correctness of Nichiren Buddhism in view of Shijo Kingo's stance and behavior.

The writing we are studying this time was sent to Kingo along with this petition. In "A Warning against Begrudging One's Fief," Nichiren praises this loyal follower for resolutely pledging never to submit such an oath or discard the Lotus Sutra.

Those who continue to uphold their beliefs through adversity are truly admirable; they are people of the highest caliber.

How sublime and noble is a life dedicated to struggling together with one's teacher in faith for the sake of *kosen-rufu*. The same mighty conviction Nichiren possessed undoubtedly pulsed vibrantly in Kingo's heart. Through studying this writing, let us deepen our understanding of faith based on the shared commitment of mentor and disciple.

THE NOBLE CHALLENGE OF UPHOLDING FAITH IN THE LOTUS SUTRA IN THE EVIL AGE OF THE LATTER DAY

Highlights

- Nichiren unstintingly commends Kingo for his staunch faith, because it is extremely rare for an ordinary person in the evil age of the Latter Day to undertake the difficult challenge of maintaining faith in the Lotus Sutra and standing up for *kosen-rufu*.

- Remaining steadfast in faith means battling the ignorance in the depths of our lives.

- This is an extremely arduous path because those who pursue it are certain to be assailed by the three obstacles and four devils, along with the three powerful enemies.

- We can only truly attain Buddhahood by defeating these obstacles and steadfastly working on our inner transformation.

In the struggle to defend the correct teaching, Nichiren Daishonin always responded with lightning speed. As soon as he saw any of his disciples facing adversity, he promptly took action to offer wholehearted encouragement to dispel the darkness of ignorance[8] from their hearts and infuse their lives with the fresh breeze of faith. Further, he battled each onslaught of negative functions and raised high the banner of the correct teaching for all to see. Inspired by his swift and impassioned words of encouragement, one disciple after another stood up, and *kosen-rufu* began to move forward momentously.

In the first part of this writing, Nichiren praises Shijo Kingo, who had resolved to persevere in his faith. He especially lauds the assistance that his disciple has given him, going so far as to say that it must have been due to "Bodhisattva Superior Practices taking possession of Shijo Kingo," or to "the design of Shakyamuni Buddha, the lord of teachings."

He unstintingly commends Kingo for his staunch faith, because it is extremely rare for an ordinary person in the evil age of the Latter Day to undertake the difficult challenge of maintaining faith in the Lotus Sutra and standing up for *kosen-rufu*.

This challenge is so difficult because remaining steadfast in faith means battling the ignorance or darkness in the depths of our lives—in other words, making continuous efforts to transform our lives on a fundamental level. This is an extremely arduous path because those who pursue it are certain to be assailed by the three obstacles and four devils,[9] along with the three powerful enemies.[10] However, we can only truly attain Buddhahood by defeating these obstacles and steadfastly working on our inner transformation. Nichiren no doubt praised Kingo because the latter had struggled alongside him as a great pioneer on the path of "attaining Buddhahood as an ordinary person" in the Latter Day of the Law.

THWARTING THE SCHEMES OF THE DEVIL KING THROUGH RESOLUTE FAITH

Highlights

- The devil king of the sixth heaven can be relentless, devious and determined.

- Nichiren observes, "Those possessed by a great devil will, once they succeed in persuading a believer to recant, use that person as a means for making many others abandon their faith."

- To protect each person by defeating the negative functions that seek to take advantage of them is to safeguard *kosen-rufu*.

- Devilish functions seek to bring down the "pillars," or the mainstays of the Buddhist community of believers. This is precisely why such people must stand firm.

In this writing, Nichiren Daishonin declares that the slanderous allegations were definitely the result of the scheming of Ryokan of Gokuraku-ji temple and his cohort Ryuzo-bo. These and other malicious people wanted to force Shijo Kingo to abandon his faith so that they could circulate the news throughout Kamakura to sow doubt in the hearts of the Daishonin's other followers and cause them all to stop practicing.

This episode represented a manifestation of the workings of the devil king of the sixth heaven,[11] which can be truly relentless, devious and determined. During such grave obstacles as the Tatsunokuchi Persecution and subsequent Sado Exile, Nichiren had completely triumphed over this ultimate devilish function. Next, however, the vanquished devil king sought to drive the Daishonin's followers into quitting their faith and thereby destroy the community of believers.

As he observes in another writing, "Those possessed by a great devil will, once they succeed in persuading a believer to recant, use that person as a means for making many others abandon their faith" ("The Workings of Brahma and Shakra," WND-1, 800). Causing one person to stop practicing so as to make many others lose their faith is how the devil king operates. In that sense, too, each person is extremely important. To protect each person by defeating the negative functions that seek to take advantage of them is to safeguard *kosen-rufu*. Shijo Kingo's profound resolve not to discard his faith thwarted the scheming of the devil king. This is one reason why the Daishonin praises him.

Devilish functions seek to bring down the "pillars," or the mainstays of the Buddhist community of believers. This is precisely why such people must stand firm. In particular, the members of the men's division—the golden pillars of *kosen-rufu*—have a mission to secure the path established by the Daishonin and carry through with faith that would win his praise, just as their great predecessor Shijo Kingo had.

In many writings, the Daishonin guides and encourages Kingo, a key figure among his followers, to live out his life as a worthy or sage. In this present letter, too, he tells him: "It is the nature of ordinary people not to know what awaits them in the future. Those who have a full understanding of this are called worthies or sages" (WND-1, 824).

To not know what will happen to us in the future is our lot as ordinary people. However, by maintaining faith in the Mystic Law, we can make our way through life as worthies or sages based on the Buddhist wisdom that we can tap from within. President Toda said that we can develop the life-state of "an ordinary person enlightened from time without beginning." This is because faith in the Mystic Law enables us to draw forth from the depths of our lives fundamental wisdom equal to that of the Buddha.

THE ETERNITY OF LIFE

Nichiren Daishonin writes: "[Life] is neither existence nor nonexistence, yet exhibits the qualities of both. It is the mystic entity of the Middle Way that is the ultimate reality," ("On Attaining Buddhahood in This Lifetime," WND-1, 4). Buddhism rejects the concepts of annihilation (life extinguished upon death) and permanence (an unchanging immortal soul). It teaches instead that while individual lifetimes begin and end, life itself is inextinguishable. We are born and we die, but death is not the end of life itself. The cycle of birth and death repeats without end, and a person's life is at once both unique and inseparable from the universe.

The correct view of life's importance is inclusive of the fleeting present moment and incalculable eternity. Though temporary, the present lifetime is unique and irreplaceable. To devalue the present moment because it is transitory robs us of volition. To cling unreasonably to temporary phenomena can lead us to lose perspective of the grand and unending nature of existence.

Nichiren writes, "However many times I were to repeat the cycle of birth and death, no life could be as fortunate as this" ("Earthly Desires Are Enlightenment," WND-1, 317). While life is unending, our present lifetime offers a unique opportunity to change our karma *now* and create a positive orientation for future lives.

CONSTRUCTING ETERNAL HAPPINESS IN OUR LIVES DURING THIS PRESENT EXISTENCE

Highlights

- From the perspective of the eternity of life, a single lifetime is like a dream, and in this brief, fleeting existence, we never know what tomorrow might bring.

- This present life is in fact the decisive moment. It is essential that we uphold faith in the Mystic Law to seize this opportunity now to establish a life-state of absolute freedom for all eternity.

"This life is like a dream. One cannot be sure that one will live until tomorrow" (WND-1, 824)—I always bear these words closely in mind.

From the perspective of the eternity of life, a single lifetime is like a dream.

Moreover, in this brief, fleeting existence, we never know what tomorrow might bring. That is our reality as ordinary people. The worldly honor, position and wealth we may gain in this lifetime are all ephemeral.

This present life that is like a passing dream is in fact the decisive moment that determines whether we will attain a state of eternal happiness. Therefore, it is essential that we uphold faith in the Mystic Law if we wish to seize this opportunity now to establish a life-state of absolute freedom for all eternity.

Transforming our inner state of life is not something that can be accomplished by means of science, economics or politics. Only Buddhism makes this transformation possible on the most fundamental level. Since we have been fortunate enough to encounter this great teaching in this lifetime, we should resolutely persevere in faith. This is the Daishonin's conclusion.

Transforming our inner state of life is not something that can be accomplished by means of science, economics or politics. Only Buddhism makes this transformation possible on the most fundamental level.

"NEVER DISGRACE THE LOTUS SUTRA"

Highlights

- No matter how painful our circumstances, as long as we persevere in faith undaunted, we are by no means bringing disgrace upon the Lotus Sutra.

- What brings "disgrace to the Lotus Sutra" is giving in to our situation and being defeated by ourselves.

- Common to all those who have brought "disgrace to the Lotus Sutra" is that they lost their faith and succumbed to their attachment to social standing or wealth.

- Craven self-interest, conceit and arrogance plunge us directly into this darkness.

- The purpose of Nichiren Buddhism is to develop an indestructible life-state as vast as the universe, while remaining unswayed by praise or censure.

The Daishonin teaches Shijo Kingo a crucial aspect of faith with the line, "However wretched a beggar you might become, never disgrace the Lotus Sutra" (WND-1, 824). Many members have engraved this line, expressing the essence of faith in their hearts. I think it would be no exaggeration to say that today this spirit can only be found in the way of practice of the Soka Gakkai.

In terms of the values of Nichiren Buddhism, to "disgrace the Lotus Sutra" is a mark of defeat in terms of faith and Buddhist practice. No matter how painful our circumstances—whether we are struggling with illness or financial difficulties—as long as we persevere in faith undaunted, we are by no means bringing disgrace upon the Lotus Sutra. What brings disgrace, if anything, is giving in to our situation, being defeated by ourselves.

Practitioners also end up denigrating the Law when they lose sight of the all-important foundation of faith, giving in to cowardice because they are afraid of what others will think or growing arrogant because they are intoxicated by worldly acclaim.

Common to all those thankless and treacherous individuals, past and present, who have brought "disgrace to the Lotus Sutra," is the fact that they lost their faith and succumbed to their attachment to social standing or wealth. They showed themselves to be sad spiritual losers whose essential faith was destroyed by the impurities of negativity and darkness in their own lives. They even lost the ability to feel any sense of shame at this. That is how frightening the fundamental darkness inherent in life can be.

Because craven self-interest, conceit and arrogance plunge us directly into this darkness, let us always be on strict guard against such tendencies.

The purpose of faith in Nichiren Buddhism is, based on our belief in the eternity of life, to develop an indestructible life-state as vast as the universe itself, while remaining unswayed by the praise or censure we encounter in this existence.

The true mission of religion is to foster towering spiritual champions.

BASING OURSELVES ON OUR GREATER SELF, NOT OUR LESSER SELF

Highlights

- Living based on our lesser self—chasing after impermanent phenomena and earthly desires—is a source of suffering.

- Nichiren Buddhism teaches how to live based on our greater self, in which our actions accord with the eternal and unchanging Mystic Law.

- When making an important or fateful choice, we should always calmly choose the way of the greater self.

- We must progress in our human revolution each day through consistent Buddhist practice to thoroughly and successfully combat ignorance and negativity.

- The vital criterion for choosing the correct course each time and for walking the path of success is to always advance with our mentor in faith.

Buddhism teaches that rather than living based on our lesser self,[12] we ought to base ourselves on our greater self.[13]

Buddhism, generally speaking, is known for emphasizing impermanence. It is certainly true that living based on our lesser self—chasing after changing and impermanent phenomena and being caught up in earthly desires[14]—is a source of suffering. Therefore, Buddhism teaches that we should discard our ego-driven lesser self. This, however, doesn't mean discarding the life we have lived or renouncing all of our roles or positions in society and living like a hermit.

Nichiren Buddhism, which discerns the essential nature of existence, teaches us how to live based on our greater self so that our actions accord with the eternal and unchanging Law that encompasses everything in this impermanent world. Living based on our greater self means breaking through our attachment to our lesser self and correctly orienting our daily lives, unswayed by changing phenomena, with a solid autonomy and life force that are one with the eternal and unchanging Law.

Accordingly, in saying, "However wretched a beggar you might become ... ," the Daishonin's implication is not that Kingo's fiefs or other affairs don't matter; rather, he is saying that when in the course of life one is called upon to make an important or fateful choice between two options, one should always calmly choose the way of the greater self, that is to say, the eternal and unchanging way of faith.

As long as we are clear about this direction, it is only natural that we should proceed with the aim of being victorious in society. Buddhism is about winning. Even if we should suffer temporary setbacks in our activities in society, we will definitely be able to win in life, so long as we earnestly continue to forge on to the very end based on faith—with the spirit of "praying to the Buddha for final victory,"[15] as expressed in one of President Toda's poems. In light of the Daishonin's teachings, our victory is absolutely assured.

Even when facing storms of karma and obstacles, those who resolutely uphold the Mystic Law, adhere to the path of mentor and disciple, support the Soka Gakkai and work to build a harmonious community of practitioners are at that moment already winners in the dimension of life. Because by basing ourselves on our greater self, we gain the strength and vigor to repel any and all hardships. This genuine victory on the spiritual level will definitely open the way to our ultimate victory in life.

That is also why we need to polish our lives and progress in our human revolution each day through our consistent Buddhist practice. For if we do so, thoroughly forging our lives, we will be able to successfully combat darkness or ignorance, which can be a dire enemy, and prevent negative or destructive forces from being activated at a crucial moment.

It all comes down to which path we choose at major crossroads in our lives. Will we choose the wise path that leads to our further growth and development as human beings? Or will we choose the foolish path in which we are constantly swayed and controlled by others' opinions? In a sense, it could be said that in life we are always at such a crossroads. That is why it is vital for us to have an unwavering criterion for choosing the correct course in life each time.

For us, that integral criterion is to always advance together with our mentor, just as Shijo Kingo chose to do with

THE TEN DEMON DAUGHTERS

The ten demon daughters appear in the "Dharani" chapter of the Lotus Sutra. Along with the Mother of Demon Children, they vow to the Buddha to shield and guard the sutra's votaries, saying, "If there are those who fail to heed our spells / and trouble and disrupt the preachers of the Law, / their heads will split into seven pieces" (*The Lotus Sutra and Its Opening and Closing Sutras*, p. 351).

These ten demon daughters represent forces that protect those who propagate the Mystic Law. The ultimate source of these forces is within us, not outside of us. They are a function of our Buddha nature.

Buddhism teaches the oneness of our lives and the surrounding environment. Therefore, our inner, life-affirming conviction will manifest itself in our surroundings.

275

the Daishonin. Those who proceed with the same spirit as their mentor when standing at a crossroads in life will definitely walk the path to success. A life of deep commitment to the way of mentor and disciple creates a great path to victory in life. This is precisely what Nichiren Buddhism, the Buddhism of mentor and disciple, teaches.

VIEWING ALL CIRCUMSTANCES FROM THE PERSPECTIVE OF FAITH AND BUDDHISM

Highlights

- It is important to live with dignity, courage and dauntless confidence, rather than seeking to flatter or curry favor with someone.

- From the Buddhist perspective, difficulties that arise while advancing *kosen-rufu* have profound meaning.

- If we are swayed amid ever-changing circumstances, then we will not accomplish a true revolution in our state of life.

- We must always believe in the Mystic Law and construct a life of good fortune and happiness that will endure eternally.

- Instead of drawing conclusions from a superficial viewpoint, we need to calmly discern the true reality and significance of things based on faith and keep pressing forward.

Throughout this writing, Nichiren Daishonin stresses to Shijo Kingo the importance of conducting himself with dignity and courage, and of making his way through life with dauntless confidence and conviction. The diametric opposite of such a way of life is one of servility and flattery. Seeking to flatter or curry favor with someone can arise from self-interest or cowardice—and, at times, even a guilty conscience. To be ruled by fear, quite bluntly, is to be caught up in the lesser self, which is readily swayed by praise or censure. In this writing, Nichiren repeatedly admonishes Kingo not to speak or act with servility—whether it be toward his lord or the magistrate acting under the latter's direction. This is guidance to base his life on his greater self.

Next, Nichiren tells him that even if his fiefs should be confiscated or he should be driven out of the Ema clan, he should regard this as due to the workings of the heavenly deities—the protective functions of the universe—and contend with these developments based on faith.

Referring to an example from his own life, the Daishonin reflects that had he not been exiled to Sado Island and instead remained in Kamakura, he would most likely have been killed at the time of the disturbance of February 1272,[16] with his enemies taking advantage of the confusion to eliminate him.

The Daishonin is urging Kingo to look at things from the perspective of faith and Buddhism. He implies: "Difficulties that confront us in the course of advancing *kosen-rufu* definitely have meaning. Their significance will become clear in time. You should be confident that the heavenly deities and Buddhas and bodhisattvas throughout the universe will most certainly protect you because you are striving in faith with the spirit of not begrudging your life."

As the Daishonin goes on to mention in the next section of this writing, if Kingo were to remain in the service of the Ema clan under these circumstances, he would be in certain danger of hostile fellow retainers making an attempt on his life. For that reason, Nichiren advises Kingo to view being ousted from the clan, should it come to pass, as the workings of the heavenly deities.

Seen from the perspective of faith and Buddhism, everything has profound meaning. There is no need whatsoever for us to vacillate between elation and despair at each turn of events. There is no such thing as a storm that will continue blowing and wreaking havoc without end. In the same way,

there is no hardship that will continue forever. There are clear days and there are rainy days. If we are swayed by our environment, rejoicing one moment and despairing the next amid ever-changing circumstances, then we will not be able to accomplish a true revolution in our state of life.

The important thing is to always believe in the Mystic Law and to enter the powerful orbit of faith, practice and study. Entering this orbit—the orbit of human revolution and of changing our karma—is the way to construct a life of good fortune and happiness that will endure throughout eternity. No matter what happens, we will enjoy the unerring protection of the Gohonzon. Instead of drawing conclusions about the world of faith from a superficial viewpoint, we need to calmly discern the true reality and significance of things and keep pressing forward. With the passage of time, it will definitely become clear that everything has unfolded in the best possible manner.

Instead of drawing conclusions about the world of faith from a superficial viewpoint, we need to calmly discern the true reality and significance of things and keep pressing forward.

In this writing, we can feel the Daishonin's wish to ensure that his followers will be able to advance with confidence on the path of attaining Buddhahood throughout the three existences of past, present and future, never giving in to any onslaught of destiny. Embraced in Nichiren's strict compassion, Shijo Kingo used the crisis he faced as a momentous turning point to usher in a brilliant dawn of victory in his life.

GREAT EVIL PORTENDS GREAT GOOD

Highlights

- When a great disaster or dire situation occurs, it is possible to turn great evil into great good through the power of the Mystic Law.

- The important thing is to have no fear, regardless of what happens.

- When encountering obstacles for the sake of the Law, we need to break through people's negativity or darkness by taking courageous action in accord with the principle of "upsetting attachments and arousing doubts," and by tenaciously affirming justice and asserting the truth with conviction.

- This requires the resolute strength and wisdom to keep evil people at a distance and not allowing devilish functions to take advantage.

In the latter half of this writing, Nichiren Daishonin gives Shijo Kingo specific guidance on how to conduct himself. He also instructs Kingo to ask one of his close disciples in Kamakura to make a clean copy of the petition he has composed on his behalf—"The Letter of Petition from Yorimoto"—and to then submit it to Lord Ema.

In the petition, Nichiren sets down the facts of what took place at the Kuwagayatsu Debate—where the erroneous doctrines of various schools were soundly rebutted—and especially brings into sharp focus the true pernicious nature of Ryokan of Gokuraku-ji temple and others allied with him. Reading the petition would make the reprehensible actions of these individuals plain to Ema or anyone else. And if these facts were to become well known in Kamakura, then they would in all likelihood come to the attention of the regent Hojo Tokimune.[17] In that scenario, a complete turnaround in circumstances was entirely conceivable, transforming the environment for *kosen-rufu* from adverse to conducive.

The Daishonin writes, "When it comes to a matter of great importance, great disaster without fail changes into great fortune" (WND-1, 824). When a great disaster or dire situation occurs, it is possible to turn great evil into great good through the power of the Mystic Law, to "change poison into medicine,"[18] as expounded in the Lotus Sutra. That's why great evil can be a portent of great good fortune. Consequently, the important thing is to have no fear, regardless of what happens. When encountering obstacles for the sake of the Law, we need to break through people's negativity or darkness by taking courageous action in accord with the principle of "upsetting attachments and arousing doubts"[19] and by tenaciously affirming justice and asserting the truth with dauntless conviction. This is the formula for achieving victory based on the Mystic Law.

Finally, in the closing section of this writing, the Daishonin gives Kingo a series of detailed instructions. He urges him, for example, to be careful to stay away from gatherings, to exercise strict caution at night, and to maintain friendly relations with the night watchmen and make them his allies. In particular, he exhorts Kingo not to lose his precious life on account of carelessness.

The Daishonin teaches that we need to possess the resolute strength and wisdom to keep evil people at a distance and not allow devilish functions to take advantage.

What, then, became of Shijo Kingo? A short time later, his circumstances suddenly changed for the better. In "The Three Kinds of Treasure," which is dated two months after this letter, the Daishonin writes, "Ryuzo-bo, whom these people count on as their pillar of strength, has already been toppled" (WND-1, 848). We can surmise from this that something untoward must have happened to Ryuzo-bo, thus radically transforming the entire situation.

SGI PRESIDENT IKEDA ON THE MENTOR AND DISCIPLE RELATIONSHIP

It is through the bond of mentor and disciple that the Law is transmitted. Buddhism is the Law of life; and the Law of life cannot be transmitted through words or concepts alone.

Nichiren reveals the spirit of the mentor–disciple relationship in Buddhism. He writes, "Nichiren has been trying to awaken all the people of Japan to faith in the Lotus Sutra so that they too can share the heritage and attain Buddhahood" ("The Heritage of the Ultimate Law of Life," WND-1, vol. 1, p. 217). This passage can be read as expressing the fundamental spirit of the Buddha of the Latter Day, which pervades Nichiren's life of momentous struggle for *kosen-rufu.*

This desire to enable all people to equally share in the heritage of attaining Buddhahood is itself the spirit of the Lotus Sutra, and also the great wish, or vow, of the Buddha described in the sutra.

Accordingly, the great vow of the Buddha and the wish of the mentor— for the enlightenment of all people and the happiness of self and others —are none other than the great vow, or wish, for *kosen-rufu* itself.

The Heritage of the Ultimate Law of Life, pp. 80–81

In addition, Ema fell ill, and Shijo Kingo was able to regain his lord's trust as a result of his earnest efforts to treat his illness. After that, Shijo Kingo was given an estate that was three times larger than the one he already held. The Daishonin's statement, "Great disaster without fail changes into great fortune," was borne out by events.

Faith based on the Law, faith of selfless devotion to the Law—which is what is indicated by the statement "never disgrace the Lotus Sutra"—will adorn our lives with nobility and splendor. Selfless dedication in faith is entirely free of any sense of waste, sacrifice or regret.

President Toda once gave the following guidance: "On our planet, people kill each other in wars; our economies are based on the survival of the fittest and do not necessarily lead to human happiness; and many of society's leaders, who by rights ought to help others, instead often look down on and exploit people. And the same kind of thing is found in such spheres as politics, science and religion. Call it humanity's karma, but society is complex and full of contradictions. Nowhere can we find a fundamental path to happiness for all people. Only Nichiren Buddhism sets forth the means for fundamentally transforming our karma. It teaches the path of eternity, happiness, true self and purity, the path of lasting fulfillment and satisfaction. There is no higher path in life than this. That is why, if you give your all for the sake of faith, you will never regret it."

True to this guidance from my mentor, I have given my all to opening the path of *kosen-rufu* and directly forging ahead along the great path of transforming the destiny of humankind.

Only Nichiren Buddhism sets forth the means for fundamentally transforming our karma. It teaches the path of eternity, happiness, true self and purity, the path of lasting fulfillment and satisfaction. There is no higher path in life than this.

I have wholeheartedly exerted myself as a dedicated disciple of President Toda and as a revolutionary of the Mystic Law. I do not have the slightest regret.

"Just what should we do?" In response to this question, David Rossi, the protagonist of the novel *The Eternal City*, which I studied with President Toda in my youth, proclaims, "Our duty ... is to remove every obstacle in the path of the people."[20] And his frame of mind is described as follows: "Henceforth he would devote himself to the people, without a thought of what might happen. Nothing should come between him and his work for humanity—nothing whatever."[21]

Let us likewise set out brightly and with dauntless confidence and conviction on the next new phase in our struggle to construct the eternal city of peace and victory that is *kosen-rufu*.

Mr. Toda declared: "The Soka Gakkai has faith. Therefore, what can we possibly have to fear!" I present this immortal lion's roar to the youthful leaders of the 21st century in Japan and around the world.

This lecture was published in the December 2008 Daibyakurenge, *the Soka Gakkai monthly study journal.*

This concludes the series "Learning From the Writings: The Hope-filled Teachings of Nichiren Daishonin."

NOTES:

1. Bodhisattva Universal Worthy and Manjushri: Two leading bodhisattvas who are depicted as attending to Shakyamuni in various sutras. Bodhisattva Universal Worthy is regarded as symbolic of the virtues of truth and practice, while Manjushri is regarded as symbolic of the virtues of wisdom and enlightenment. Generally in Buddhist art, Manjushri is shown riding a lion at the Buddha's left, and Bodhisattva Universal Worthy shown riding a white elephant at the Buddha's right.

2. Five (or seven) characters: Myoho-renge-kyo is written with five Chinese characters, while Nam-myoho-renge-kyo is written with seven (*nam*, or *namu*, is composed of two characters). The Daishonin, however, often uses Myoho-renge-kyo synonymously with Nam-myoho-renge-kyo in his writings.

3. Bodhisattvas of the Earth: Countless bodhisattvas whom Shakyamuni calls forth in the "Emerging from the Earth" chapter of the Lotus Sutra. They are led by four great bodhisattvas—Superior Practices, Boundless Practices, Pure Practices and Firmly Established Practices. In the "Supernatural Powers" chapter, Shakyamuni entrusts these bodhisattvas with the essential teaching that they are to spread in the evil age after his passing.

4. Ryokan (1217–1303): Also known as Ninsho. A priest of the True Word Precepts school in Japan. With the patronage of the Hojo clan, Ryokan became chief priest of Gokuraku-ji temple in Kamakura and commanded enormous influence both among government officials and among the people. He was hostile to Nichiren Daishonin and actively conspired with the authorities to have him and his followers persecuted.

5. Ryuzo: Also known as Ryuzo-bo. A Tendai priest who was expelled from Enryaku-ji temple on Mount Hiei, the headquarters of the Tendai school, and later came to Kamakura where he won the patronage of Ryokan.

6. Shijo Kingo (circa 1230–1300): One of Nichiren Daishonin's leading followers. His full name and title was Shijo Nakatsukasa Saburo Saemon-no-jo Yorimoto. As a samurai retainer, he served the Ema family, a branch of the ruling Hojo clan. Kingo was well versed in both medicine and the martial arts. He is said to have converted to the Daishonin's teachings around 1256. When Nichiren was taken to Tatsunokuchi to be beheaded in 1271, Shijo Kingo accompanied him, resolved to die by his side.

7. Sammi-bo: One of Nichiren Daishonin's earliest disciples. Although he was highly esteemed for his

learning and debating skill and assisted Nikko Shonin's propagation efforts in the Fuji area, he was arrogant about his knowledge and desirous of social recognition and status. The Daishonin found it necessary to admonish him about this on several occasions. During the Atsuhara Persecution, Sammi-bo renounced his belief in Nichiren's teachings and turned against him and his supporters. In several letters, the Daishonin refers to Sammi-bo's untimely and tragic death, though the details are unknown.

8. Ignorance: Also, illusion or darkness. In Buddhism, ignorance about the true nature of existence. Ignorance is the first of the twelve-linked chain of causation, the sequence of causal relationships connecting ignorance with suffering. In the concept of the twelve-linked chain of causation, ignorance is the fundamental cause of delusion, suffering and transmigration in the realm of delusion and suffering.

9. Three obstacles and four devils: Various obstacles and hindrances to the practice of Buddhism. The three obstacles are (1) the obstacle of earthly desires, (2) the obstacle of karma and (3) the obstacle of retribution. The four devils are (1) the hindrance of the earthly desires, (2) the hindrance of the five components, (3) the hindrance of death and (4) the hindrance of the devil king.

10. Three powerful enemies: Three types of arrogant people who persecute those who propagate the Lotus Sutra in the evil age after Shakyamuni Buddha's death, described in a 20-line verse section of the "Encouraging Devotion" chapter of the Lotus Sutra. The Great Teacher Miao-lo of China summarizes them as arrogant lay people, arrogant priests and arrogant false sages.

11. Devil king of the sixth heaven: Also, devil king or heavenly devil. The king of devils, who dwells in the highest or the sixth heaven of the world of desire. He is also named Freely Enjoying Things Conjured by Others, the king who makes free use of the fruits of others' efforts for his own pleasure. Served by innumerable minions, he obstructs Buddhist practice and delights in sapping the life force of other beings.

12. Lesser self: Ego-consciousness that is focused on and absorbed with one's own self, seeking only one's own self-preservation and self-advancement.

13. Greater self: Autonomy attained by breaking through attachment to the lesser self and fusing with the Mystic Law and the principle of universal coexistence. A state of life in which one desires to live in harmony, coexistence and mutual prosperity with other human beings and the natural

environment, and works actively to realize happiness for both oneself and others.

14. Earthly desires: Various illusions and sufferings that obstruct one's Buddhist practice, including greed, anger and foolishness.

15. This is a line from the last poem SGI President Ikeda received from Mr. Toda: "Winning and losing are both part of life, but I pray to the Buddha for final victory."

16. This refers to an incident known as the "Hojo Tokisuke Disturbance," civil strife that broke out in Kyoto and Kamakura in February 1272. Hojo Tokisuke, an elder half-brother of the regent Hojo Tokimune, was suspected of plotting to seize power. Tokimune reacted by ordering to have Tokisuke killed.

17. Hojo Tokimune (1251–1284): The eighth regent of the Kamakura regime and son of Tokiyori, the fifth regent. Tokimune's tenure was a time when Japan was beset with both internal and external troubles. There were frequent occurrences of extraordinary natural phenomena and outbreaks of epidemics. Because of its autocratic rule, the main branch of the Hojo clan became enmeshed in an ongoing power struggle with the shogun, with other branches of the Hojo clan and with influential vassals of the shogun. At the same time, Japan faced successive invasions by the Mongols.

18. Changing poison into medicine: The principle that the three paths of earthly desires, karma and suffering can be transformed into the Buddha's three virtues of the Dharma body, wisdom and emancipation through the power of the Mystic Law. This phrase is found in a passage from Nagarjuna's *Treatise on the Great Perfection of Wisdom*, which mentions "a great physician who can change poison into medicine." T'ien-t'ai says in *The Profound Meaning of the Lotus Sutra*: "That persons of the two vehicles were given the prophecy of their enlightenment in this [Lotus] sutra means that it can change poison into medicine." This phrase is often cited to show that any problem or suffering can be transformed eventually into a cause of the greatest happiness and fulfillment in life.

19. Upsetting attachments and arousing doubts: A means employed by the Buddha to lead people toward the true teaching. It means to disturb the mind that is attached to inferior teachings, thereby arousing doubt in those attachments and causing the person to aspire for a deeper understanding of the correct teaching.

20. Hall Caine, *The Eternal City* (New York: D. Appleton and Company, 1901), p. 292.

21. *The Eternal City*, p. 190.

INDEX

W–Z